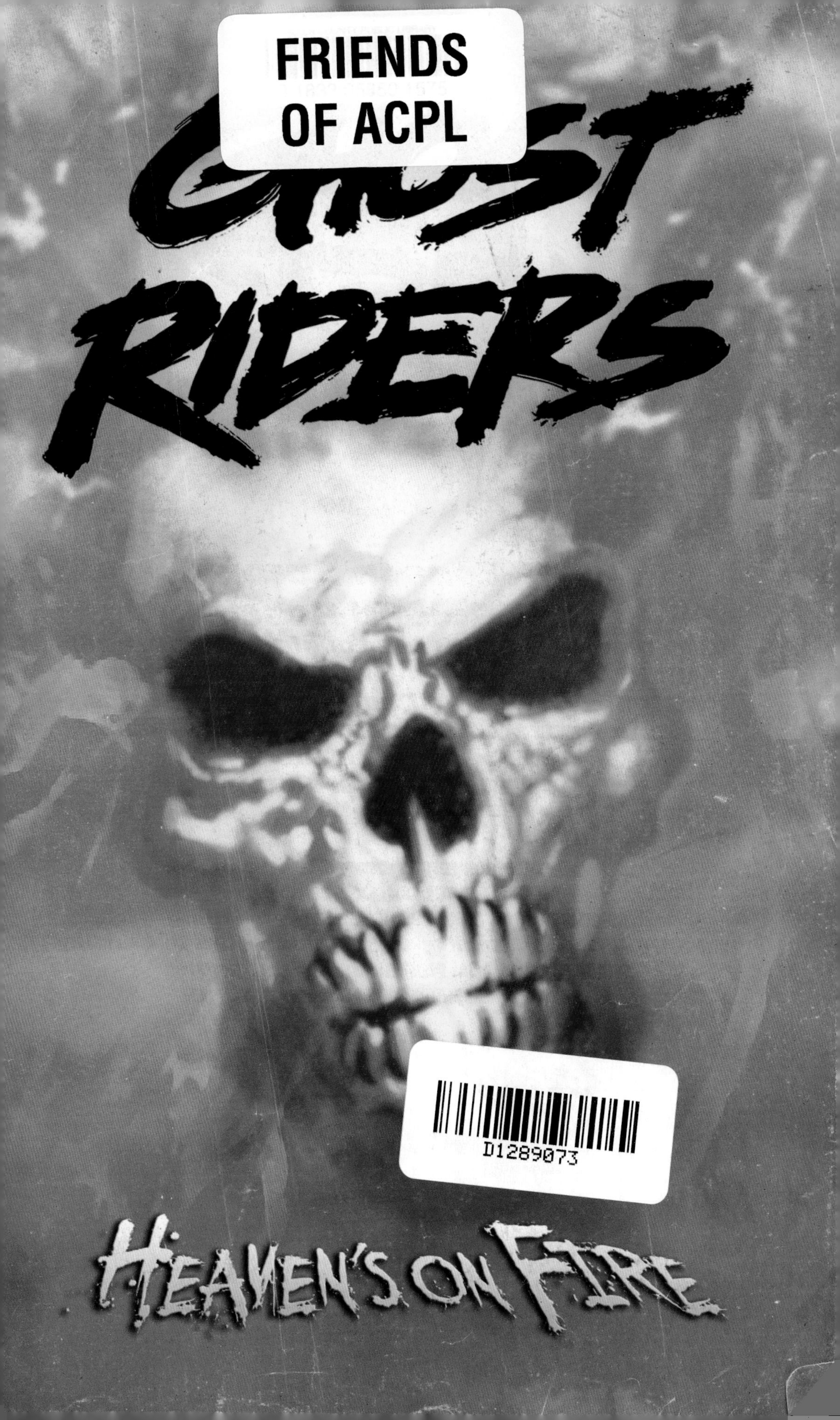
RIDERS
HEAVEN'S ON FIRE

GHOST RIDERS
HEAVEN'S ON FIRE

WRITER: **Jason Aaron**
ARTIST: **Roland Boschi**
COLORS: **Dan Brown with Lee Loughridge (Issue #6)**
LETTERER: **Virtual Calligraphy's Joe Caramagna**
COVER ARTISTS: **Jae Lee, Phil Jimenez, Das Pastoras,**
Dustin Weaver, Greg Land & Christian Nauck
EDITOR: **Sebastian Girner**
CONSULTING EDITOR: **Axel Alonso**

COLLECTION EDITOR: **Cory Levine**
ASSISTANT EDITOR: **Alex Starbuck**
ASSOCIATE EDITOR, SPECIAL PROJECTS: **John Denning**
EDITORS, SPECIAL PROJECTS: **Jennifer Grünwald & Mark D. Beazley**
SENIOR EDITOR, SPECIAL PROJECTS: **Jeff Youngquist**
SENIOR VICE PRESIDENT OF SALES: **David Gabriel**

EDITOR IN CHIEF: **Joe Quesada**
PUBLISHER: **Dan Buckley**
EXECUTIVE PRODUCER: **Alan Fine**

PREVIOUSLY:

Johnny Blaze is cursed, doomed to live life as the Ghost Rider, a brutal spirit that exists only to mete out vengeance against evil-doers. After years spent being a pawn of Hell, Blaze has recently learned that the Ghost Rider is actually a weapon of Heaven, bonded to him by the renegade angel Zadkiel. At long last, Blaze knows exactly who's responsible for ruining his life.

Johnny Blaze's brother, Danny Ketch, was recently tricked by Zadkiel into gathering together the powers of all the Ghost Riders from around the world. After Zadkiel used that power to conquer Heaven, Danny and Johnny went their separate ways. Neither of them expects the world to be around for much longer, as Zadkiel is now close to wielding ultimate power over all creation.

The odds don't look good, but that's never stopped Johnny before. With the help of Sister Sara, the last of the Caretakers, the keepers and guides of the Ghost Riders, he sets off after Zadkiel.

The only thing they've got to do is find a way to get to Heaven.

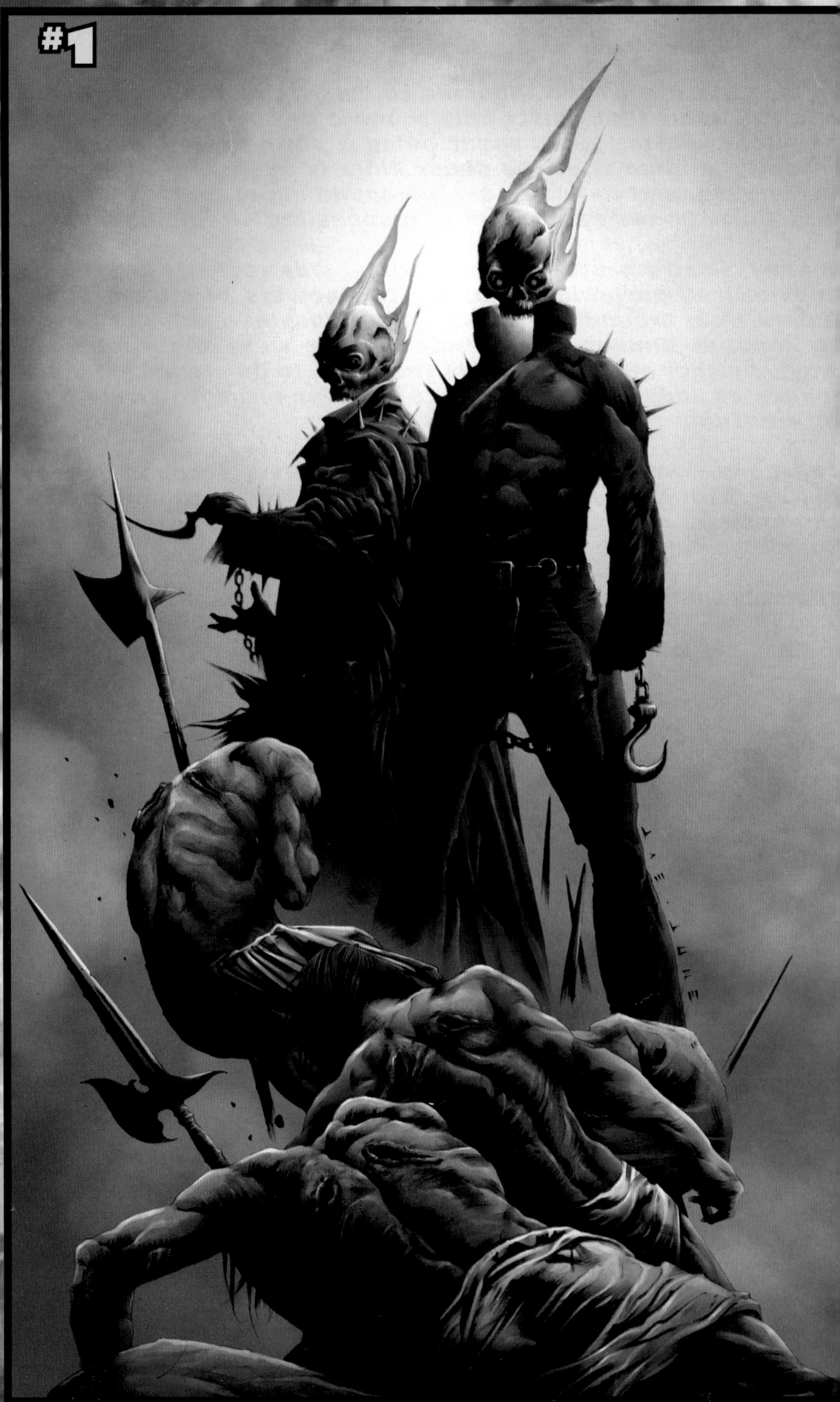
#1

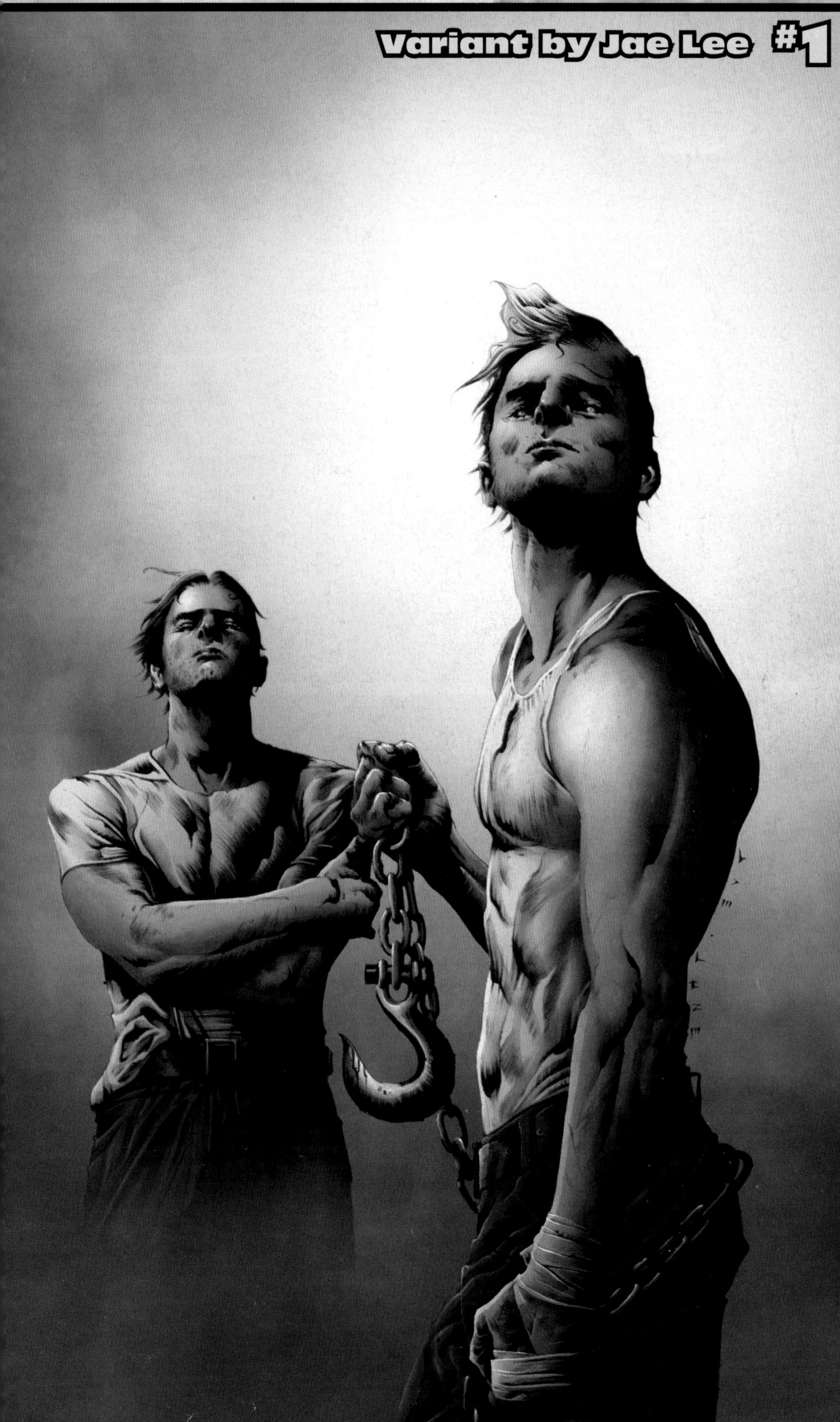
Variant by Jae Lee #1

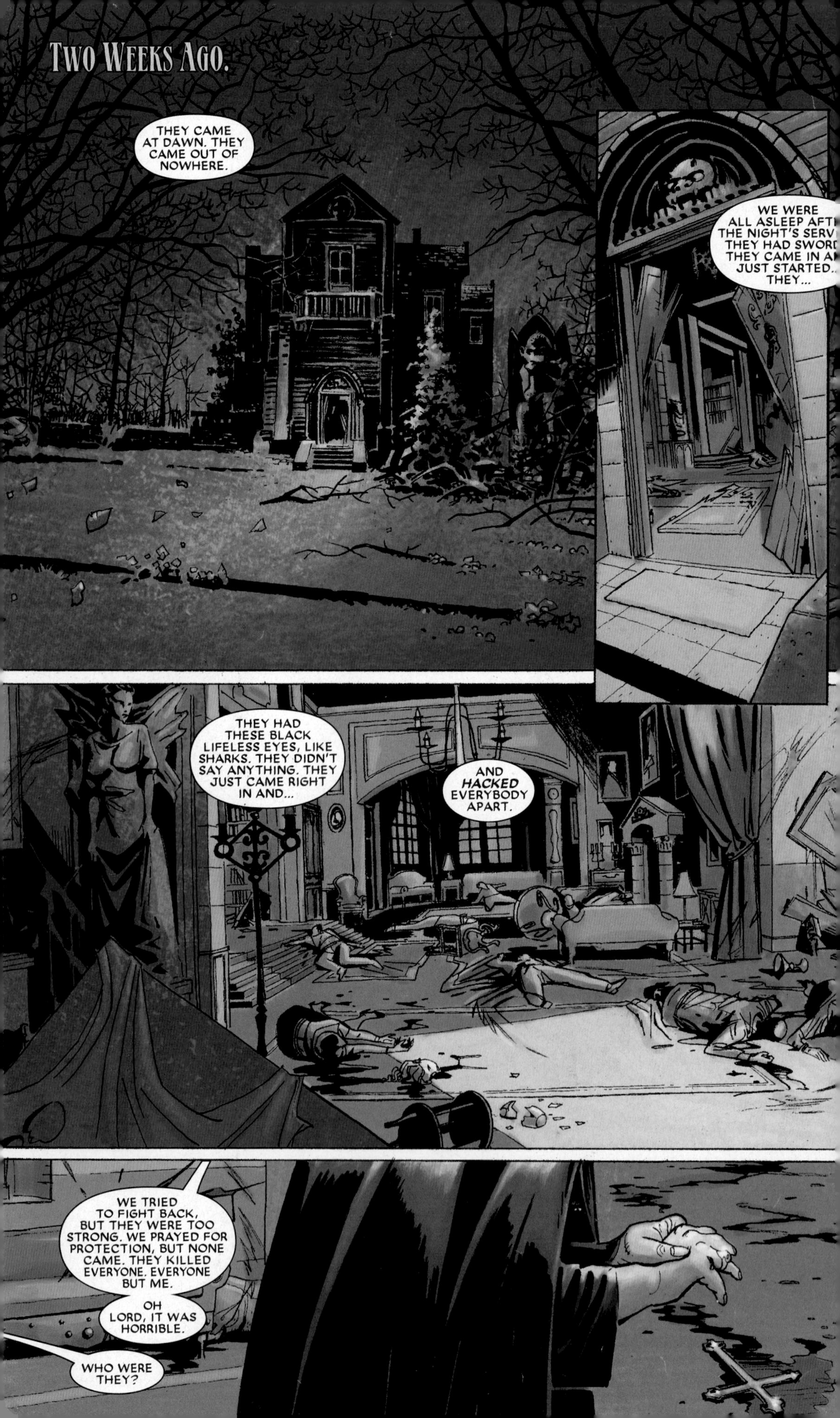
TWO WEEKS AGO.
THEY CAME AT DAWN. THEY CAME OUT OF NOWHERE.
THEY HAD THESE BLACK LIFELESS EYES, LIKE SHARKS. THEY DIDN'T SAY ANYTHING. THEY JUST CAME RIGHT IN AND...
AND *HACKED* EVERYBODY APART.
WE TRIED TO FIGHT BACK, BUT THEY WERE TOO STRONG. WE PRAYED FOR PROTECTION, BUT NONE CAME. THEY KILLED EVERYONE. EVERYONE BUT ME.
OH LORD, IT WAS HORRIBLE.
WHO WERE THEY?

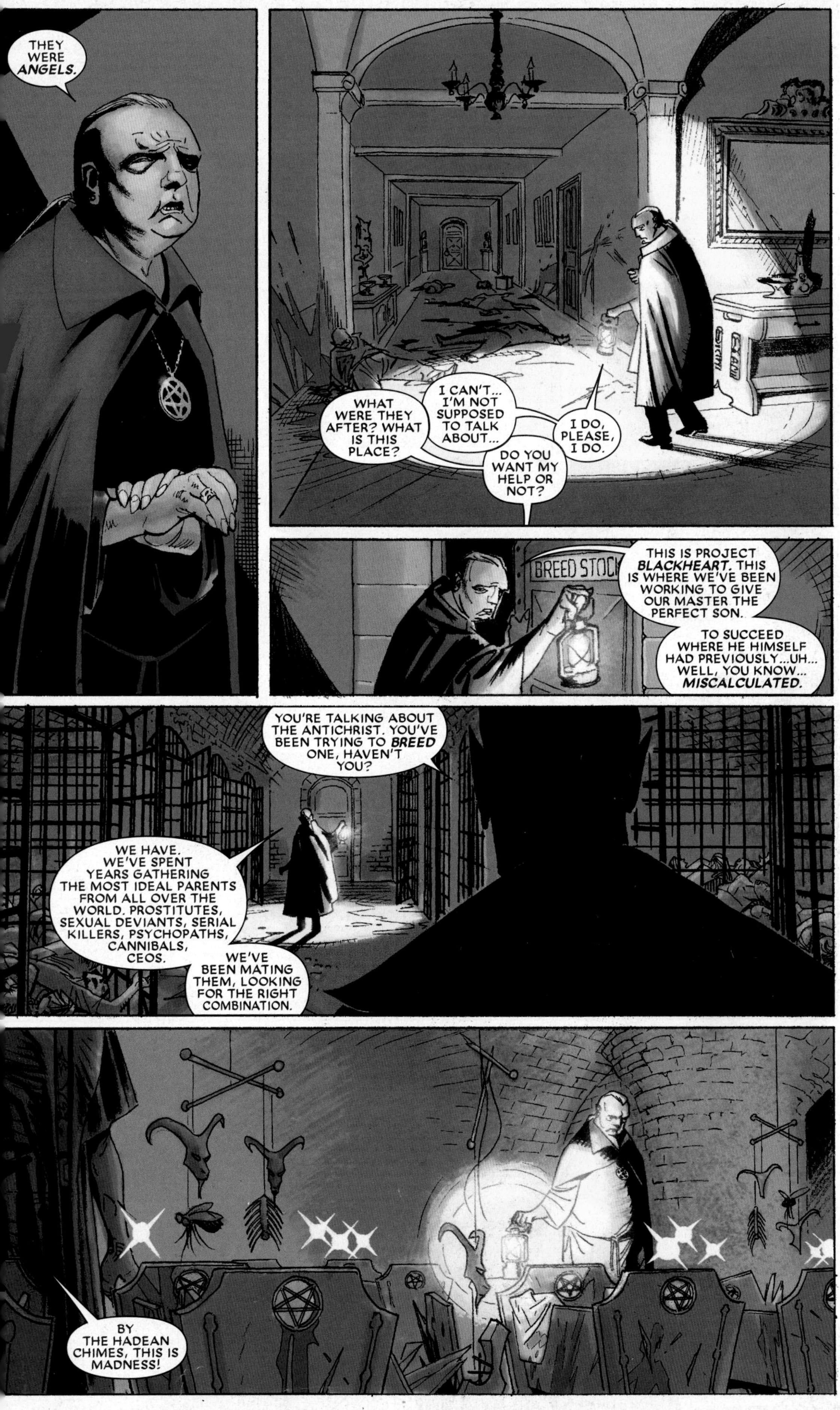
THEY WERE ANGELS.
WHAT WERE THEY AFTER? WHAT IS THIS PLACE?
I CAN'T... I'M NOT SUPPOSED TO TALK ABOUT...
I DO, PLEASE, I DO.
DO YOU WANT MY HELP OR NOT?
BREED STOCK
THIS IS PROJECT BLACKHEART. THIS IS WHERE WE'VE BEEN WORKING TO GIVE OUR MASTER THE PERFECT SON.
TO SUCCEED WHERE HE HIMSELF HAD PREVIOUSLY...UH... WELL, YOU KNOW... MISCALCULATED.
YOU'RE TALKING ABOUT THE ANTICHRIST. YOU'VE BEEN TRYING TO BREED ONE, HAVEN'T YOU?
WE HAVE. WE'VE SPENT YEARS GATHERING THE MOST IDEAL PARENTS FROM ALL OVER THE WORLD. PROSTITUTES, SEXUAL DEVIANTS, SERIAL KILLERS, PSYCHOPATHS, CANNIBALS, CEOS.
WE'VE BEEN MATING THEM, LOOKING FOR THE RIGHT COMBINATION.
BY THE HADEAN CHIMES, THIS IS MADNESS!

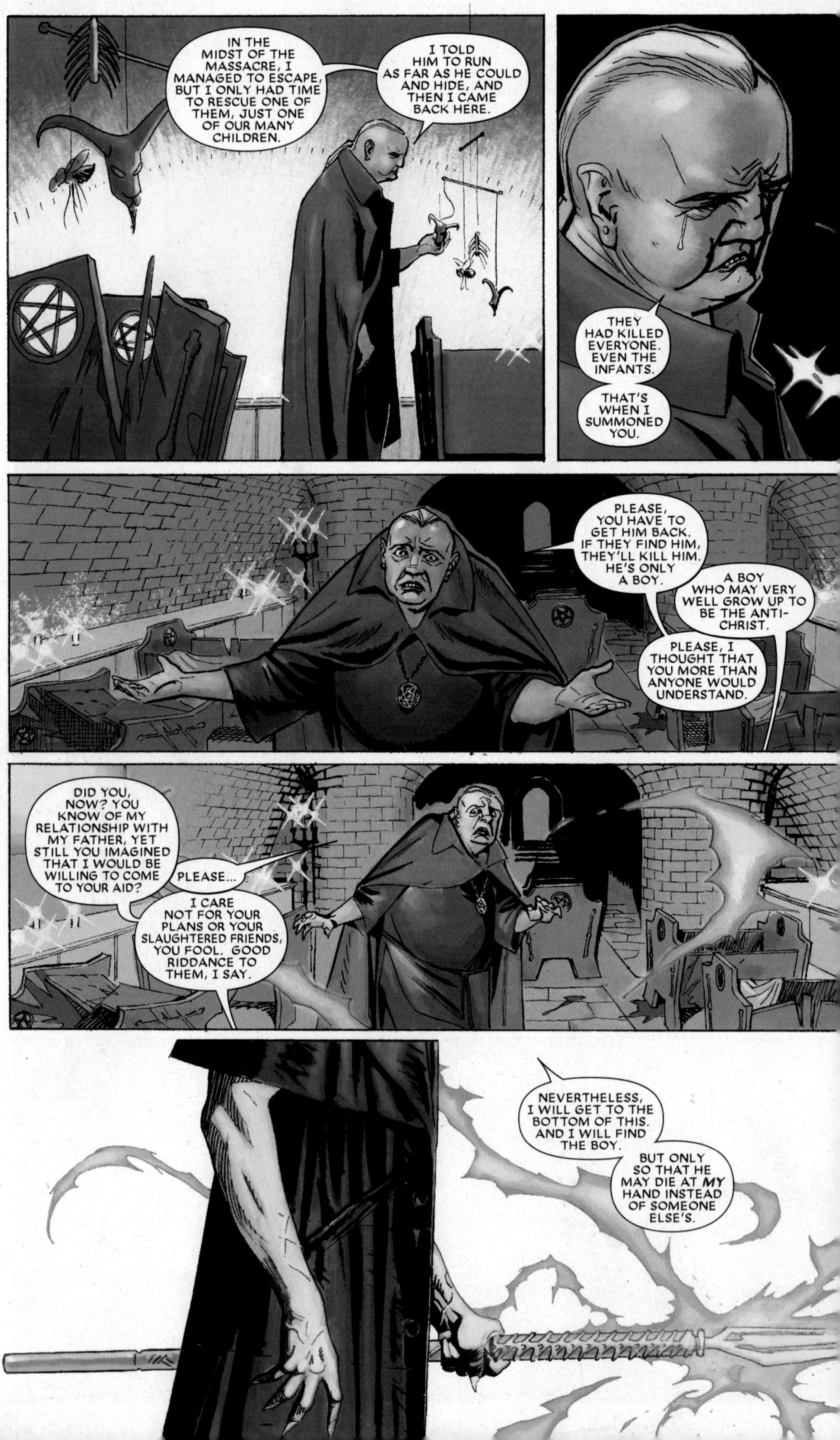
IN THE MIDST OF THE MASSACRE, I MANAGED TO ESCAPE, BUT I ONLY HAD TIME TO RESCUE ONE OF THEM, JUST ONE OF OUR MANY CHILDREN.
I TOLD HIM TO RUN AS FAR AS HE COULD AND HIDE, AND THEN I CAME BACK HERE.
THEY HAD KILLED EVERYONE. EVEN THE INFANTS.
THAT'S WHEN I SUMMONED YOU.
PLEASE, YOU HAVE TO GET HIM BACK. IF THEY FIND HIM, THEY'LL KILL HIM. HE'S ONLY A BOY.
A BOY WHO MAY VERY WELL GROW UP TO BE THE ANTI-CHRIST.
PLEASE, I THOUGHT THAT YOU MORE THAN ANYONE WOULD UNDERSTAND.
DID YOU, NOW? YOU KNOW OF MY RELATIONSHIP WITH MY FATHER, YET STILL YOU IMAGINED THAT I WOULD BE WILLING TO COME TO YOUR AID?
PLEASE...
I CARE NOT FOR YOUR PLANS OR YOUR SLAUGHTERED FRIENDS, YOU FOOL. GOOD RIDDANCE TO THEM, I SAY.
NEVERTHELESS, I WILL GET TO THE BOTTOM OF THIS. AND I WILL FIND THE BOY.
BUT ONLY SO THAT HE MAY DIE AT MY HAND INSTEAD OF SOMEONE ELSE'S.

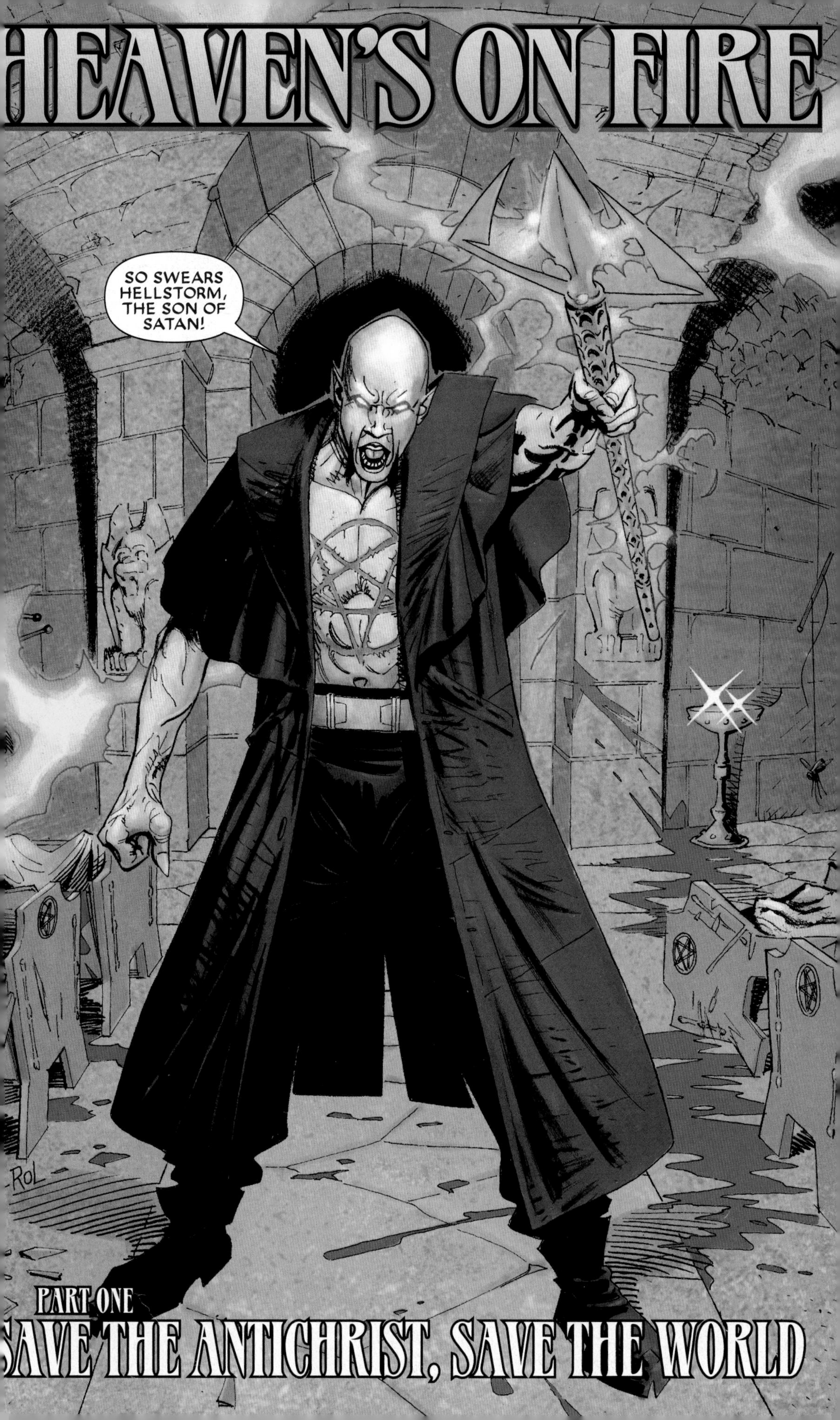
HEAVEN'S ON FIRE
SO SWEARS HELLSTORM, THE SON OF SATAN!
ROL
PART ONE
SAVE THE ANTICHRIST, SAVE THE WORLD

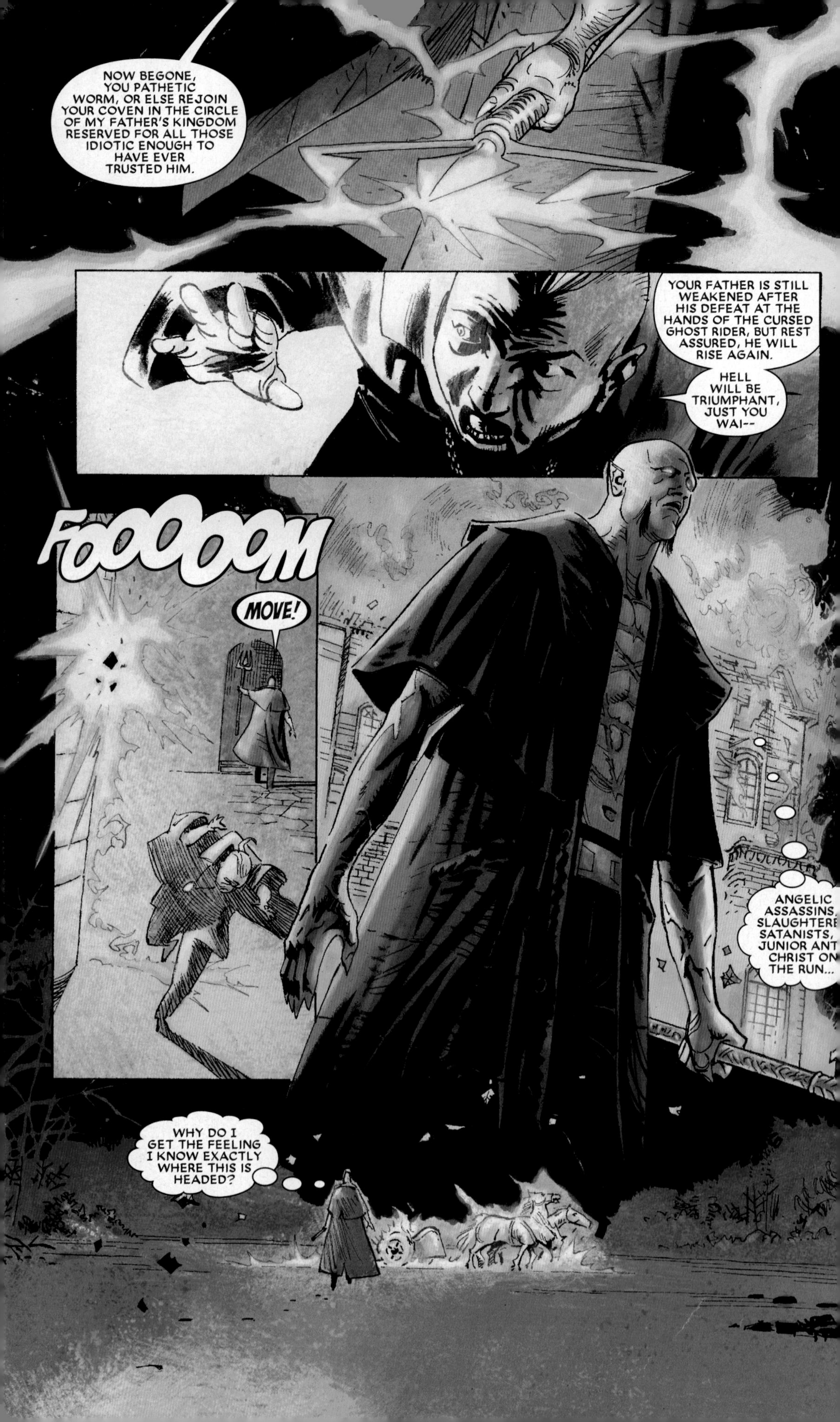
NOW BEGONE, YOU PATHETIC WORM, OR ELSE REJOIN YOUR COVEN IN THE CIRCLE OF MY FATHER'S KINGDOM RESERVED FOR ALL THOSE IDIOTIC ENOUGH TO HAVE EVER TRUSTED HIM.
YOUR FATHER IS STILL WEAKENED AFTER HIS DEFEAT AT THE HANDS OF THE CURSED GHOST RIDER, BUT REST ASSURED, HE WILL RISE AGAIN.
HELL WILL BE TRIUMPHANT, JUST YOU WAI--
FOOOOOM
MOVE!
ANGELIC ASSASSINS, SLAUGHTERE SATANISTS, JUNIOR ANT CHRIST ON THE RUN...
WHY DO I GET THE FEELING I KNOW EXACTLY WHERE THIS IS HEADED?

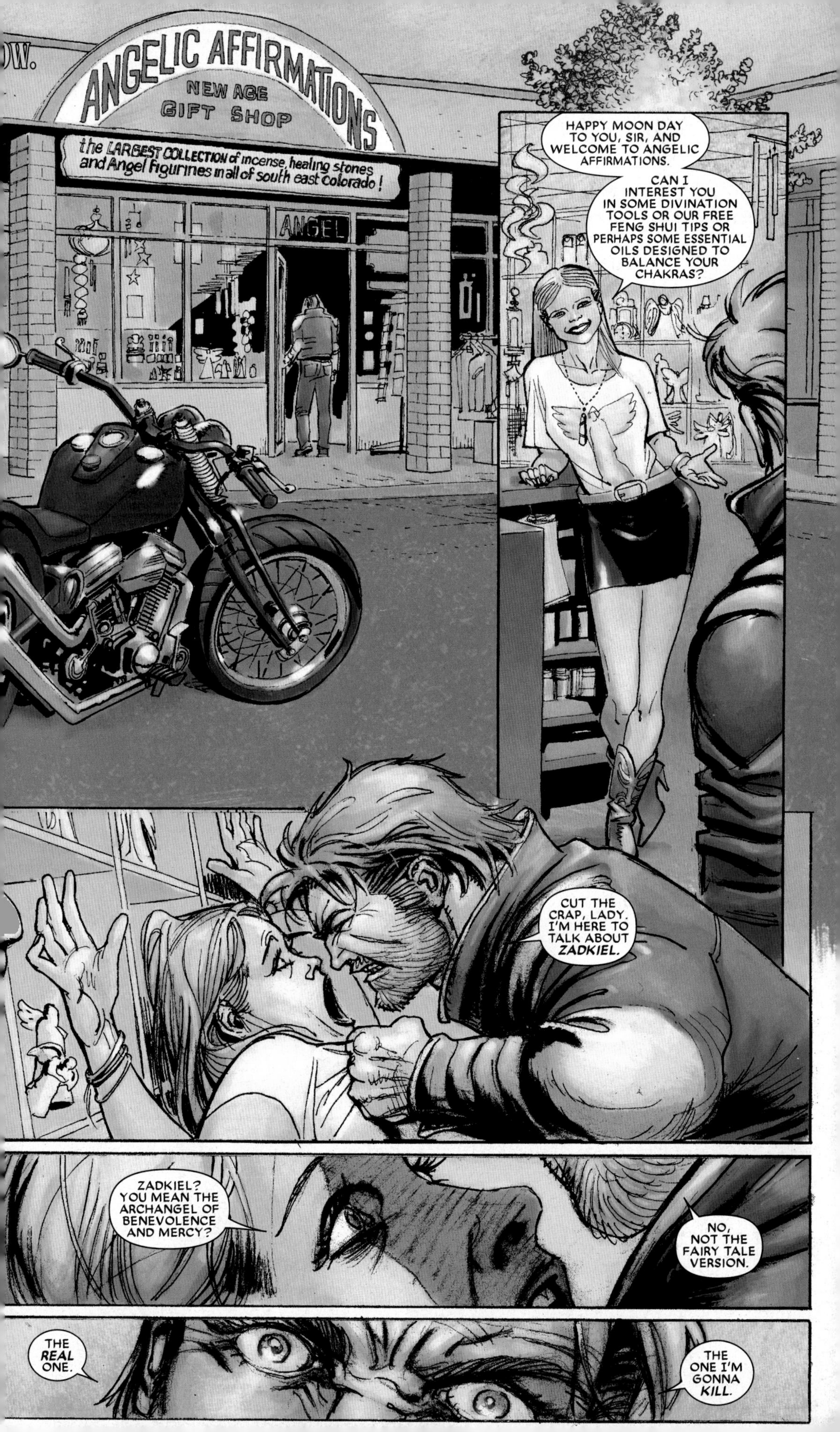

ANGELIC AFFIRMATIONS
NEW AGE GIFT SHOP
the LARGEST COLLECTION of incense, healing stones and Angel figurines in all of south east colorado!
ANGEL
HAPPY MOON DAY TO YOU, SIR, AND WELCOME TO ANGELIC AFFIRMATIONS.
CAN I INTEREST YOU IN SOME DIVINATION TOOLS OR OUR FREE FENG SHUI TIPS OR PERHAPS SOME ESSENTIAL OILS DESIGNED TO BALANCE YOUR CHAKRAS?
CUT THE CRAP, LADY. I'M HERE TO TALK ABOUT ZADKIEL.
ZADKIEL? YOU MEAN THE ARCHANGEL OF BENEVOLENCE AND MERCY?
NO, NOT THE FAIRY TALE VERSION.
THE REAL ONE.
THE ONE I'M GONNA KILL.

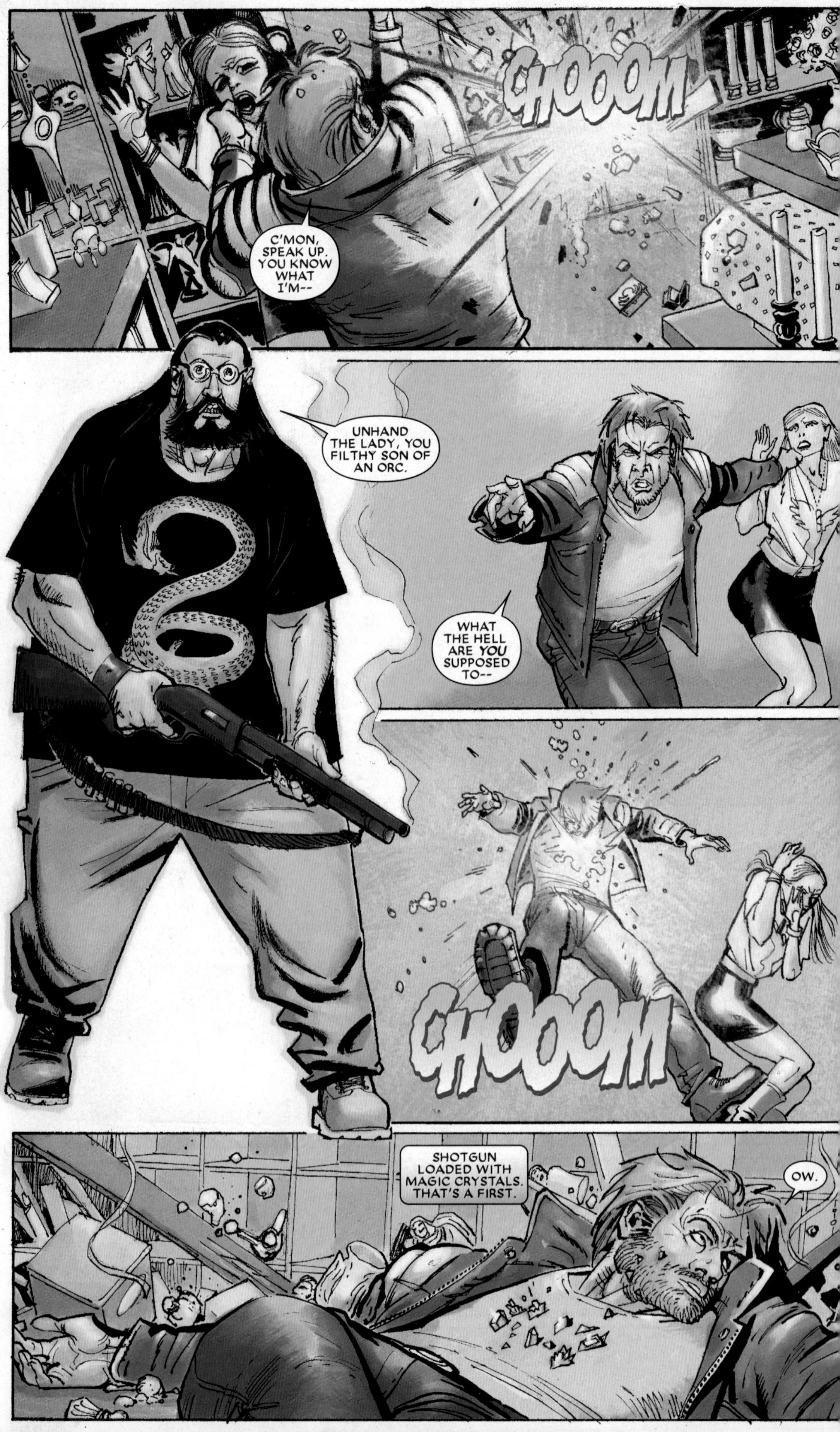
CHOOOM
C'MON, SPEAK UP. YOU KNOW WHAT I'M--
UNHAND THE LADY, YOU FILTHY SON OF AN ORC.
WHAT THE HELL ARE *YOU* SUPPOSED TO--
CHOOOM
SHOTGUN LOADED WITH MAGIC CRYSTALS. THAT'S A FIRST.
OW.

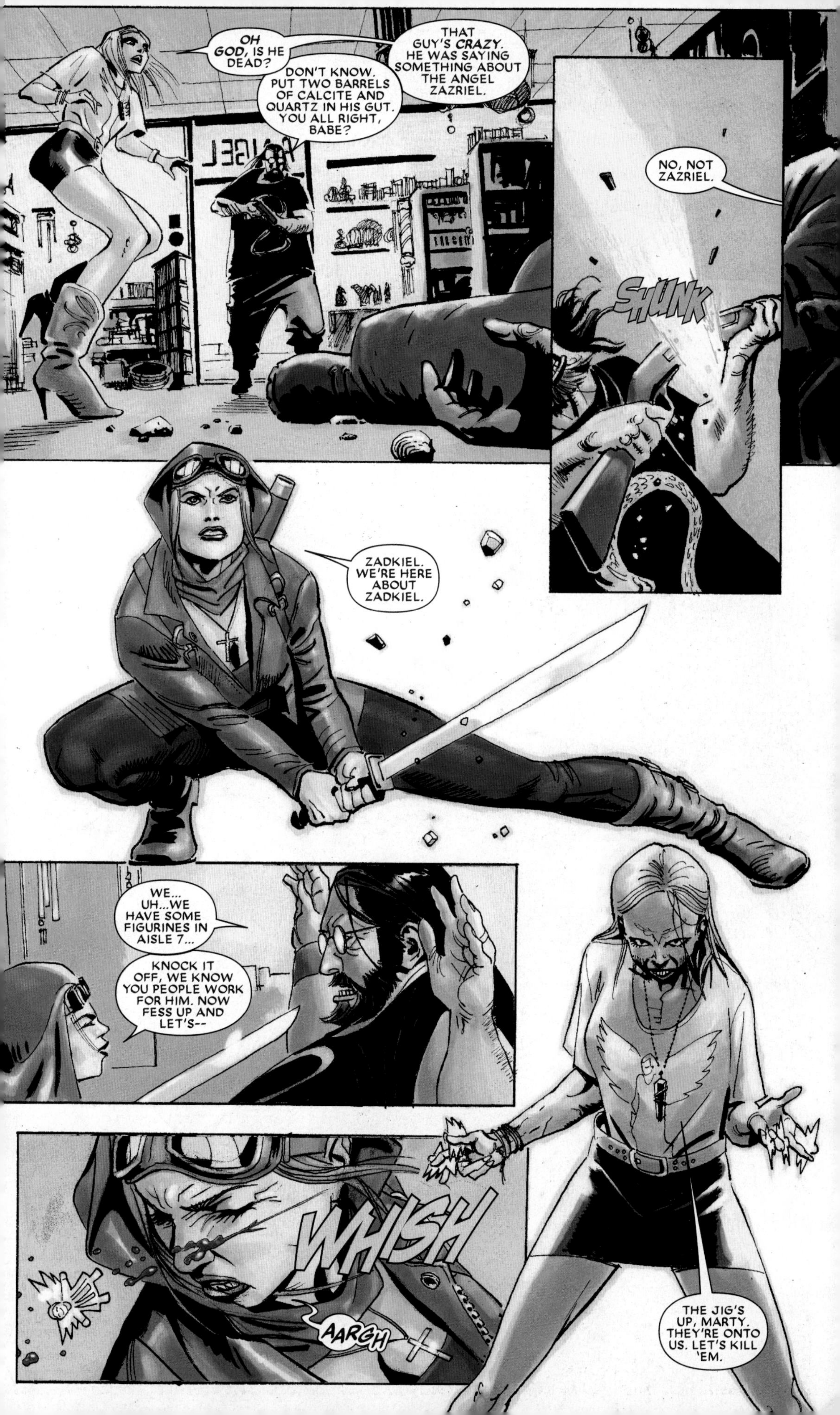
OH GOD, IS HE DEAD?
THAT GUY'S CRAZY. HE WAS SAYING SOMETHING ABOUT THE ANGEL ZAZRIEL.
DON'T KNOW. PUT TWO BARRELS OF CALCITE AND QUARTZ IN HIS GUT. YOU ALL RIGHT, BABE?
NO, NOT ZAZRIEL.
SHUNK
ZADKIEL. WE'RE HERE ABOUT ZADKIEL.
WE... UH...WE HAVE SOME FIGURINES IN AISLE 7...
KNOCK IT OFF, WE KNOW YOU PEOPLE WORK FOR HIM. NOW FESS UP AND LET'S--
WHISH
AARGH
THE JIG'S UP, MARTY. THEY'RE ONTO US. LET'S KILL 'EM.

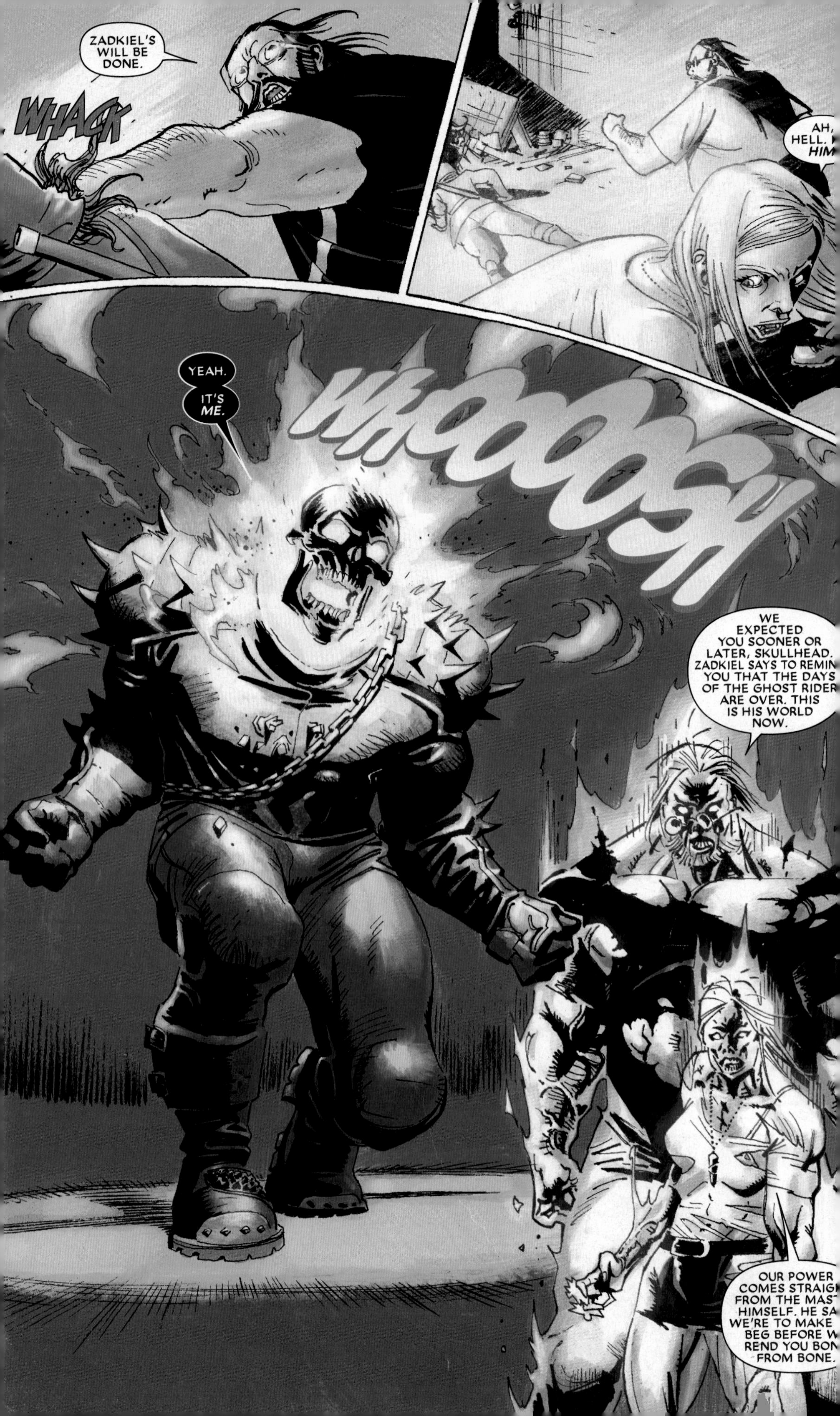
ZADKIEL'S WILL BE DONE.
WHACK
AH, HELL. HIM
YEAH.
IT'S ME.
WHOOOSH
WE EXPECTED YOU SOONER OR LATER, SKULLHEAD. ZADKIEL SAYS TO REMIN YOU THAT THE DAYS OF THE GHOST RIDER ARE OVER. THIS IS HIS WORLD NOW.
OUR POWER COMES STRAIG FROM THE MAS HIMSELF. HE SA WE'RE TO MAKE BEG BEFORE W REND YOU BON FROM BONE.

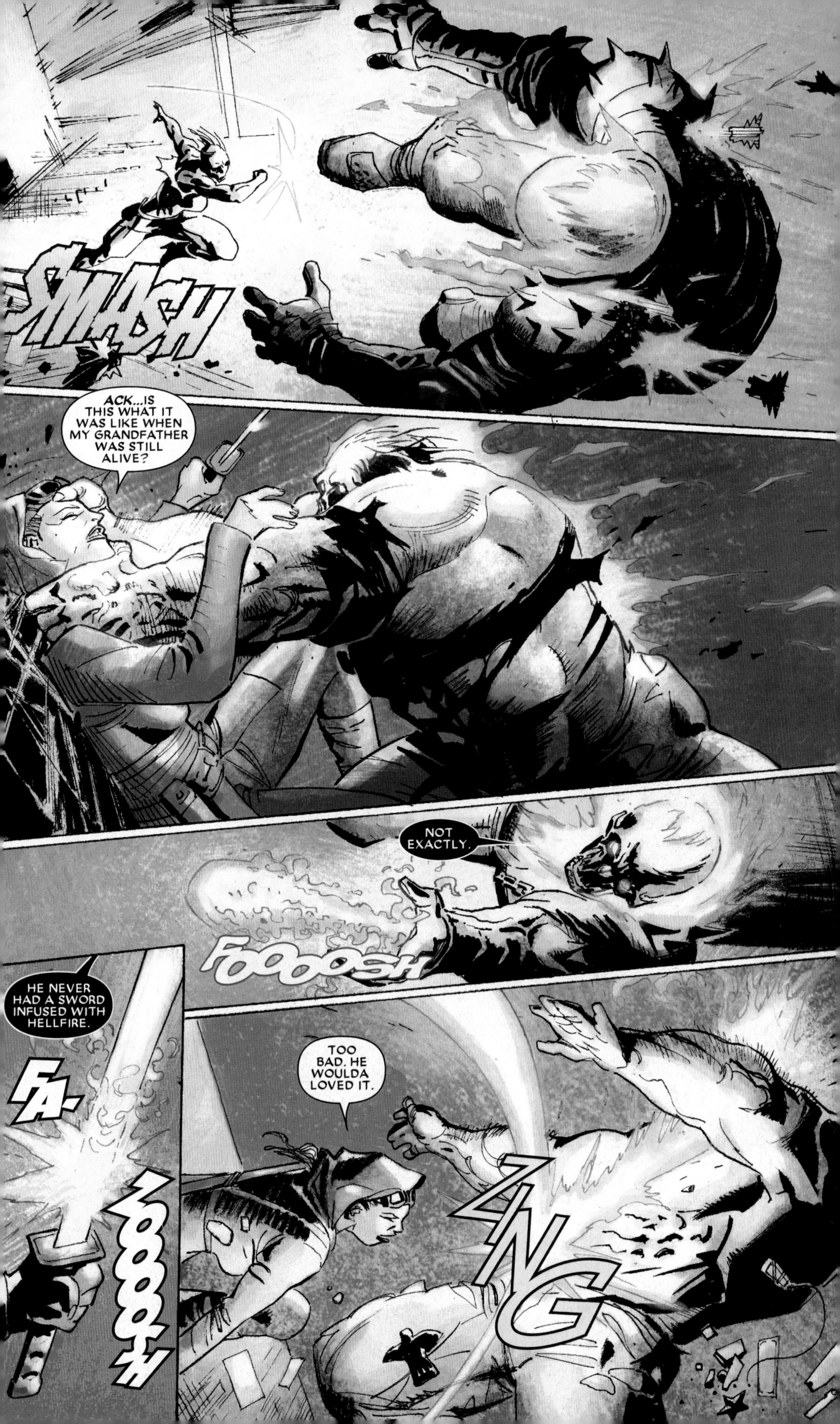
SMASH
ACK...IS THIS WHAT IT WAS LIKE WHEN MY GRANDFATHER WAS STILL ALIVE?
NOT EXACTLY.
FOOOOSH
HE NEVER HAD A SWORD INFUSED WITH HELLFIRE.
TOO BAD. HE WOULDA LOVED IT.
FA-WOOOOSH
ZING

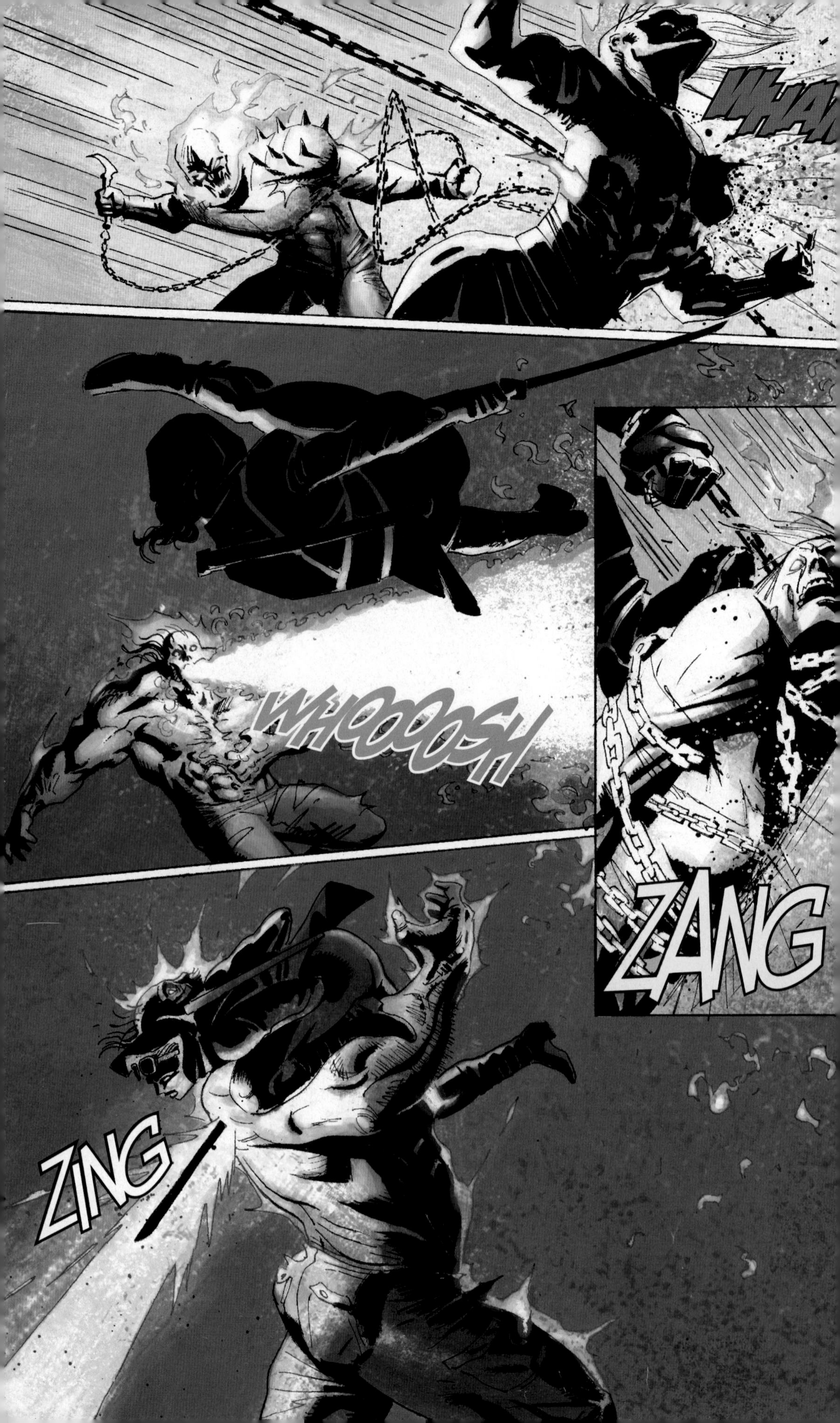
WHAM
WHOOOOSH
ZANG
ZING

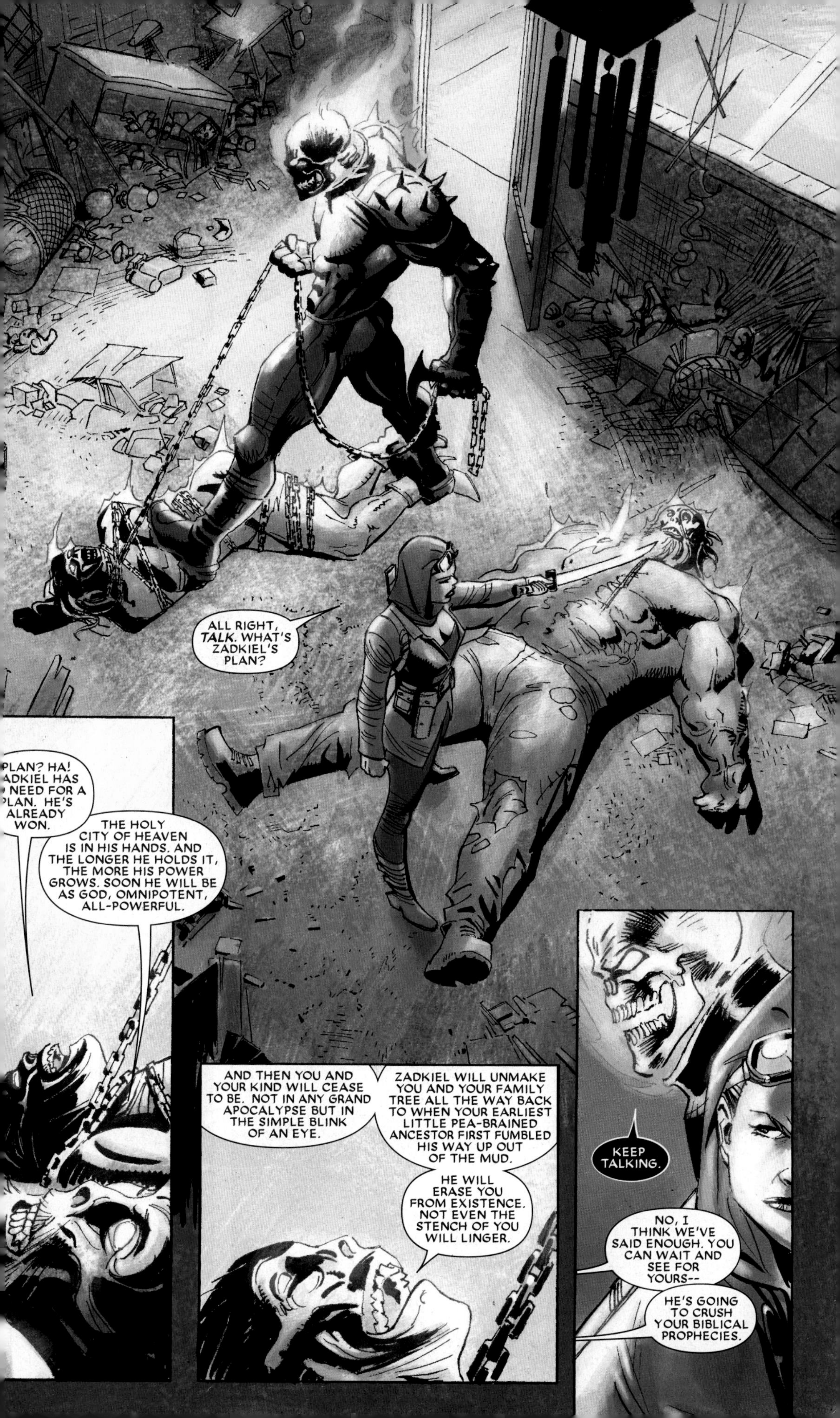
ALL RIGHT, TALK. WHAT'S ZADKIEL'S PLAN?
PLAN? HA! ADKIEL HAS NEED FOR A PLAN. HE'S ALREADY WON.
THE HOLY CITY OF HEAVEN IS IN HIS HANDS. AND THE LONGER HE HOLDS IT, THE MORE HIS POWER GROWS. SOON HE WILL BE AS GOD, OMNIPOTENT, ALL-POWERFUL.
AND THEN YOU AND YOUR KIND WILL CEASE TO BE. NOT IN ANY GRAND APOCALYPSE BUT IN THE SIMPLE BLINK OF AN EYE.
ZADKIEL WILL UNMAKE YOU AND YOUR FAMILY TREE ALL THE WAY BACK TO WHEN YOUR EARLIEST LITTLE PEA-BRAINED ANCESTOR FIRST FUMBLED HIS WAY UP OUT OF THE MUD.
HE WILL ERASE YOU FROM EXISTENCE. NOT EVEN THE STENCH OF YOU WILL LINGER.
KEEP TALKING.
NO, I THINK WE'VE SAID ENOUGH. YOU CAN WAIT AND SEE FOR YOURS--
HE'S GOING TO CRUSH YOUR BIBLICAL PROPHECIES.

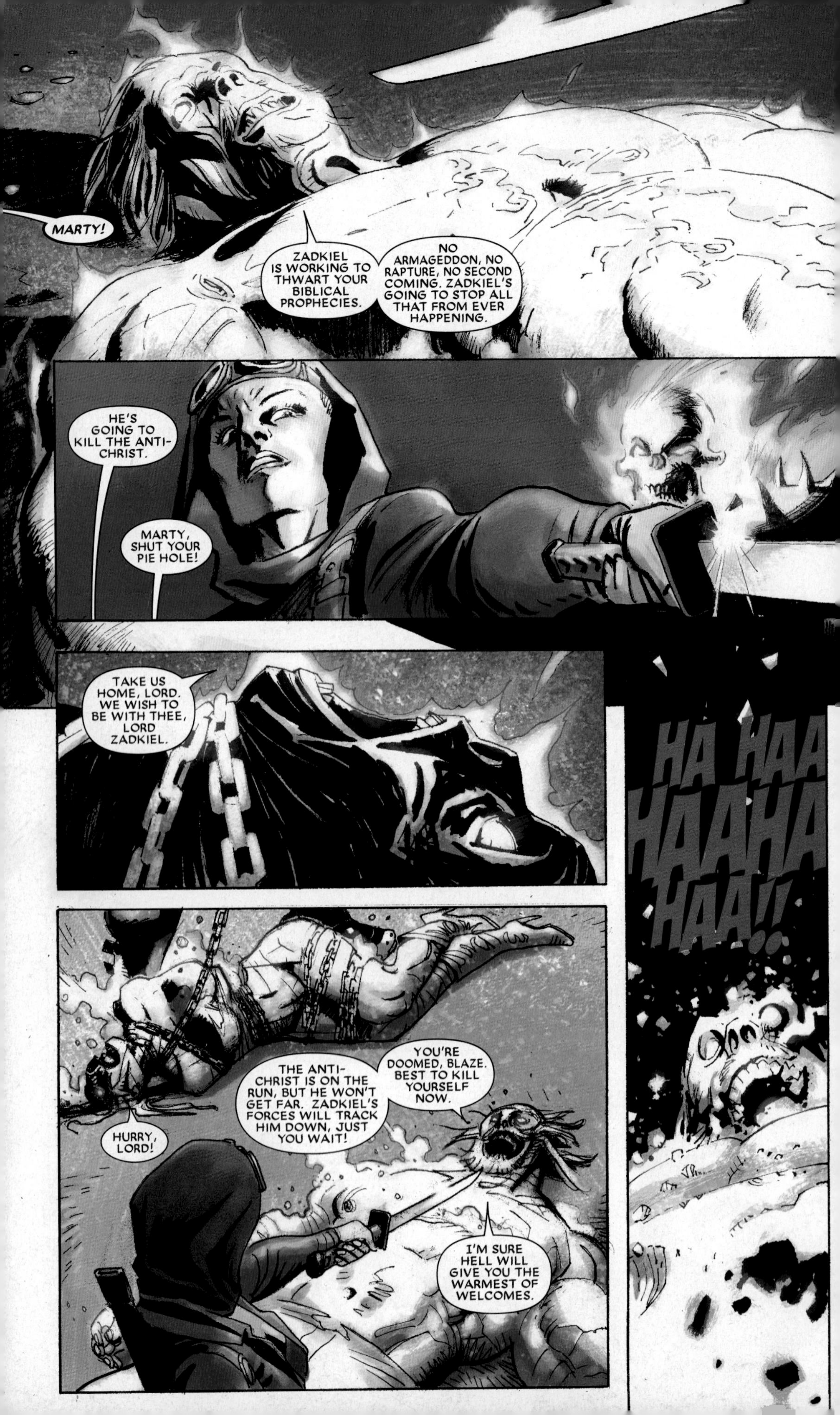
MARTY!
ZADKIEL IS WORKING TO THWART YOUR BIBLICAL PROPHECIES.
NO ARMAGEDDON, NO RAPTURE, NO SECOND COMING. ZADKIEL'S GOING TO STOP ALL THAT FROM EVER HAPPENING.
HE'S GOING TO KILL THE ANTI-CHRIST.
MARTY, SHUT YOUR PIE HOLE!
TAKE US HOME, LORD. WE WISH TO BE WITH THEE, LORD ZADKIEL.
HA HAA HAAHA HAA!!
HURRY, LORD!
THE ANTI-CHRIST IS ON THE RUN, BUT HE WON'T GET FAR. ZADKIEL'S FORCES WILL TRACK HIM DOWN, JUST YOU WAIT!
YOU'RE DOOMED, BLAZE. BEST TO KILL YOURSELF NOW.
I'M SURE HELL WILL GIVE YOU THE WARMEST OF WELCOMES.

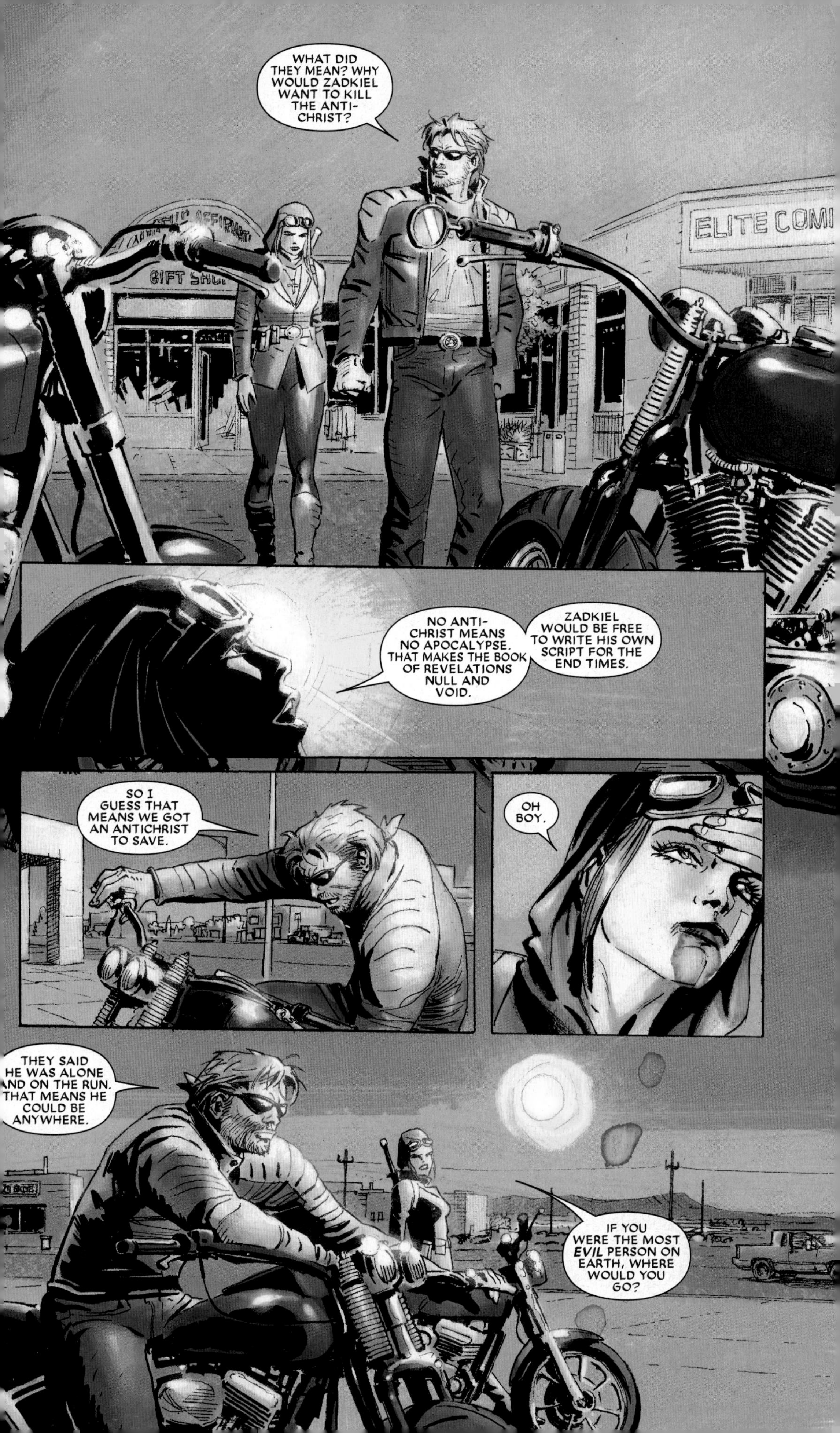
WHAT DID THEY MEAN? WHY WOULD ZADKIEL WANT TO KILL THE ANTI-CHRIST?
ELITE COMI
GIFT SHO
NO ANTI-CHRIST MEANS NO APOCALYPSE. THAT MAKES THE BOOK OF REVELATIONS NULL AND VOID.
ZADKIEL WOULD BE FREE TO WRITE HIS OWN SCRIPT FOR THE END TIMES.
SO I GUESS THAT MEANS WE GOT AN ANTICHRIST TO SAVE.
OH BOY.
THEY SAID HE WAS ALONE AND ON THE RUN. THAT MEANS HE COULD BE ANYWHERE.
IF YOU WERE THE MOST *EVIL* PERSON ON EARTH, WHERE WOULD YOU GO?

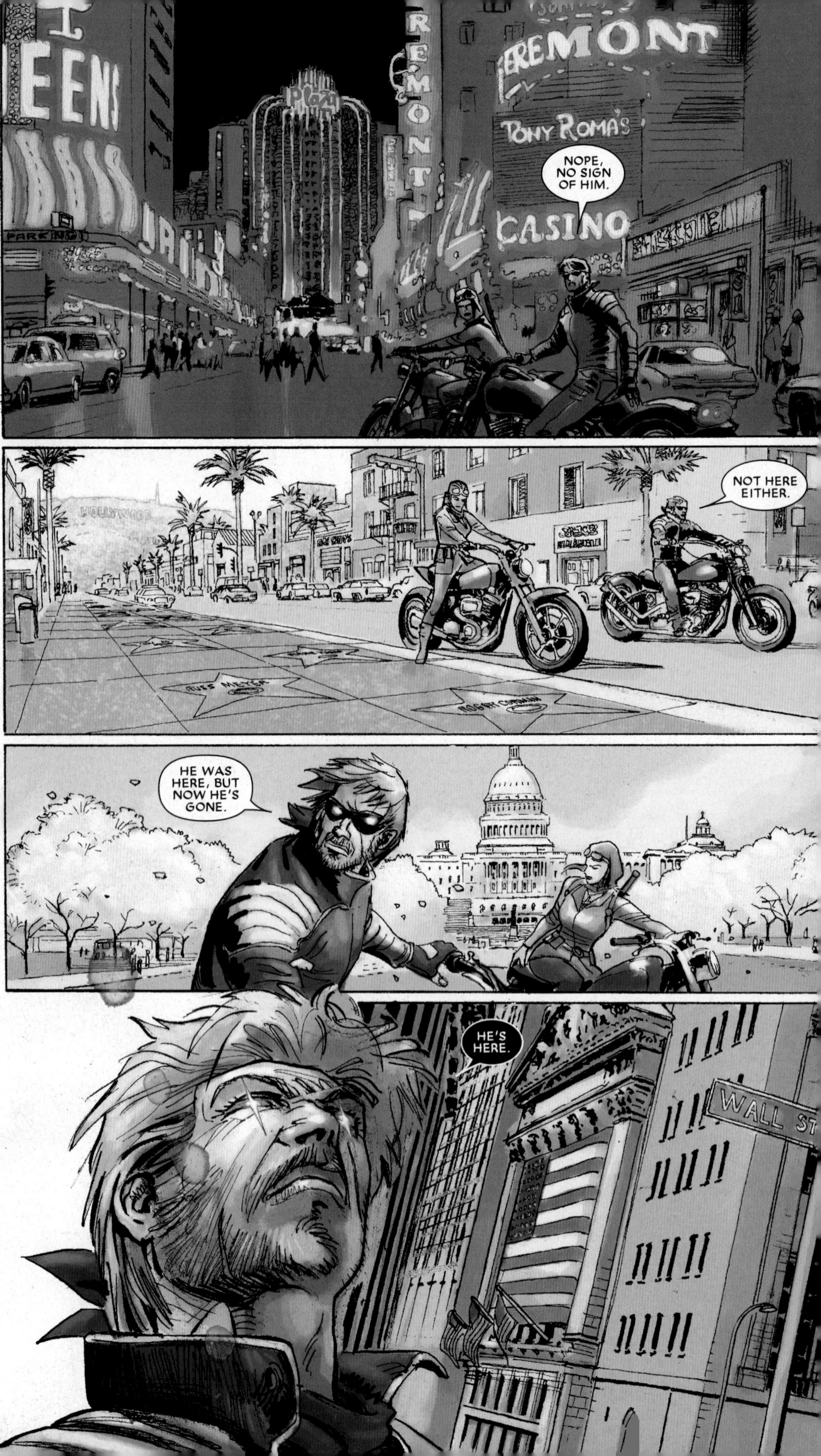

FREMONT
TONY ROMA'S
CASINO
NOPE, NO SIGN OF HIM.
NOT HERE EITHER.
HE WAS HERE, BUT NOW HE'S GONE.
HE'S HERE.
WALL ST

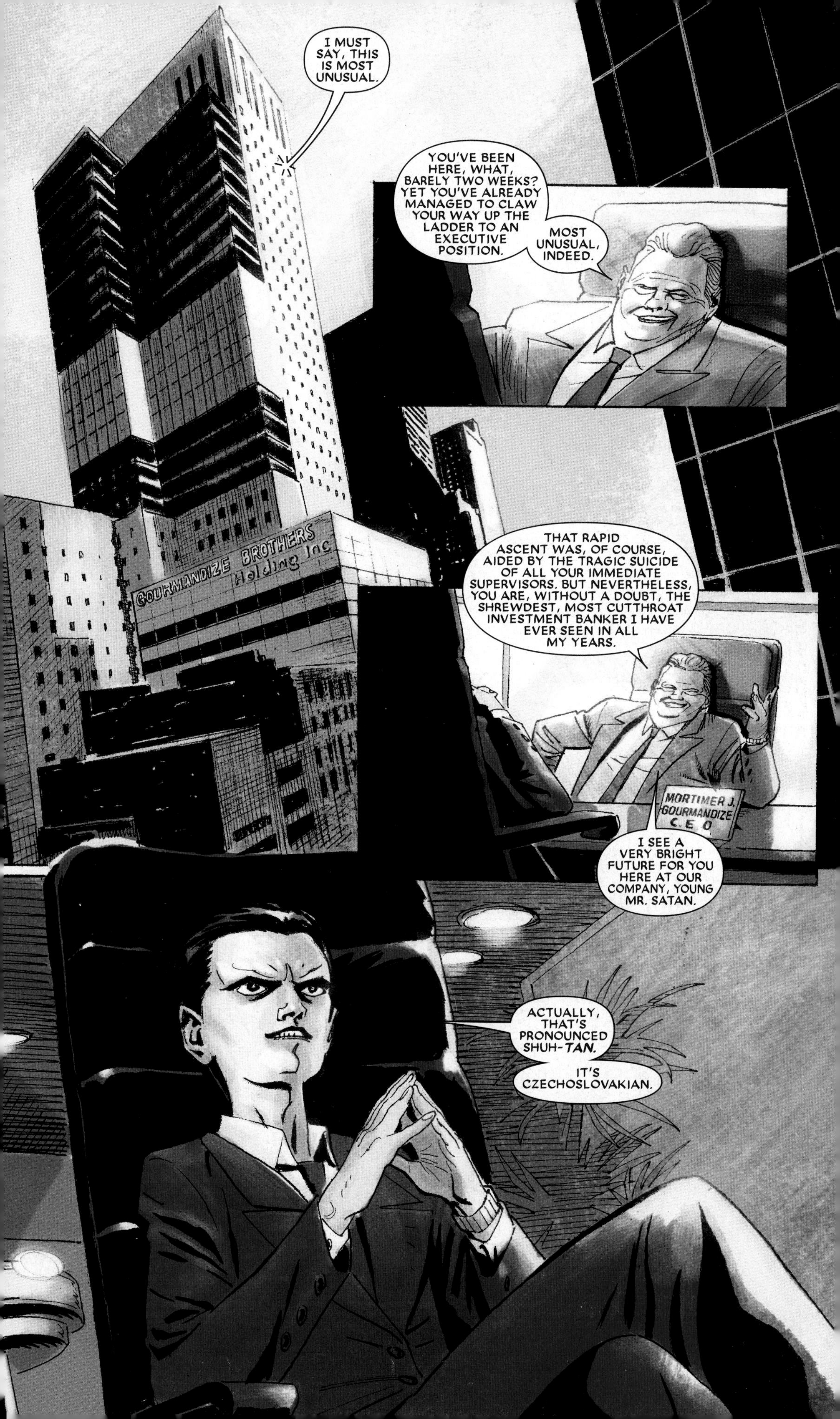
I MUST SAY, THIS IS MOST UNUSUAL.
YOU'VE BEEN HERE, WHAT, BARELY TWO WEEKS? YET YOU'VE ALREADY MANAGED TO CLAW YOUR WAY UP THE LADDER TO AN EXECUTIVE POSITION.
MOST UNUSUAL, INDEED.
GOURMANDIZE BROTHERS Holding Inc
THAT RAPID ASCENT WAS, OF COURSE, AIDED BY THE TRAGIC SUICIDE OF ALL YOUR IMMEDIATE SUPERVISORS. BUT NEVERTHELESS, YOU ARE, WITHOUT A DOUBT, THE SHREWDEST, MOST CUTTHROAT INVESTMENT BANKER I HAVE EVER SEEN IN ALL MY YEARS.
MORTIMER J. GOURMANDIZE C.E.O.
I SEE A VERY BRIGHT FUTURE FOR YOU HERE AT OUR COMPANY, YOUNG MR. SATAN.
ACTUALLY, THAT'S PRONOUNCED SHUH-*TAN.*
IT'S CZECHOSLOVAKIAN.

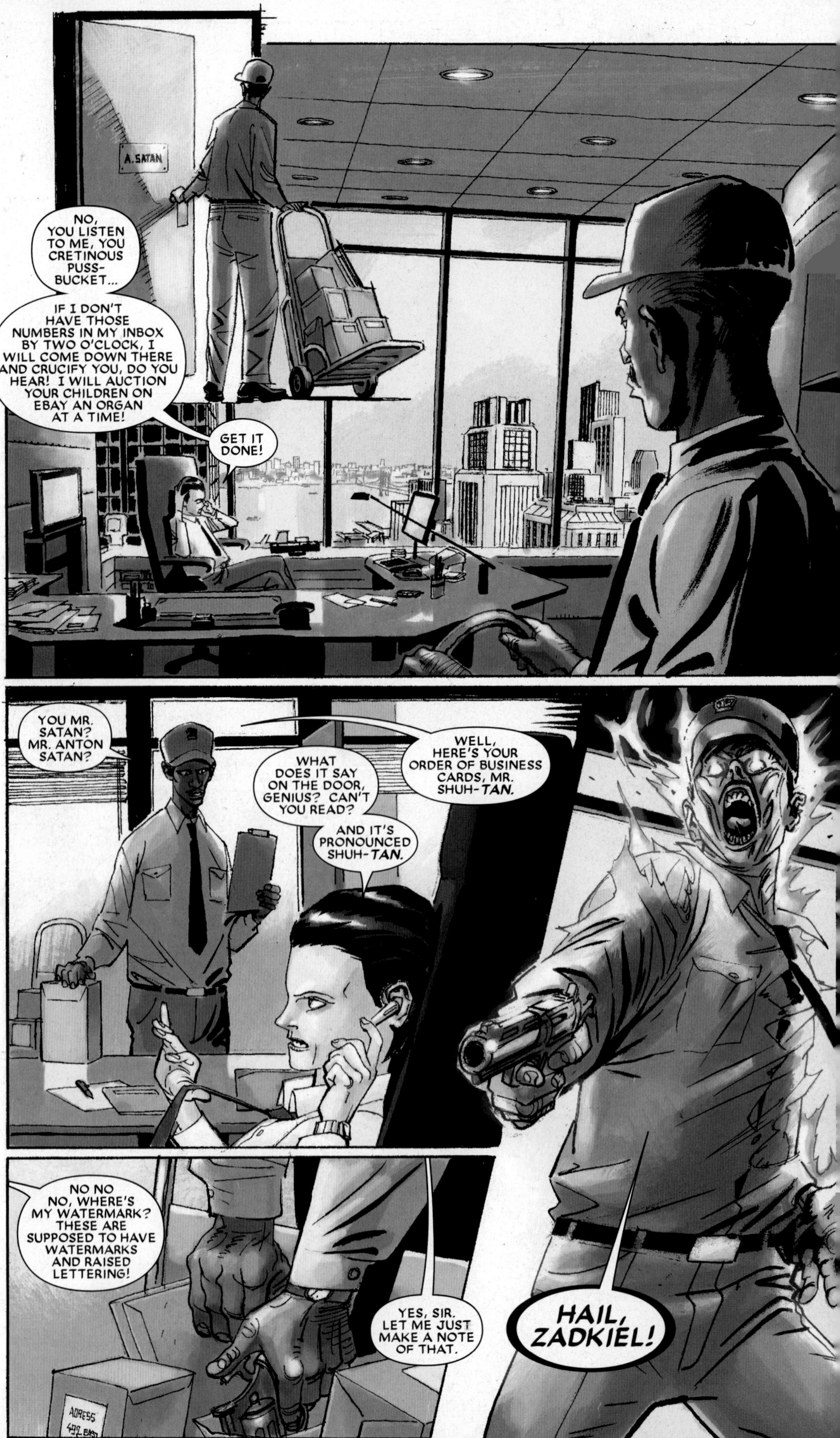

A. SATAN
NO, YOU LISTEN TO ME, YOU CRETINOUS PUSS-BUCKET...
IF I DON'T HAVE THOSE NUMBERS IN MY INBOX BY TWO O'CLOCK, I WILL COME DOWN THERE AND CRUCIFY YOU, DO YOU HEAR! I WILL AUCTION YOUR CHILDREN ON EBAY AN ORGAN AT A TIME!
GET IT DONE!
YOU MR. SATAN? MR. ANTON SATAN?
WHAT DOES IT SAY ON THE DOOR, GENIUS? CAN'T YOU READ?
AND IT'S PRONOUNCED SHUH-TAN.
WELL, HERE'S YOUR ORDER OF BUSINESS CARDS, MR. SHUH-TAN.
NO NO NO, WHERE'S MY WATERMARK? THESE ARE SUPPOSED TO HAVE WATERMARKS AND RAISED LETTERING!
YES, SIR. LET ME JUST MAKE A NOTE OF THAT.
HAIL, ZADKIEL!

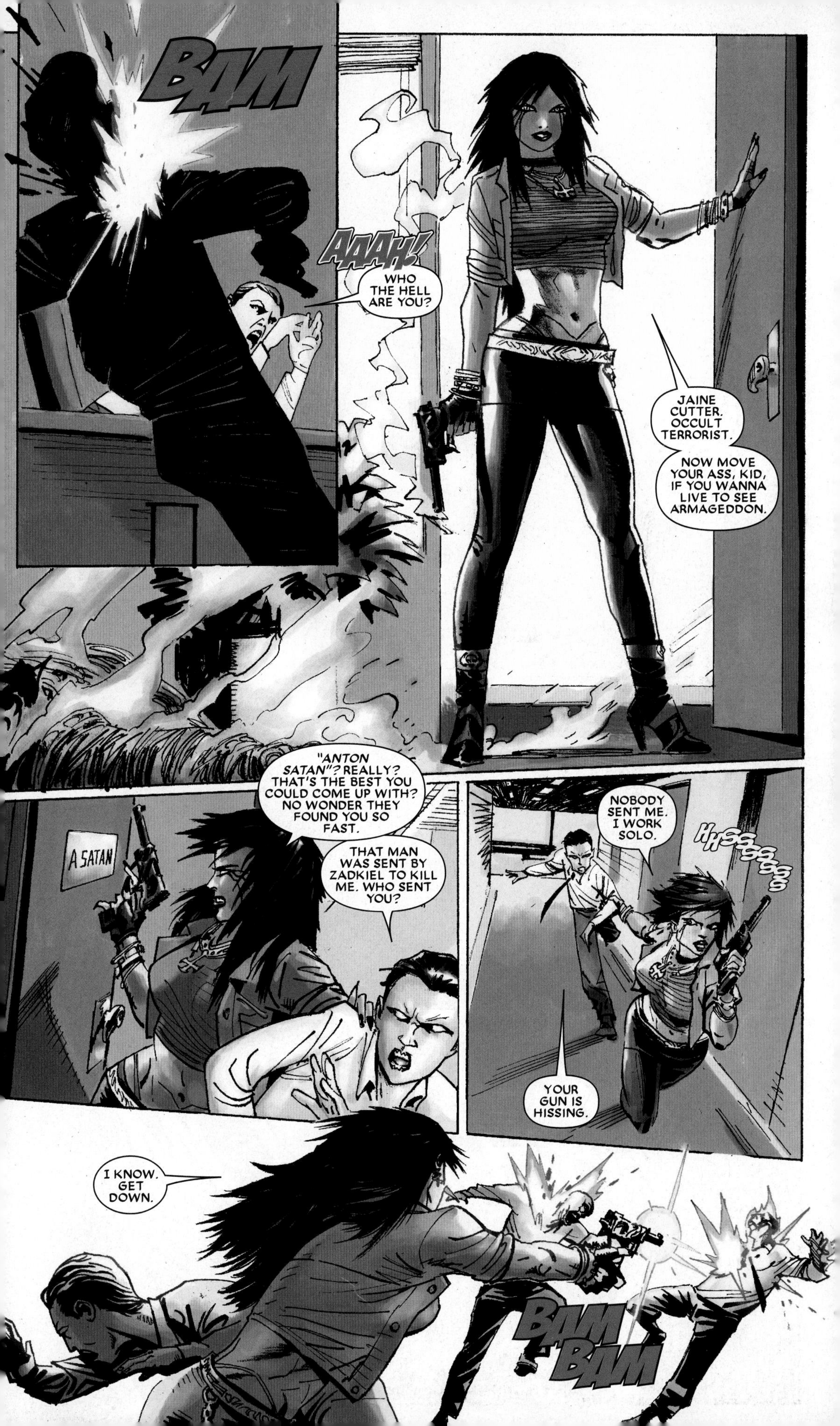
BAM
AAAH!
WHO THE HELL ARE YOU?
JAINE CUTTER. OCCULT TERRORIST.
NOW MOVE YOUR ASS, KID, IF YOU WANNA LIVE TO SEE ARMAGEDDON.
A SATAN
"ANTON SATAN"? REALLY? THAT'S THE BEST YOU COULD COME UP WITH? NO WONDER THEY FOUND YOU SO FAST.
THAT MAN WAS SENT BY ZADKIEL TO KILL ME. WHO SENT YOU?
NOBODY SENT ME. I WORK SOLO.
HHSSSSSSS
YOUR GUN IS HISSING.
I KNOW. GET DOWN.
BAM BAM

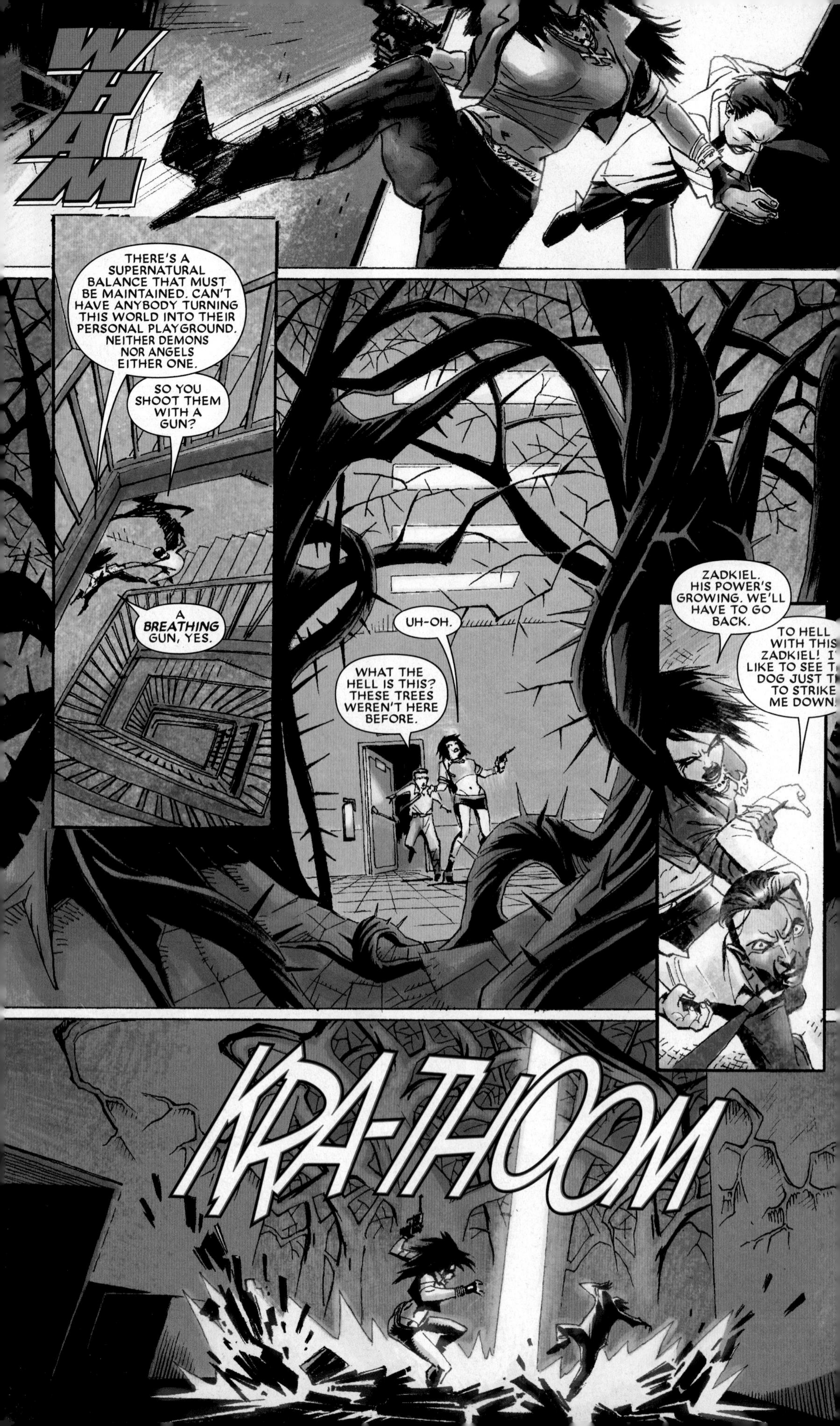
WHAM
THERE'S A SUPERNATURAL BALANCE THAT MUST BE MAINTAINED. CAN'T HAVE ANYBODY TURNING THIS WORLD INTO THEIR PERSONAL PLAYGROUND. NEITHER DEMONS NOR ANGELS EITHER ONE.
SO YOU SHOOT THEM WITH A GUN?
A BREATHING GUN, YES.
UH-OH.
WHAT THE HELL IS THIS? THESE TREES WEREN'T HERE BEFORE.
ZADKIEL. HIS POWER'S GROWING. WE'LL HAVE TO GO BACK.
TO HELL WITH THIS ZADKIEL!
KRA-THOOM

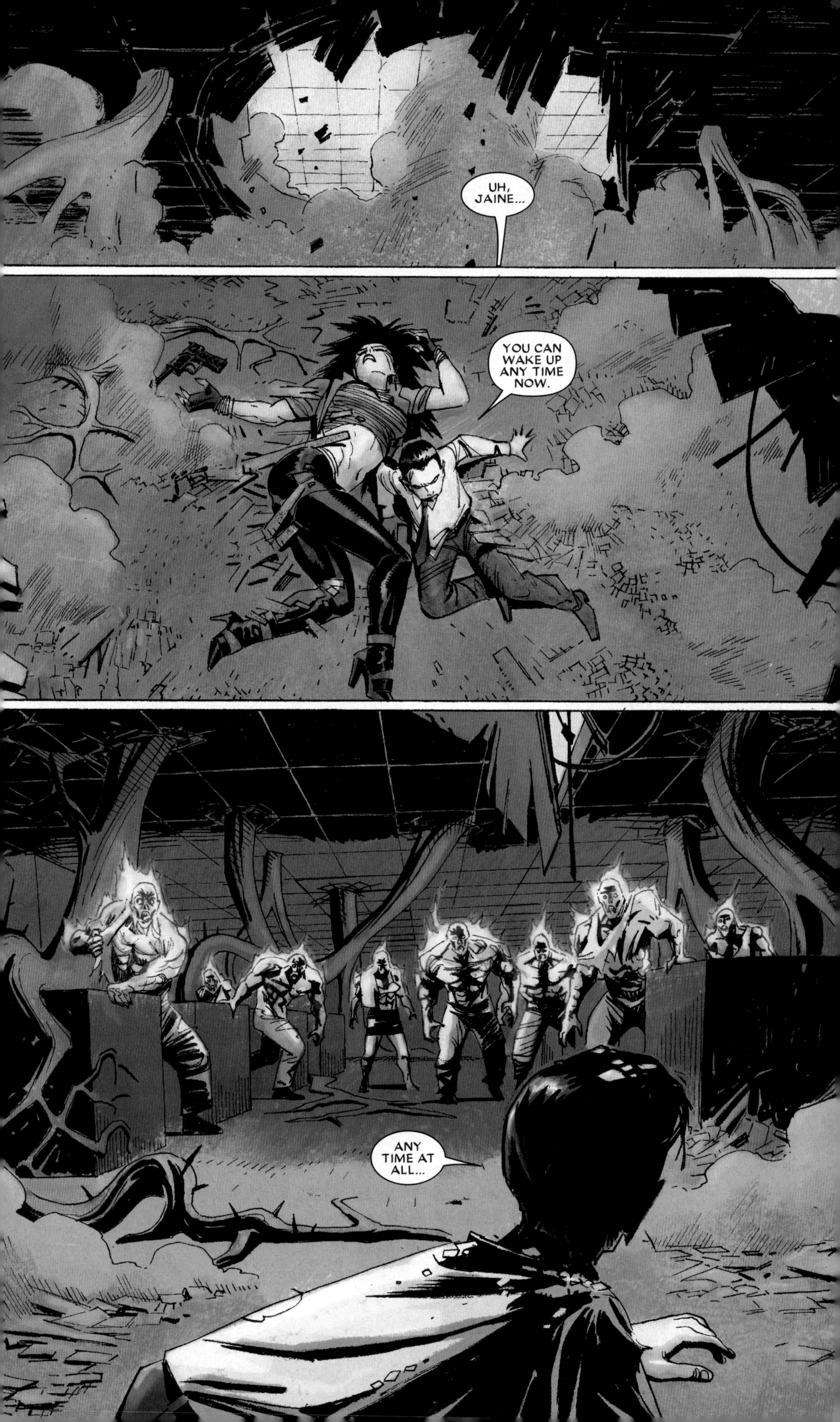
UH, JAINE...
YOU CAN WAKE UP ANY TIME NOW.
ANY TIME AT ALL...

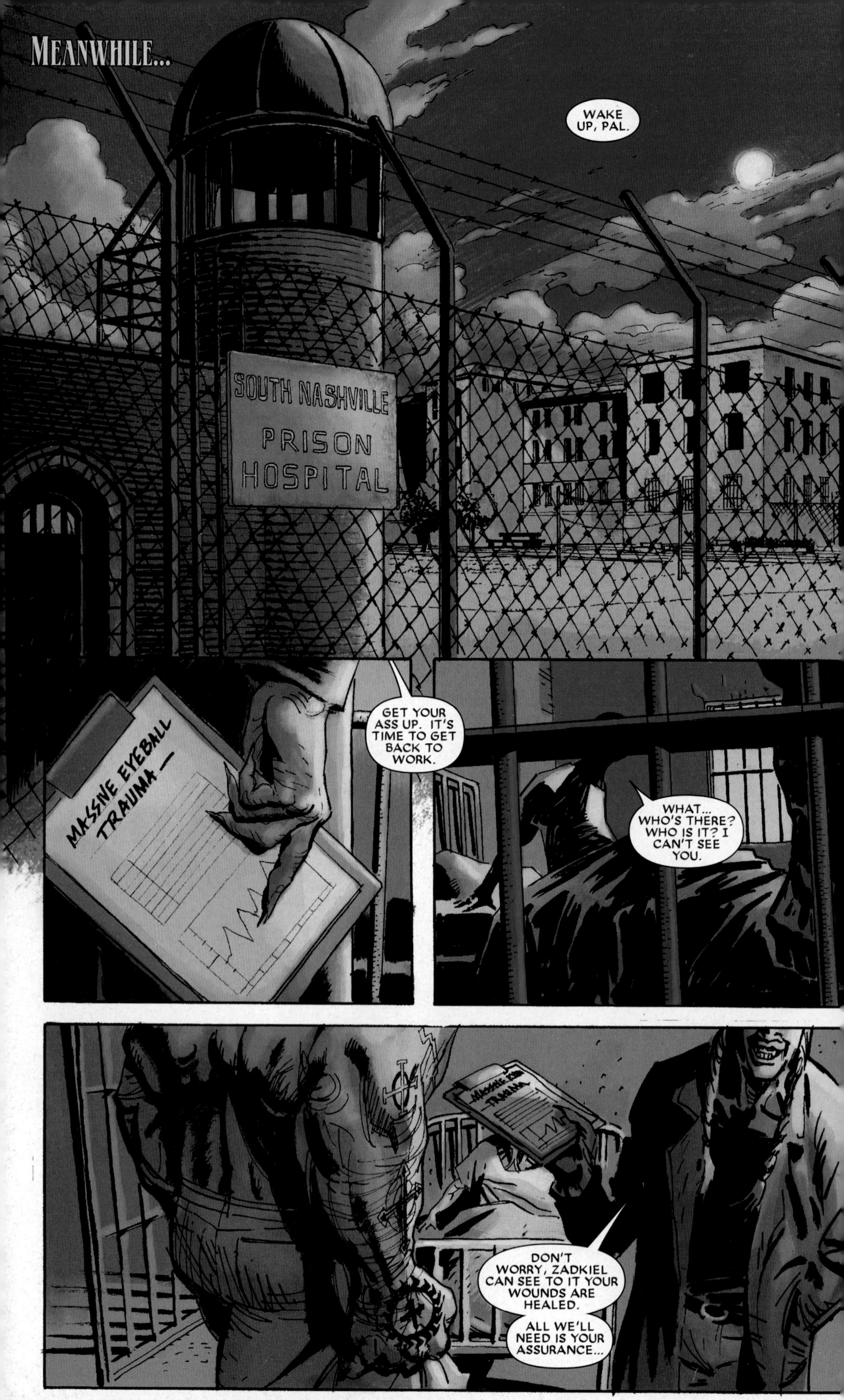
MEANWHILE...
WAKE UP, PAL.
SOUTH NASHVILLE PRISON HOSPITAL
MASSIVE EYEBALL TRAUMA
GET YOUR ASS UP. IT'S TIME TO GET BACK TO WORK.
WHAT... WHO'S THERE? WHO IS IT? I CAN'T SEE YOU.
DON'T WORRY, ZADKIEL CAN SEE TO IT YOUR WOUNDS ARE HEALED.
ALL WE'LL NEED IS YOUR ASSURANCE...

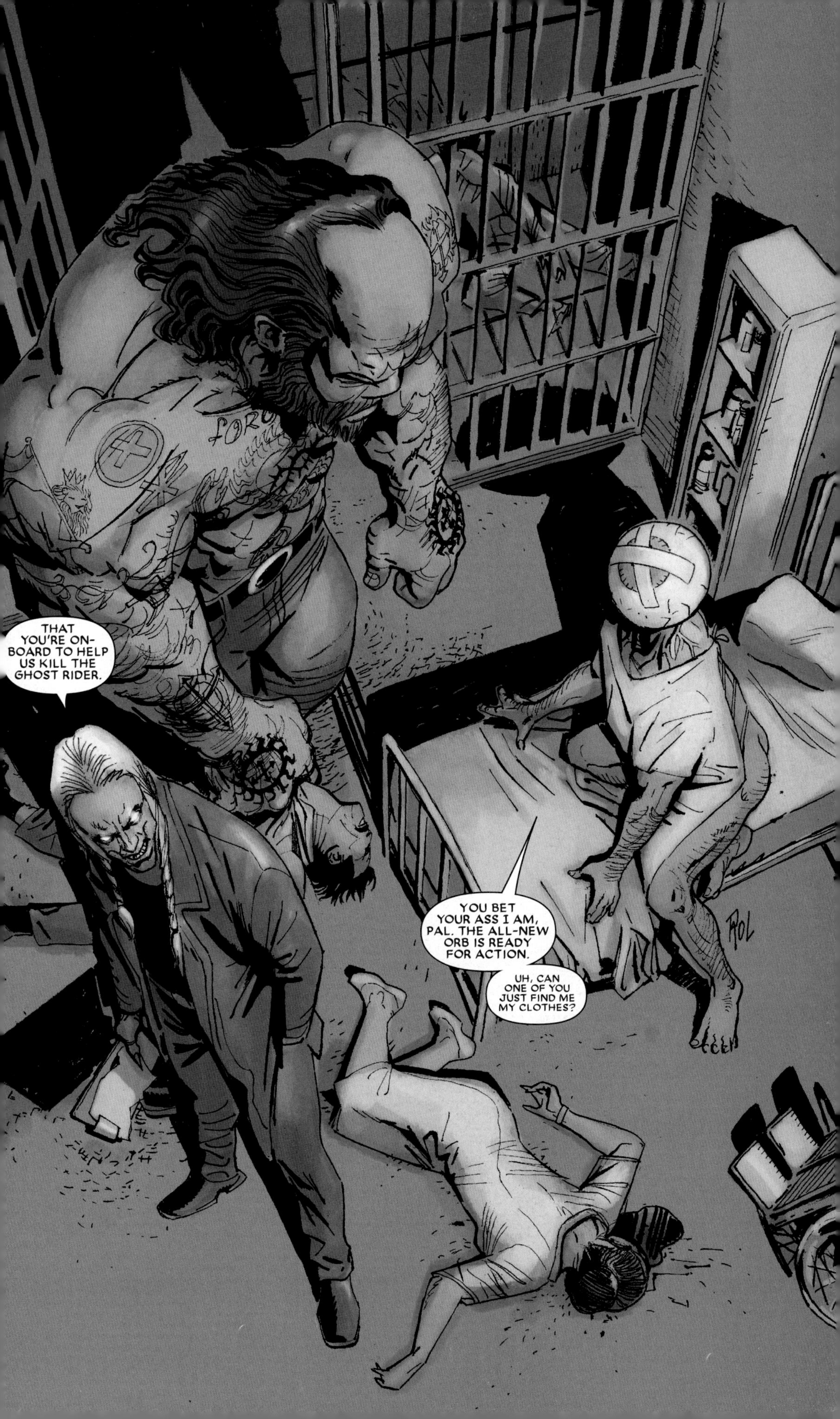
THAT YOU'RE ON-BOARD TO HELP US KILL THE GHOST RIDER.
YOU BET YOUR ASS I AM, PAL. THE ALL-NEW ORB IS READY FOR ACTION.
UH, CAN ONE OF YOU JUST FIND ME MY CLOTHES?

#2

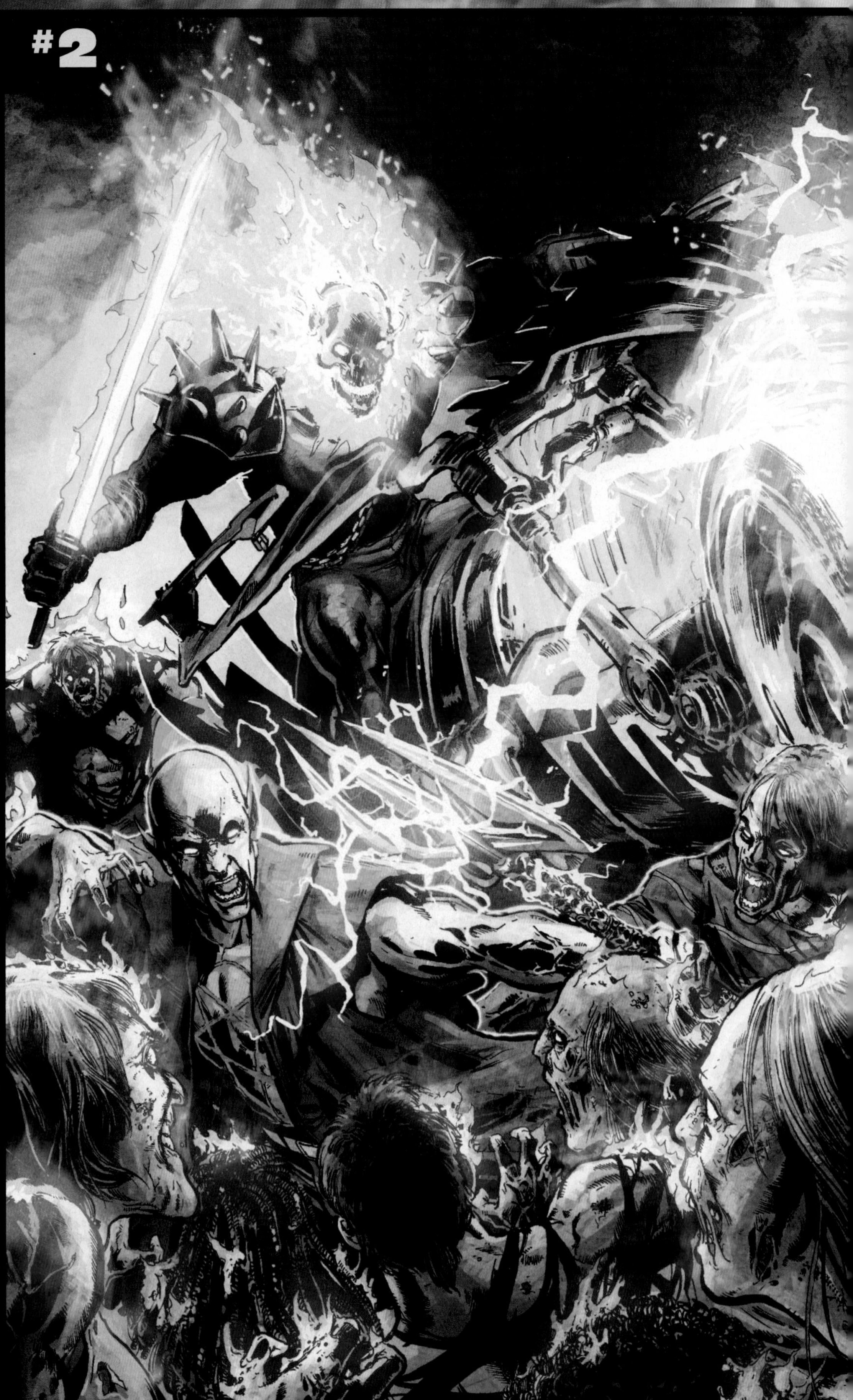

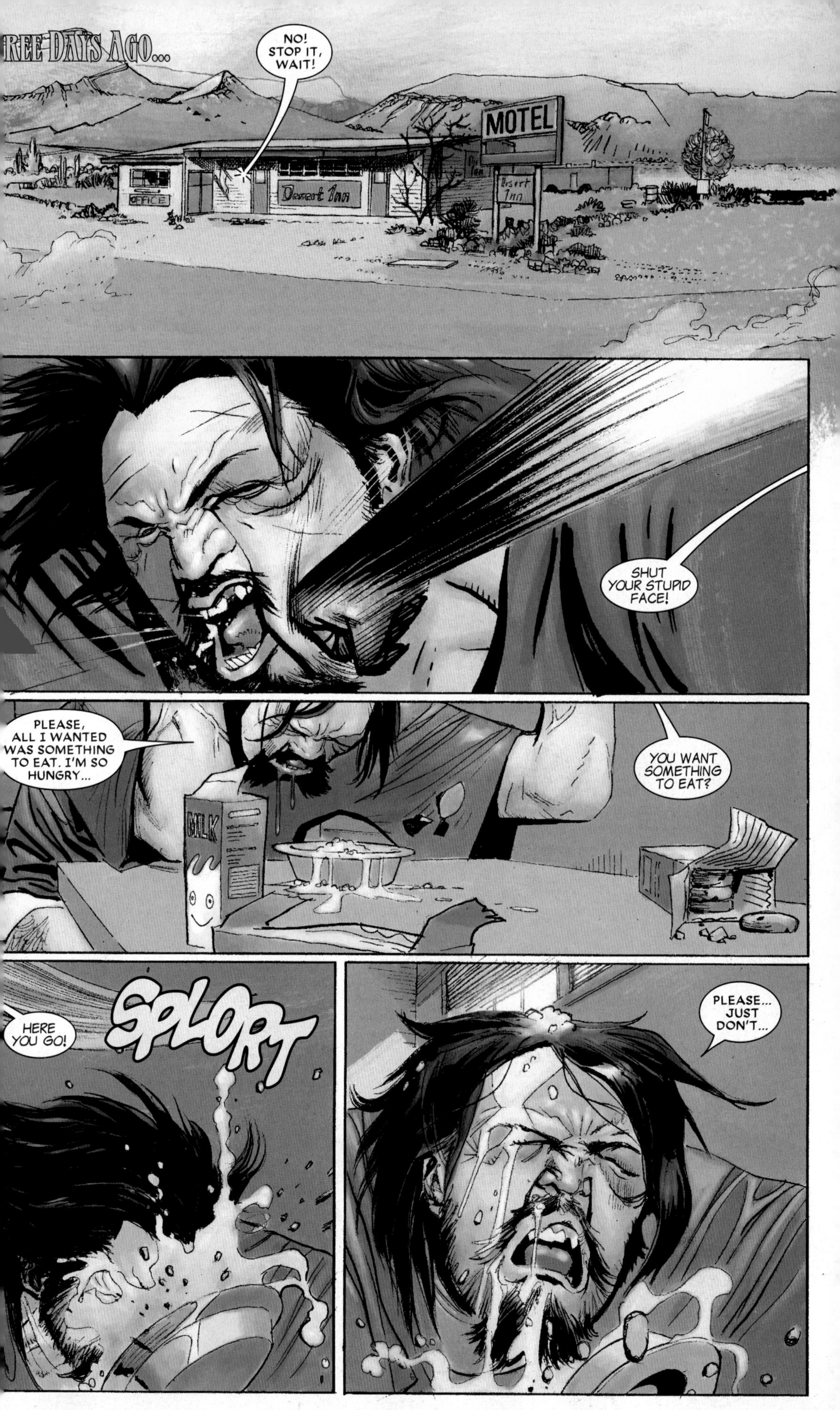
REE DAYS AGO...
NO! STOP IT, WAIT!
MOTEL
OFFICE
Desert Inn
Desert Inn
SHUT YOUR STUPID FACE!
PLEASE, ALL I WANTED WAS SOMETHING TO EAT. I'M SO HUNGRY...
YOU WANT SOMETHING TO EAT?
MILK
HERE YOU GO!
SPLORT
PLEASE... JUST DON'T...

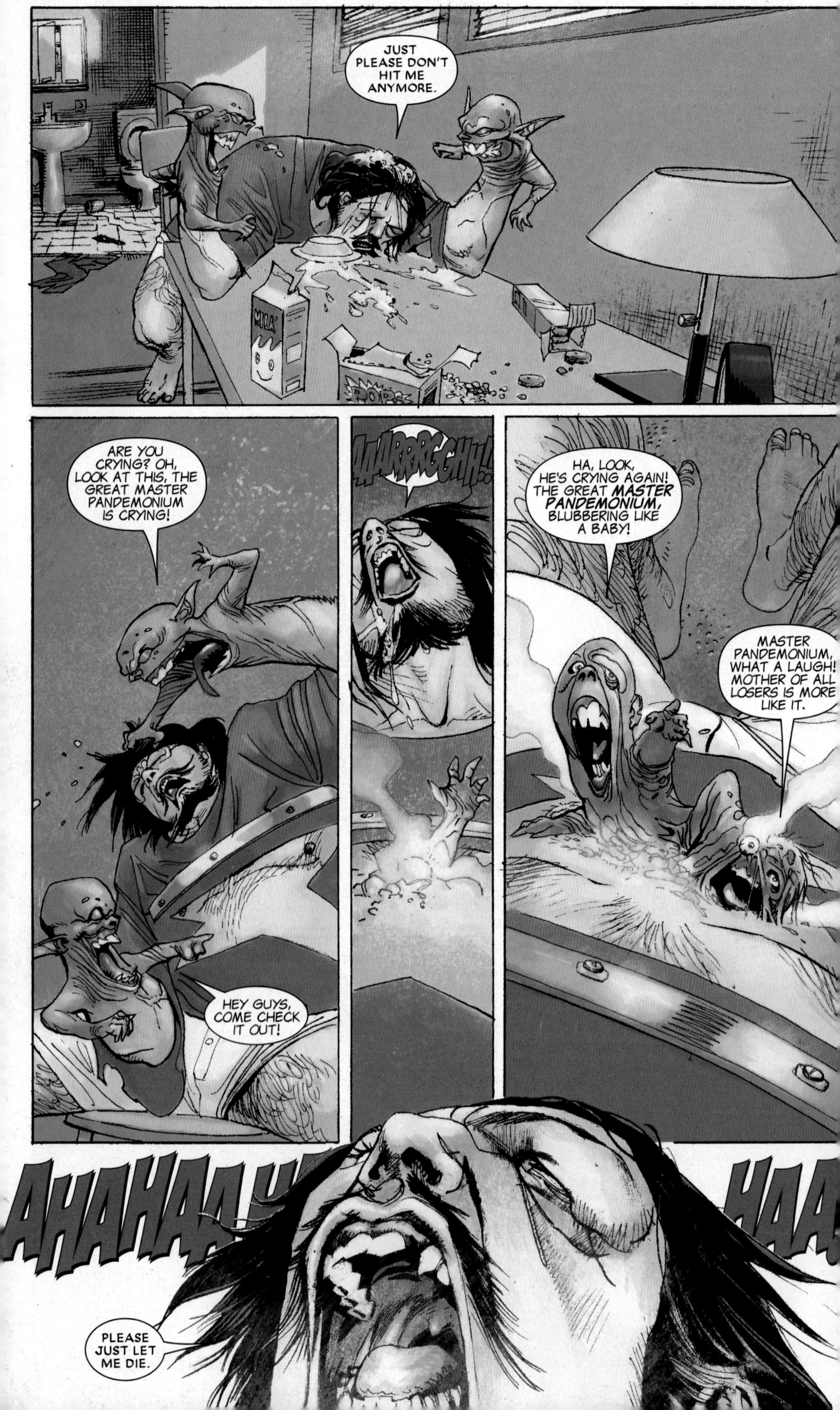
JUST PLEASE DON'T HIT ME ANYMORE.
ARE YOU CRYING? OH, LOOK AT THIS, THE GREAT MASTER PANDEMONIUM IS CRYING!
HEY GUYS, COME CHECK IT OUT!
AAARRRGGHH!!
HA, LOOK, HE'S CRYING AGAIN! THE GREAT ***MASTER PANDEMONIUM,*** BLUBBERING LIKE A BABY!
MASTER PANDEMONIUM, WHAT A LAUGH! MOTHER OF ALL LOSERS IS MORE LIKE IT.
AHAHAA
HAA
PLEASE JUST LET ME DIE.

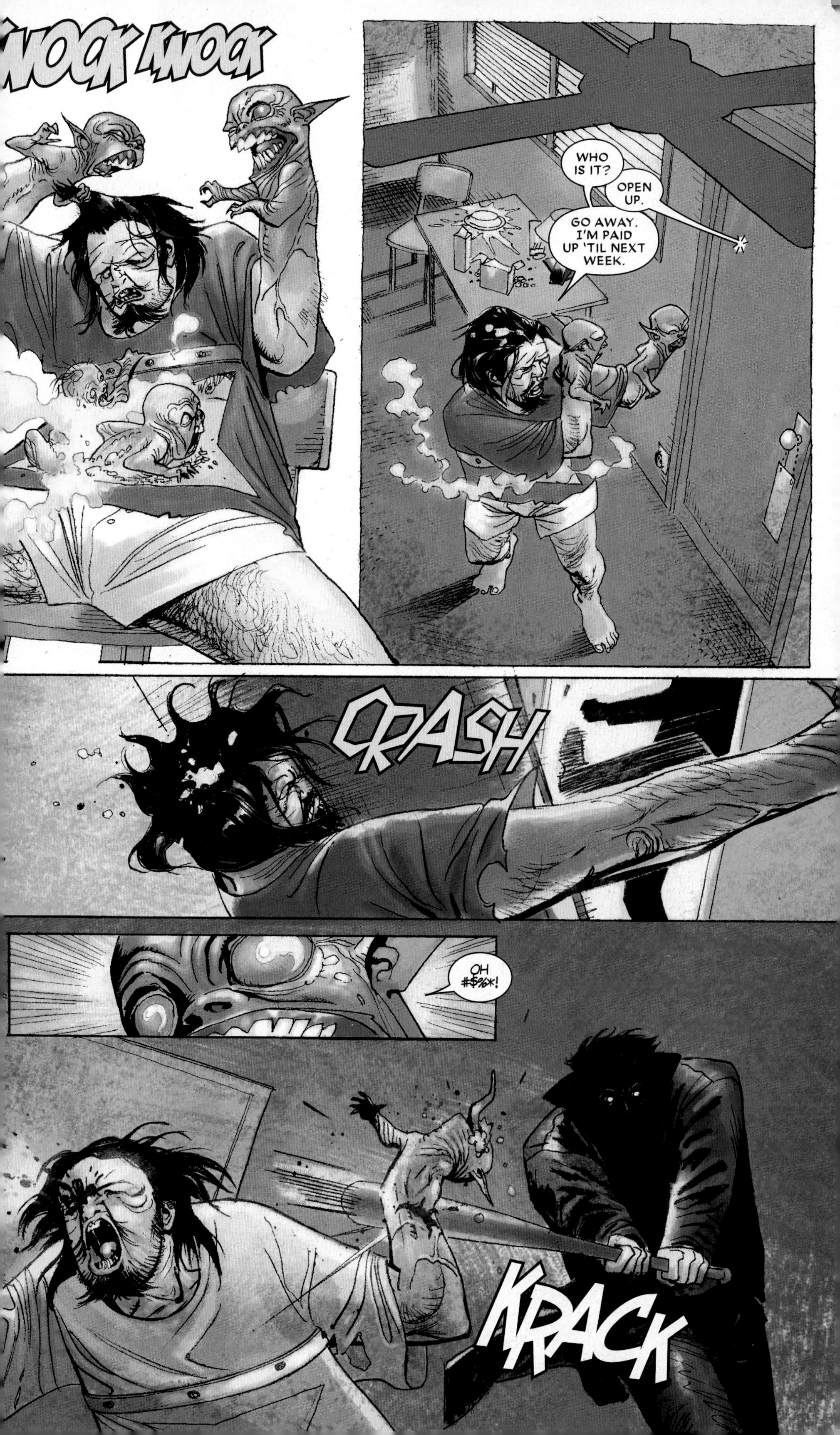
KNOCK KNOCK
WHO IS IT?
OPEN UP.
GO AWAY. I'M PAID UP 'TIL NEXT WEEK.
CRASH
OH #$%*!
KRACK

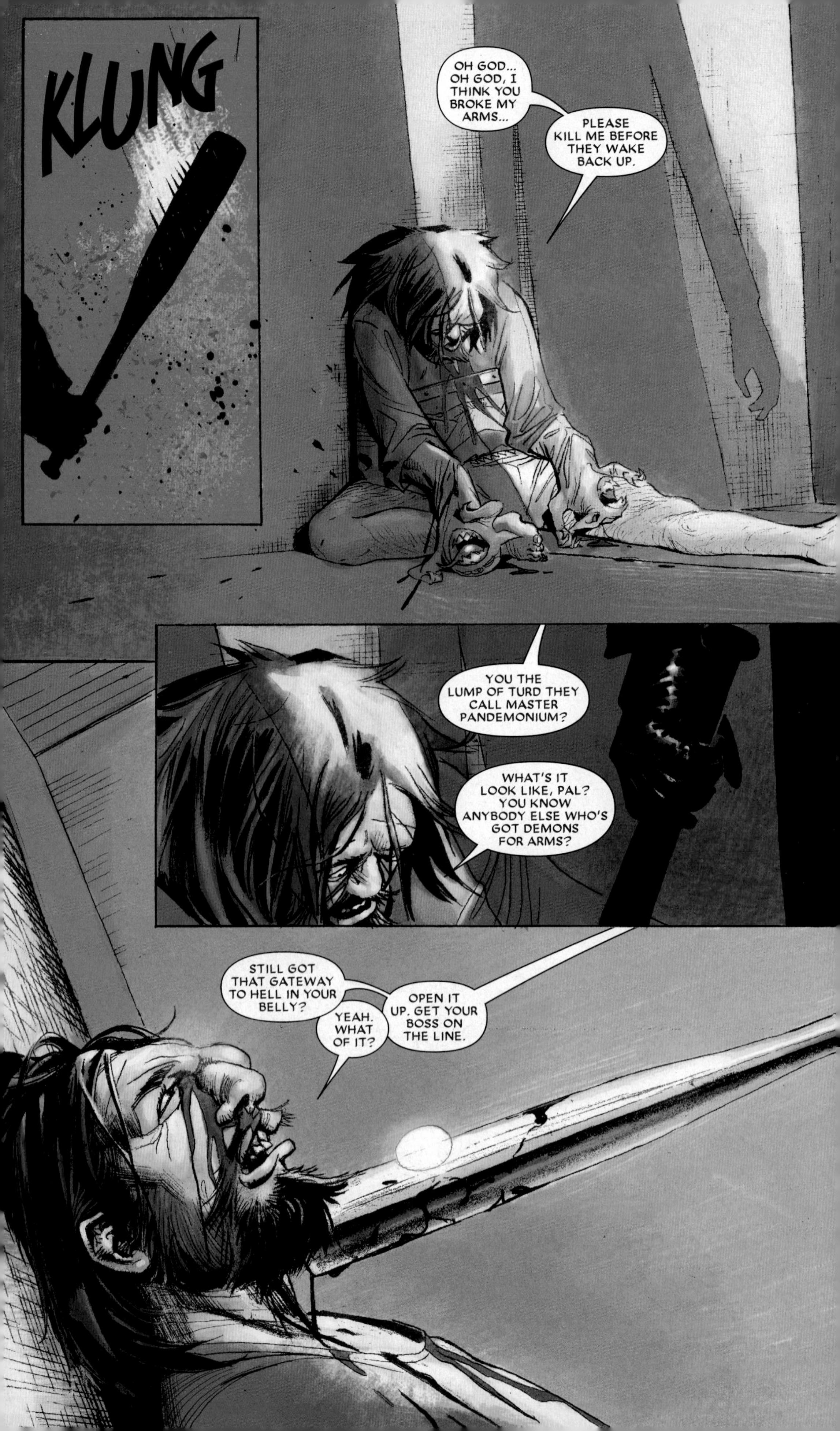
KLUNG
OH GOD... OH GOD, I THINK YOU BROKE MY ARMS...
PLEASE KILL ME BEFORE THEY WAKE BACK UP.
YOU THE LUMP OF TURD THEY CALL MASTER PANDEMONIUM?
WHAT'S IT LOOK LIKE, PAL? YOU KNOW ANYBODY ELSE WHO'S GOT DEMONS FOR ARMS?
STILL GOT THAT GATEWAY TO HELL IN YOUR BELLY?
YEAH. WHAT OF IT?
OPEN IT UP. GET YOUR BOSS ON THE LINE.

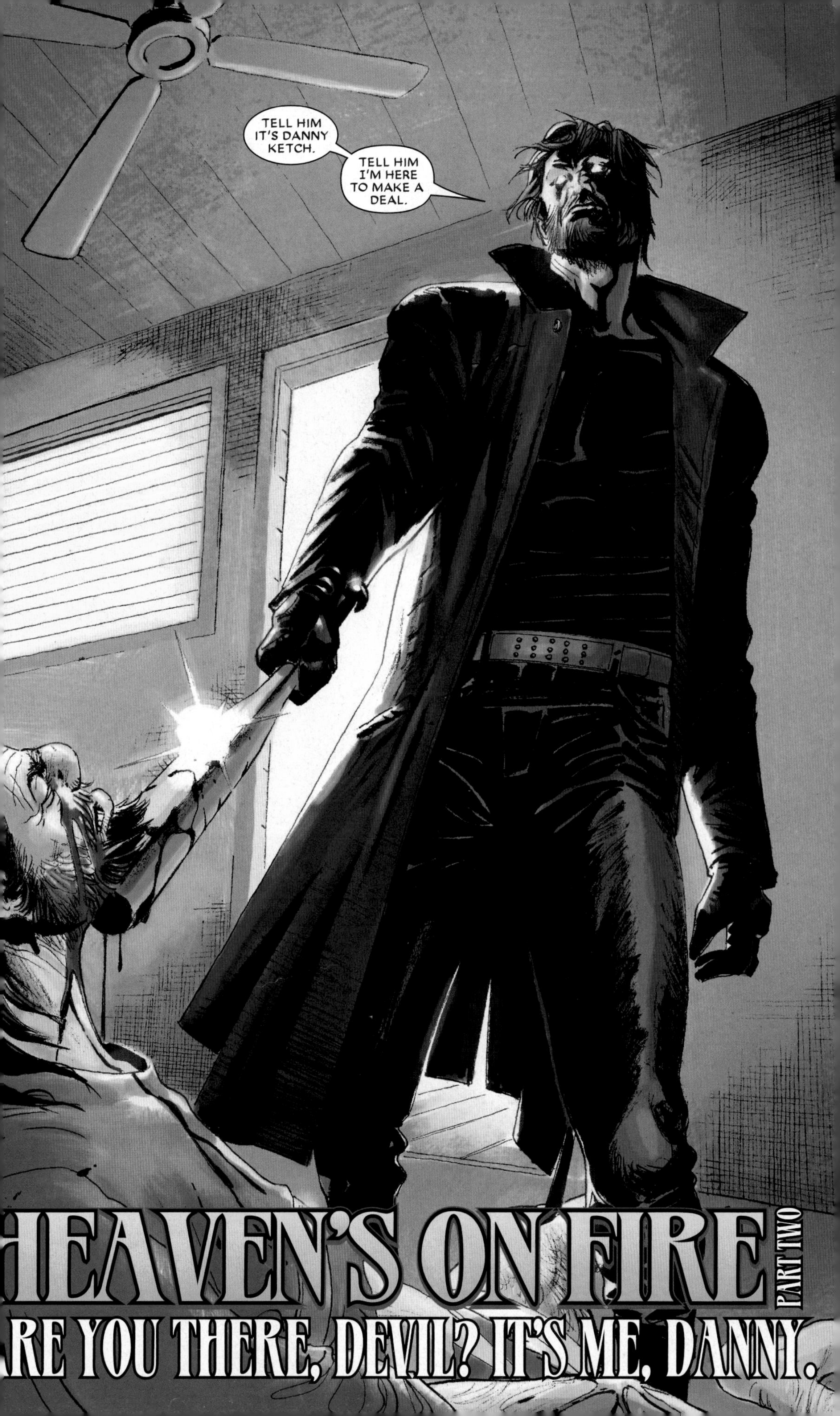
TELL HIM IT'S DANNY KETCH.
TELL HIM I'M HERE TO MAKE A DEAL.
EAVEN'S ON FIRE
PART TWO
RE YOU THERE, DEVIL? IT'S ME, DANNY.

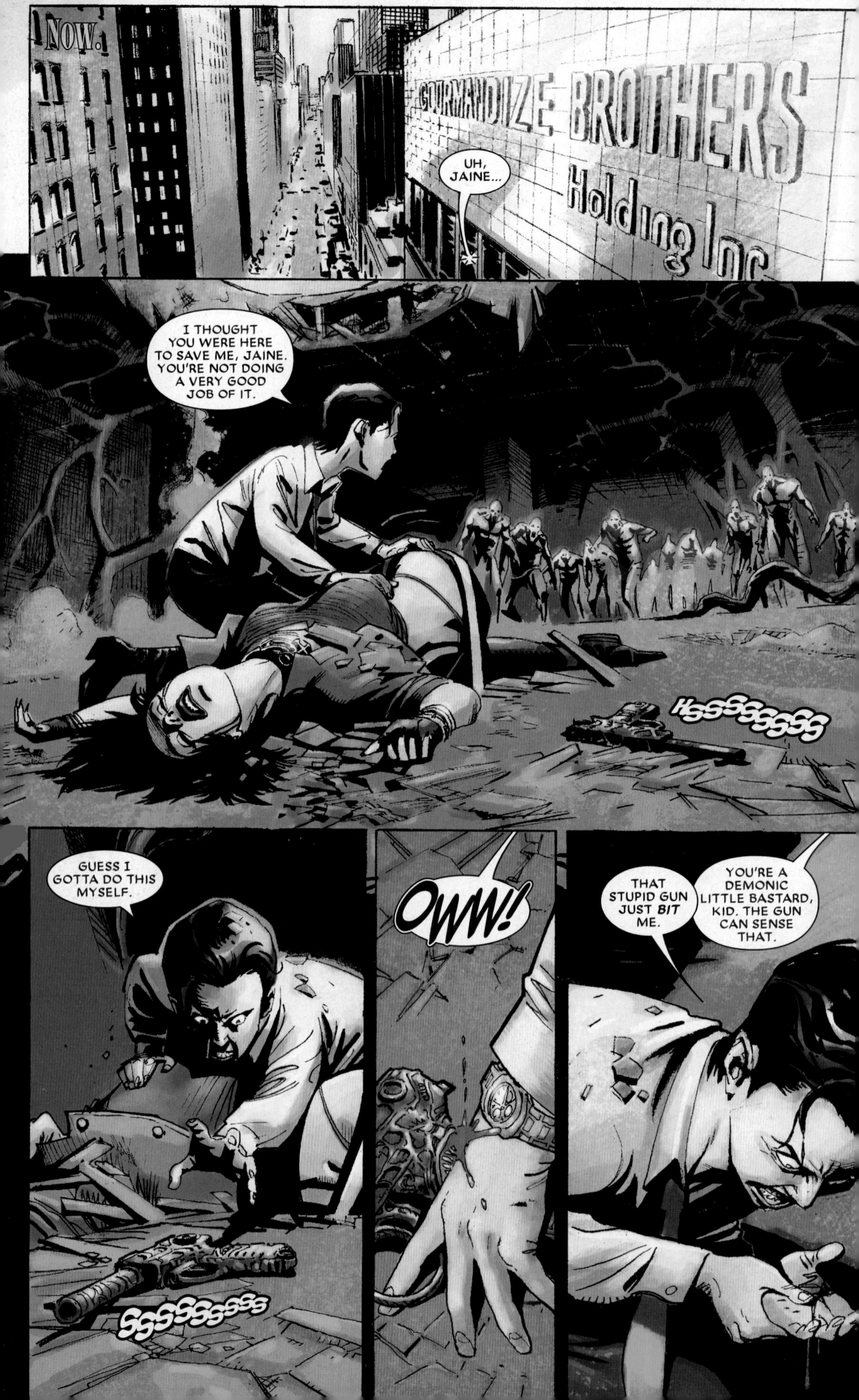
NOW.
GOURMANDIZE BROTHERS Holding Inc
UH, JAINE...
I THOUGHT YOU WERE HERE TO SAVE ME, JAINE. YOU'RE NOT DOING A VERY GOOD JOB OF IT.
HSSSSSSSS
GUESS I GOTTA DO THIS MYSELF.
SSSSSSSSS
OWW!
THAT STUPID GUN JUST *BIT* ME.
YOU'RE A DEMONIC LITTLE BASTARD, KID. THE GUN CAN SENSE THAT.

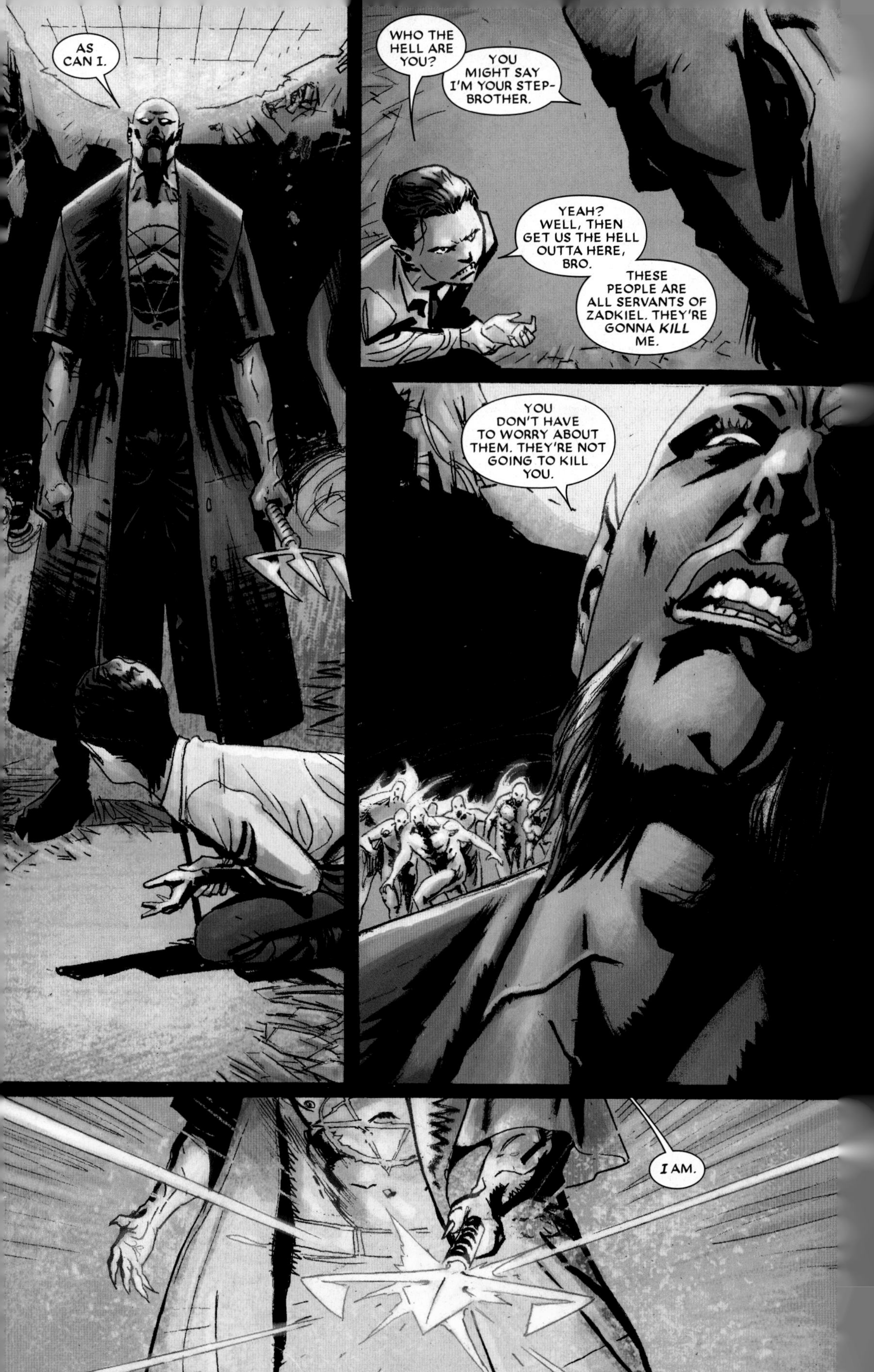
AS CAN I.
WHO THE HELL ARE YOU?
YOU MIGHT SAY I'M YOUR STEP-BROTHER.
YEAH? WELL, THEN GET US THE HELL OUTTA HERE, BRO.
THESE PEOPLE ARE ALL SERVANTS OF ZADKIEL. THEY'RE GONNA KILL ME.
YOU DON'T HAVE TO WORRY ABOUT THEM. THEY'RE NOT GOING TO KILL YOU.
I AM.

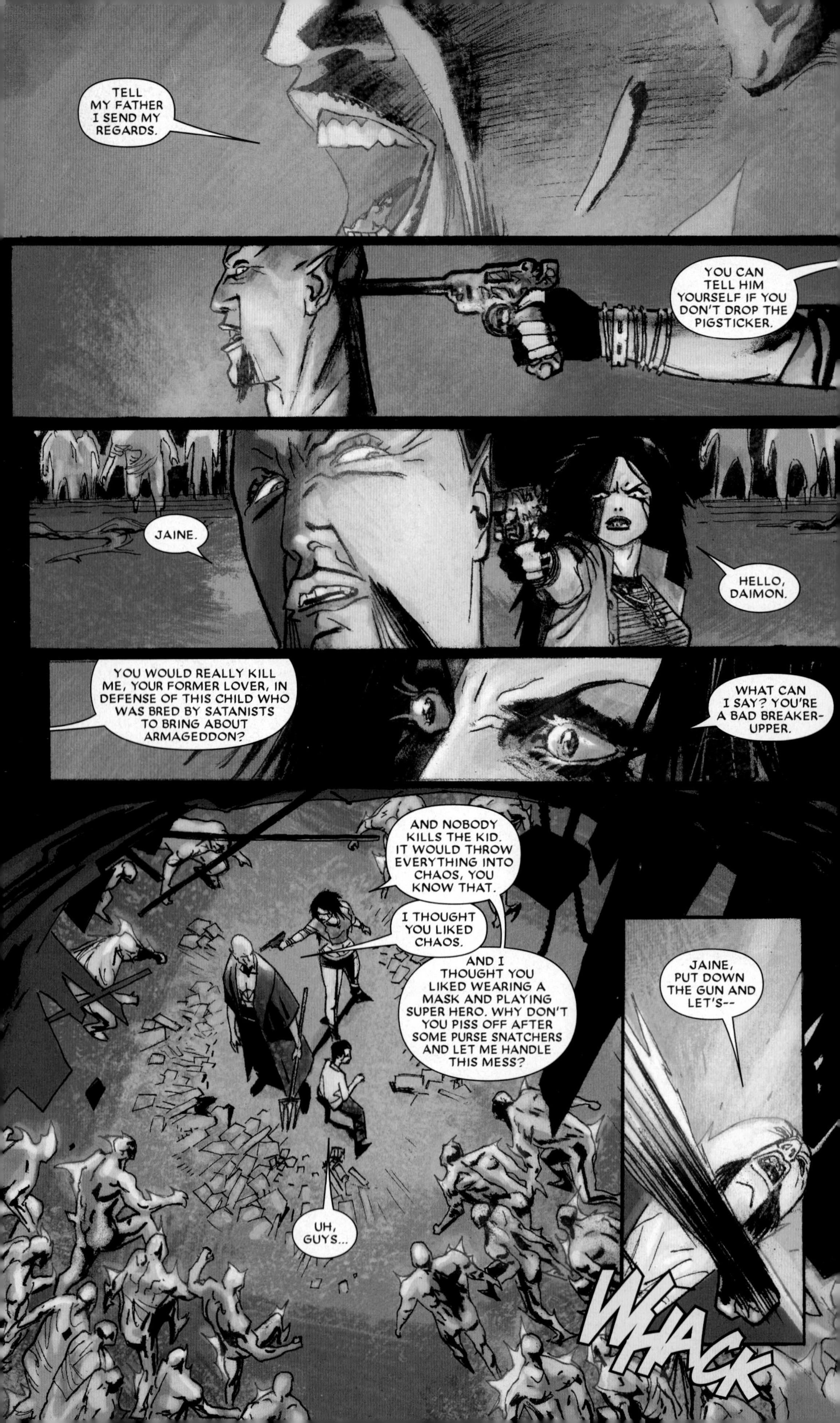
TELL MY FATHER I SEND MY REGARDS.
YOU CAN TELL HIM YOURSELF IF YOU DON'T DROP THE PIGSTICKER.
JAINE.
HELLO, DAIMON.
YOU WOULD REALLY KILL ME, YOUR FORMER LOVER, IN DEFENSE OF THIS CHILD WHO WAS BRED BY SATANISTS TO BRING ABOUT ARMAGEDDON?
WHAT CAN I SAY? YOU'RE A BAD BREAKER-UPPER.
AND NOBODY KILLS THE KID. IT WOULD THROW EVERYTHING INTO CHAOS, YOU KNOW THAT.
I THOUGHT YOU LIKED CHAOS.
AND I THOUGHT YOU LIKED WEARING A MASK AND PLAYING SUPER HERO. WHY DON'T YOU PISS OFF AFTER SOME PURSE SNATCHERS AND LET ME HANDLE THIS MESS?
UH, GUYS...
JAINE, PUT DOWN THE GUN AND LET'S--
WHACK

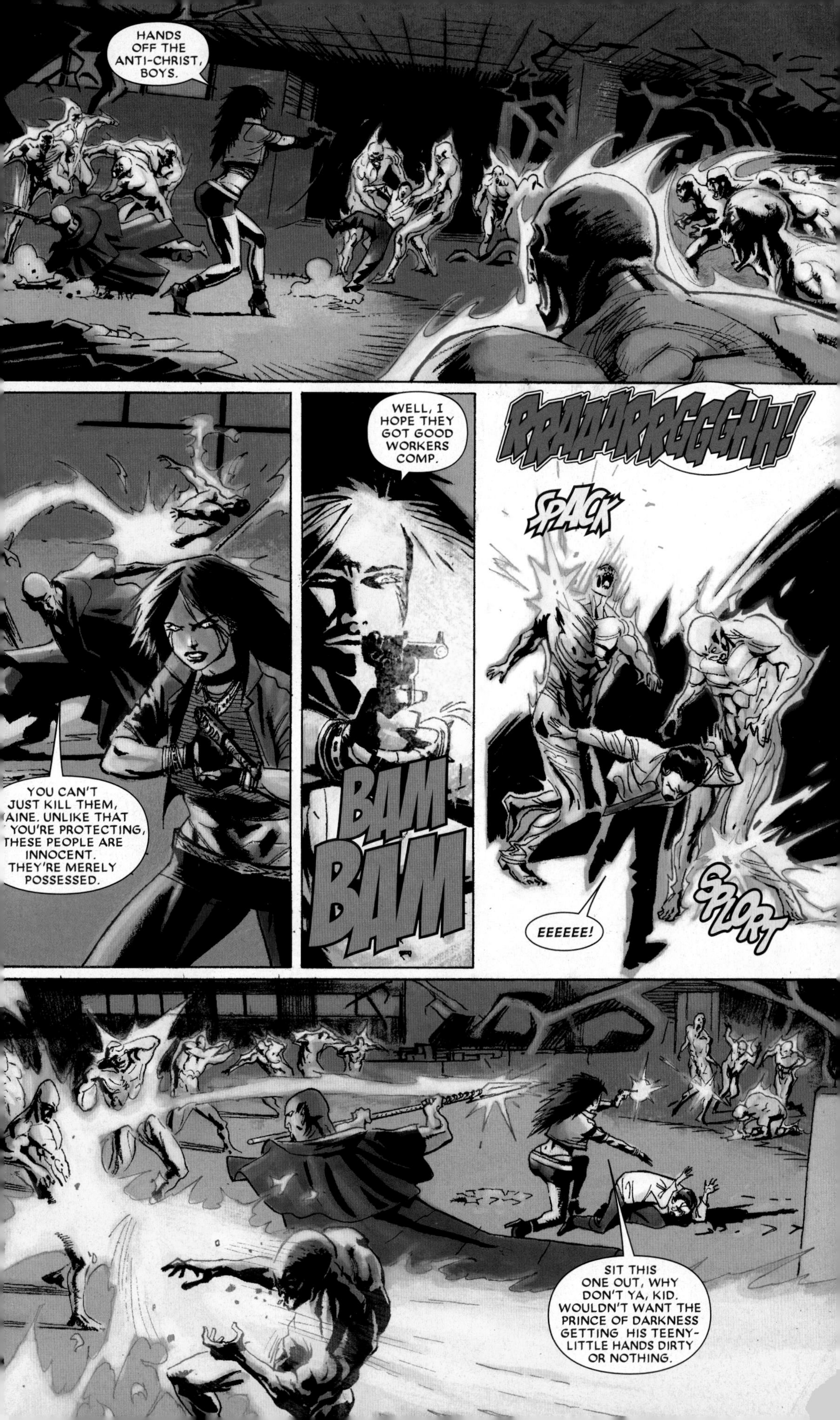
HANDS OFF THE ANTI-CHRIST, BOYS.
YOU CAN'T JUST KILL THEM, AINE. UNLIKE THAT YOU'RE PROTECTING, THESE PEOPLE ARE INNOCENT. THEY'RE MERELY POSSESSED.
WELL, I HOPE THEY GOT GOOD WORKERS COMP.
BAM BAM
RRAAAARRGGGHH!
SPACK
EEEEEE!
SPLORT
SIT THIS ONE OUT, WHY DON'T YA, KID. WOULDN'T WANT THE PRINCE OF DARKNESS GETTING HIS TEENY-LITTLE HANDS DIRTY OR NOTHING.

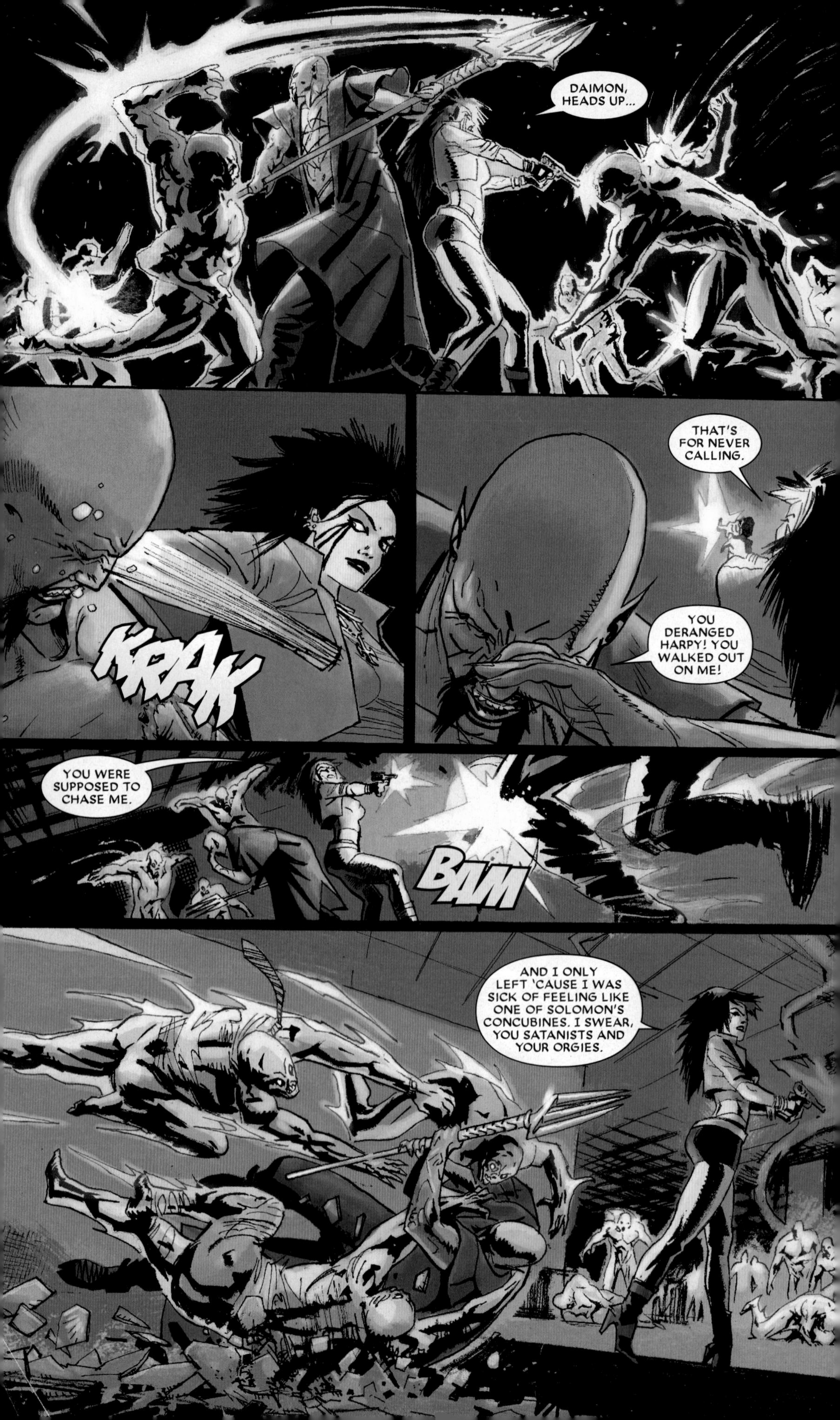
DAIMON, HEADS UP...
KRAK
THAT'S FOR NEVER CALLING.
YOU DERANGED HARPY! YOU WALKED OUT ON ME!
YOU WERE SUPPOSED TO CHASE ME.
BAM
AND I ONLY LEFT 'CAUSE I WAS SICK OF FEELING LIKE ONE OF SOLOMON'S CONCUBINES. I SWEAR, YOU SATANISTS AND YOUR ORGIES.

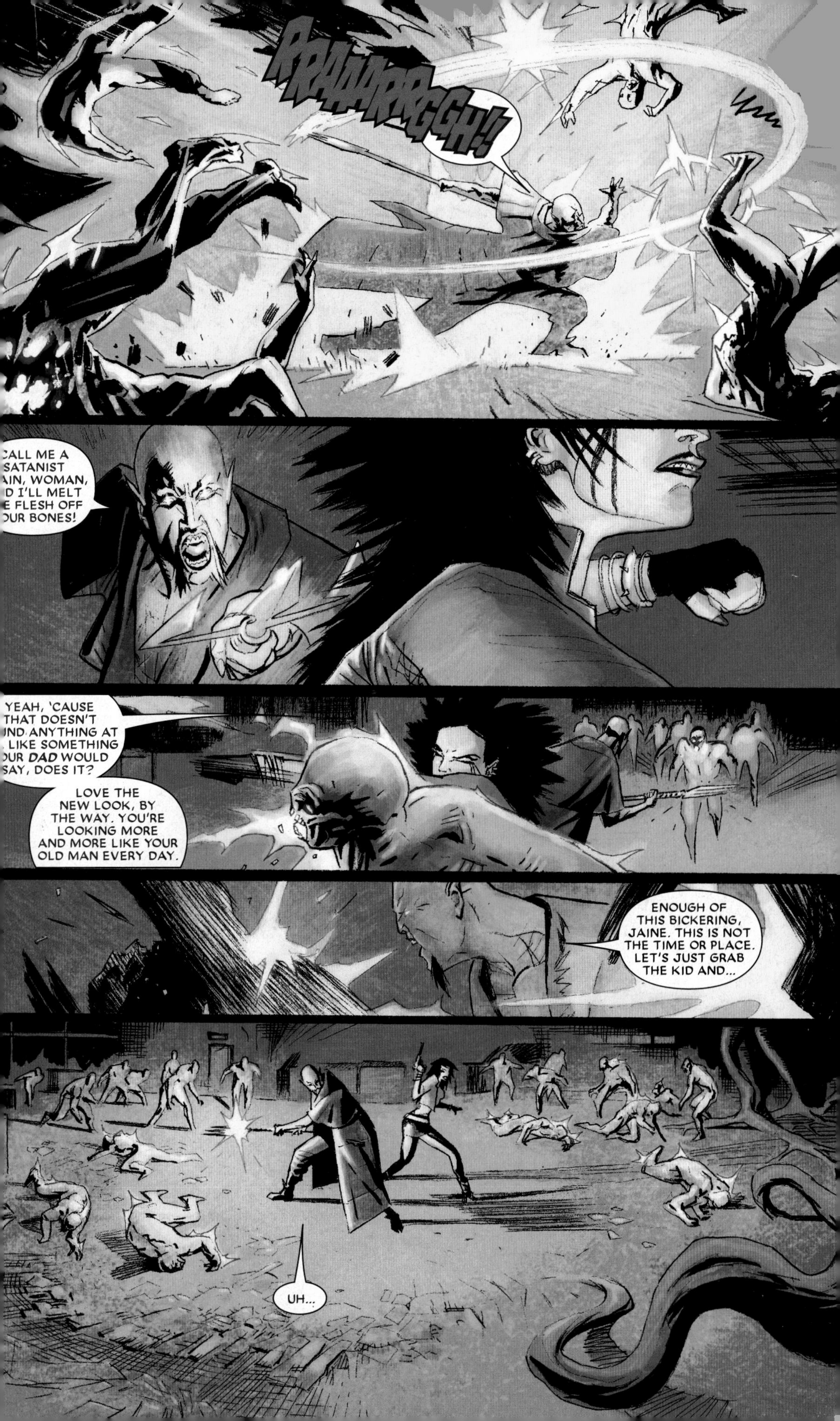
RRAAARRGGH!!
CALL ME A SATANIST AIN, WOMAN, D I'LL MELT E FLESH OFF OUR BONES!
YEAH, 'CAUSE THAT DOESN'T UND ANYTHING AT LIKE SOMETHING OUR DAD WOULD SAY, DOES IT?
LOVE THE NEW LOOK, BY THE WAY. YOU'RE LOOKING MORE AND MORE LIKE YOUR OLD MAN EVERY DAY.
ENOUGH OF THIS BICKERING, JAINE. THIS IS NOT THE TIME OR PLACE. LET'S JUST GRAB THE KID AND...
UH...

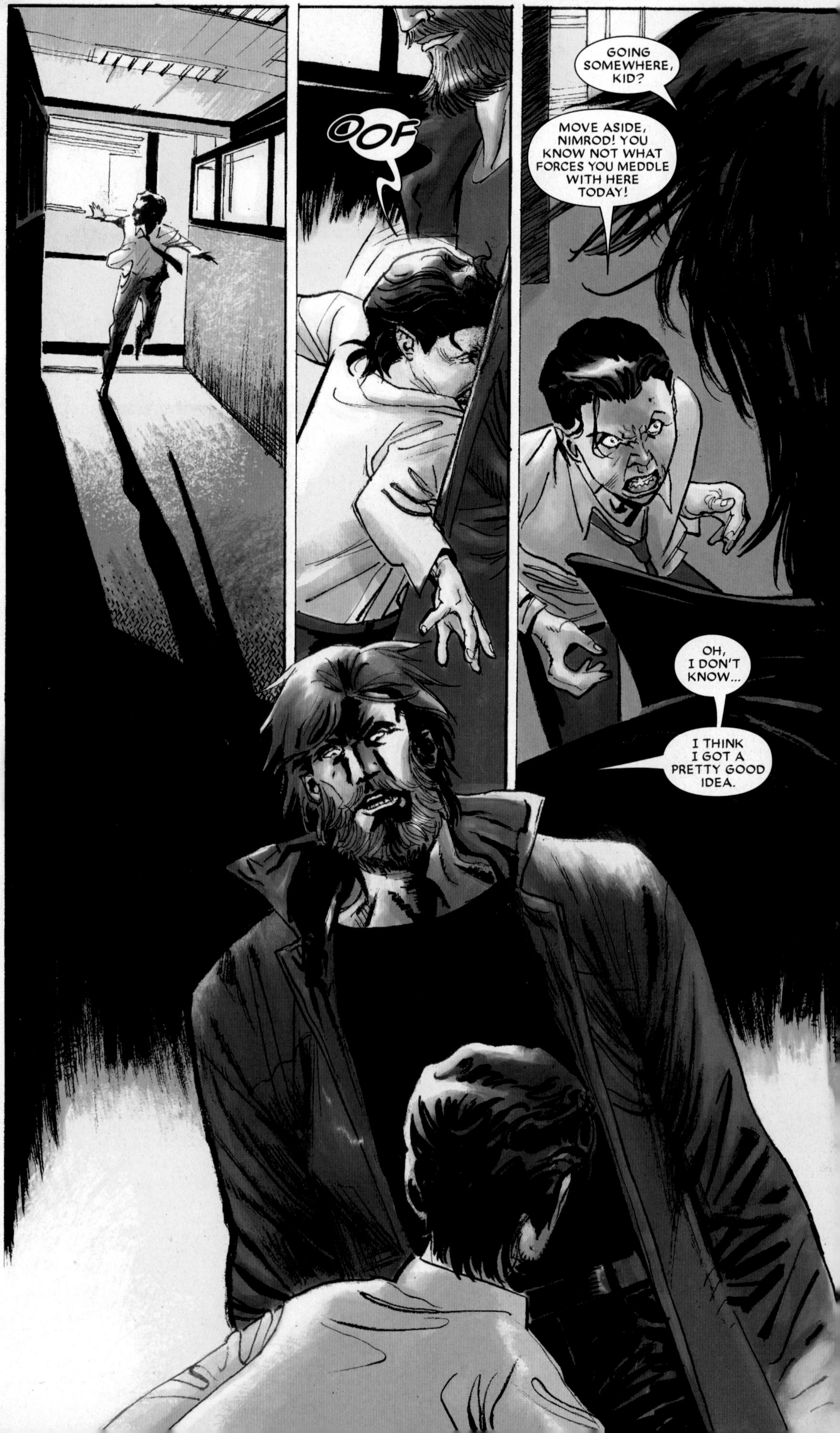
OOF
GOING SOMEWHERE, KID?
MOVE ASIDE, NIMROD! YOU KNOW NOT WHAT FORCES YOU MEDDLE WITH HERE TODAY!
OH, I DON'T KNOW...
I THINK I GOT A PRETTY GOOD IDEA.

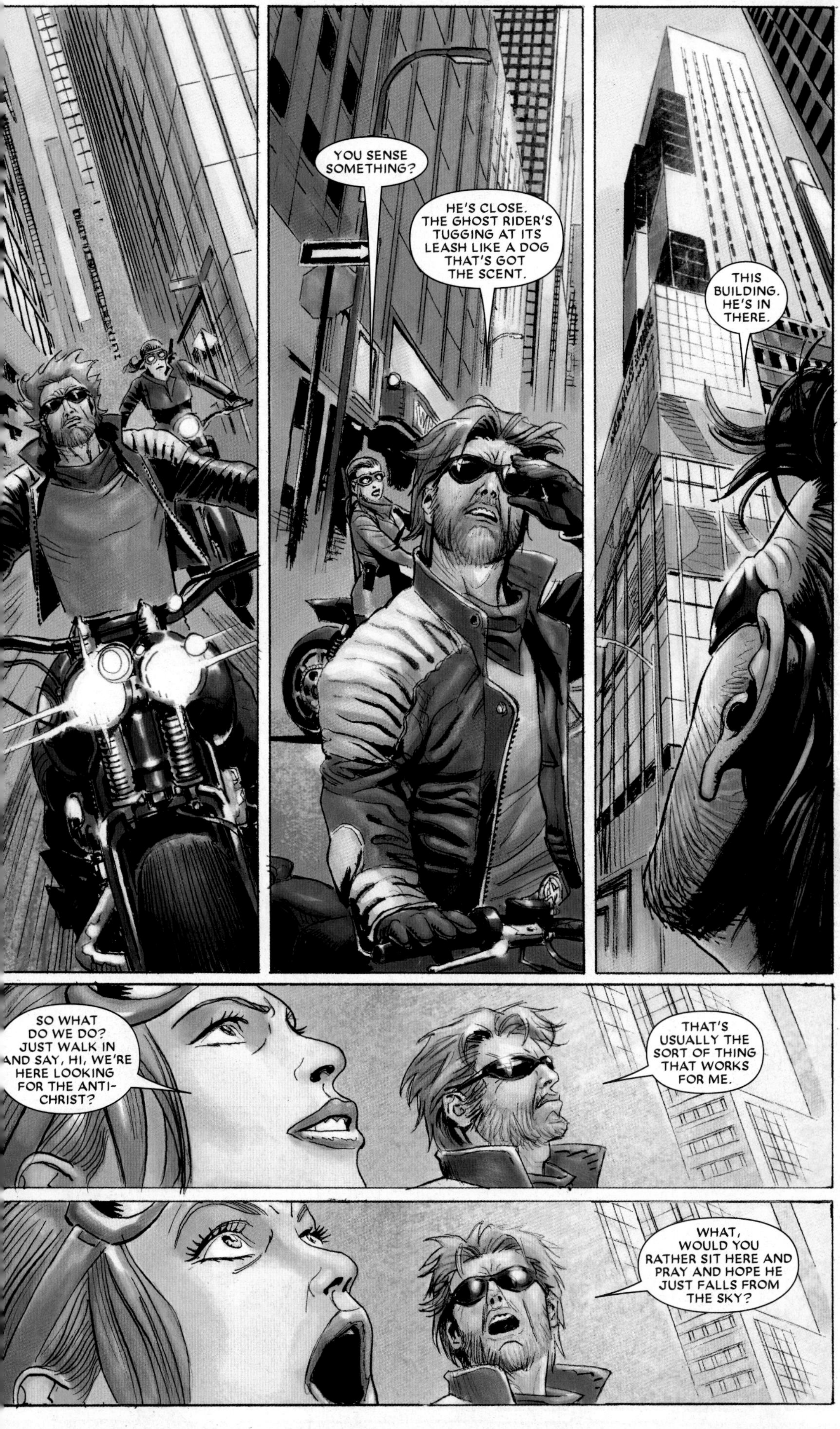
YOU SENSE SOMETHING?
HE'S CLOSE. THE GHOST RIDER'S TUGGING AT ITS LEASH LIKE A DOG THAT'S GOT THE SCENT.
THIS BUILDING. HE'S IN THERE.
SO WHAT DO WE DO? JUST WALK IN AND SAY, HI, WE'RE HERE LOOKING FOR THE ANTI-CHRIST?
THAT'S USUALLY THE SORT OF THING THAT WORKS FOR ME.
WHAT, WOULD YOU RATHER SIT HERE AND PRAY AND HOPE HE JUST FALLS FROM THE SKY?

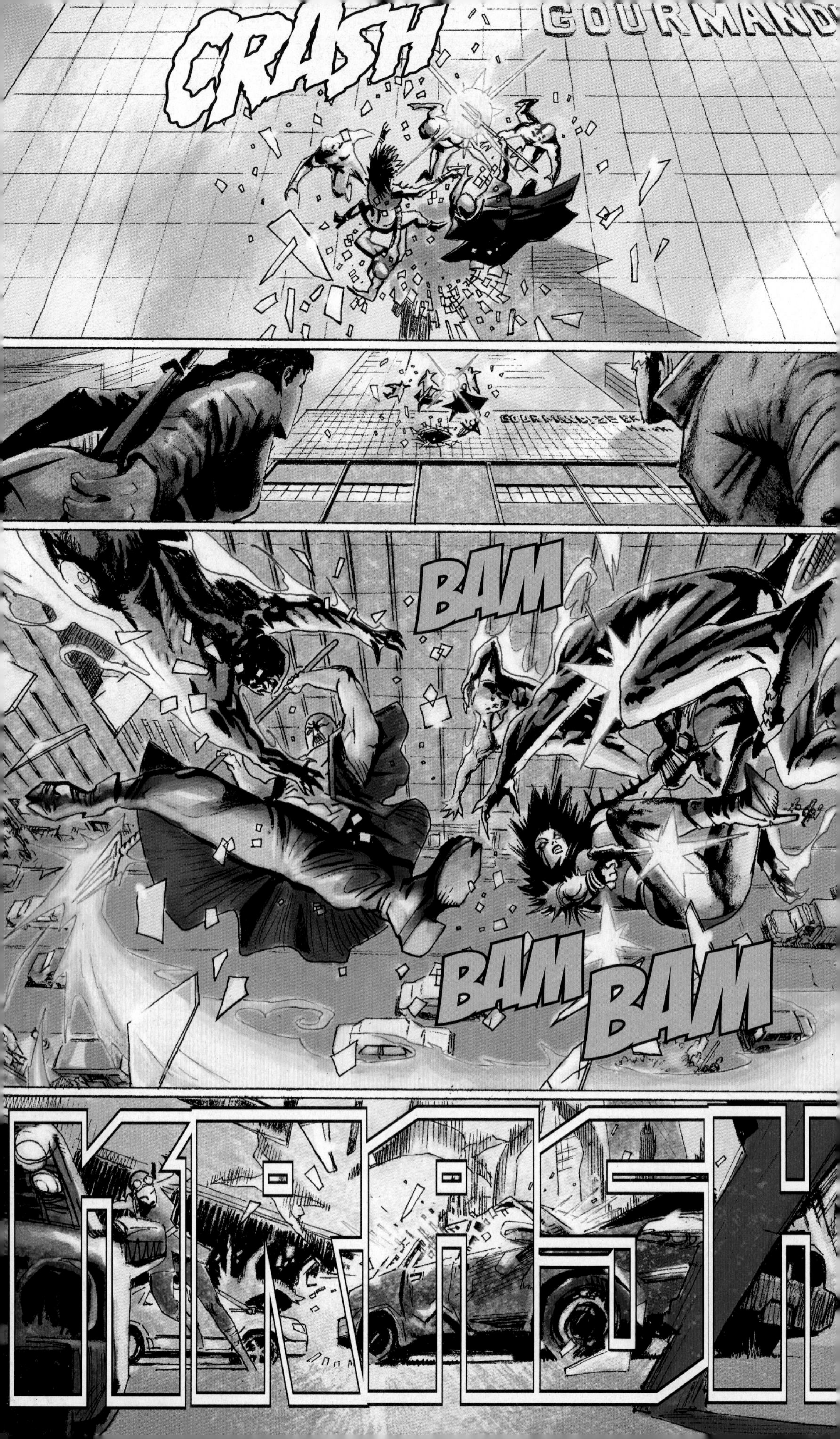
CRASH
GOURMAND
BAM
BAM
BAM

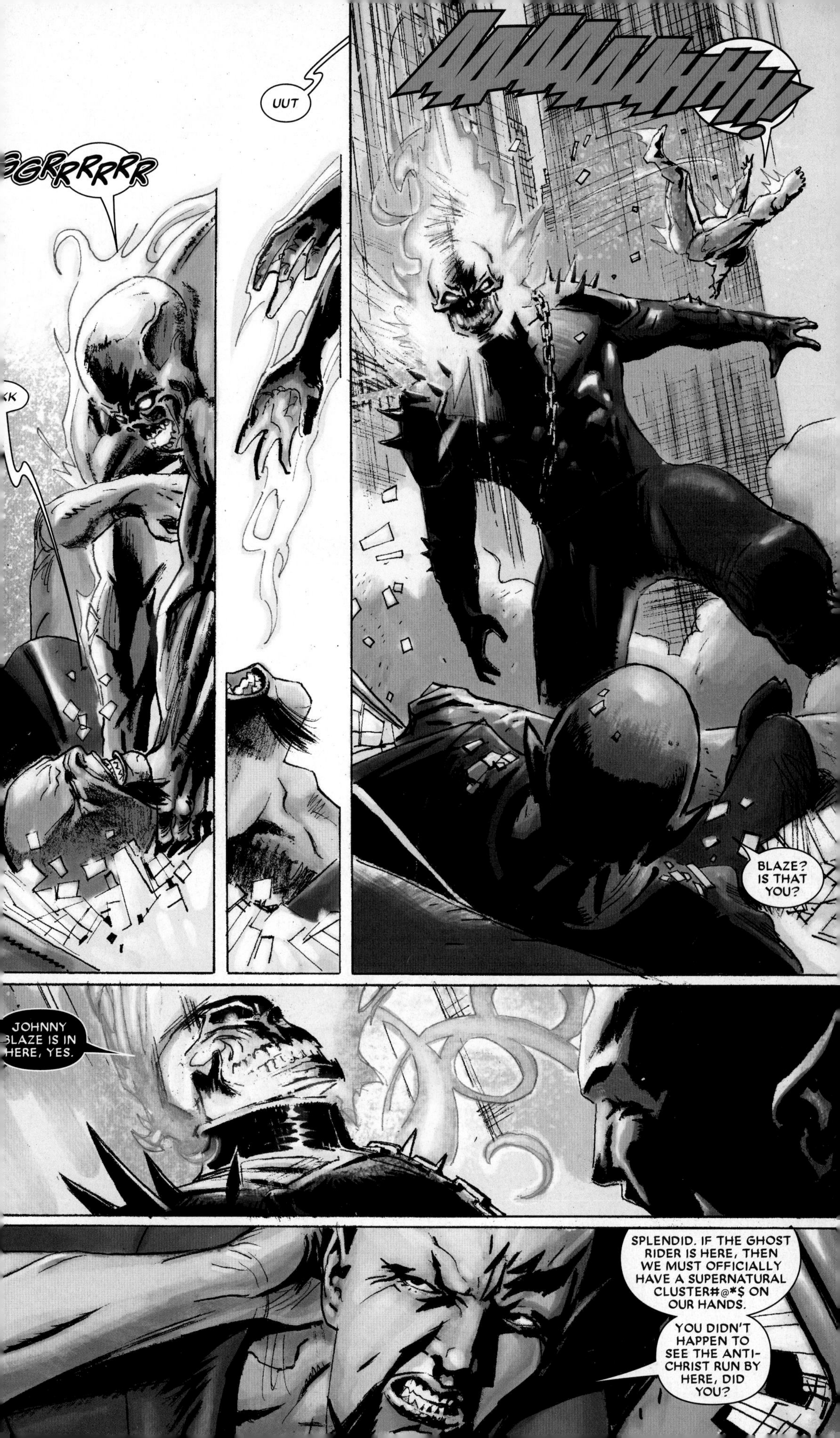

UUT
AAAAAAHHH!
GRRRRRRR
KK
BLAZE? IS THAT YOU?
JOHNNY BLAZE IS IN HERE, YES.
SPLENDID. IF THE GHOST RIDER IS HERE, THEN WE MUST OFFICIALLY HAVE A SUPERNATURAL CLUSTER#@*$ ON OUR HANDS.
YOU DIDN'T HAPPEN TO SEE THE ANTI-CHRIST RUN BY HERE, DID YOU?

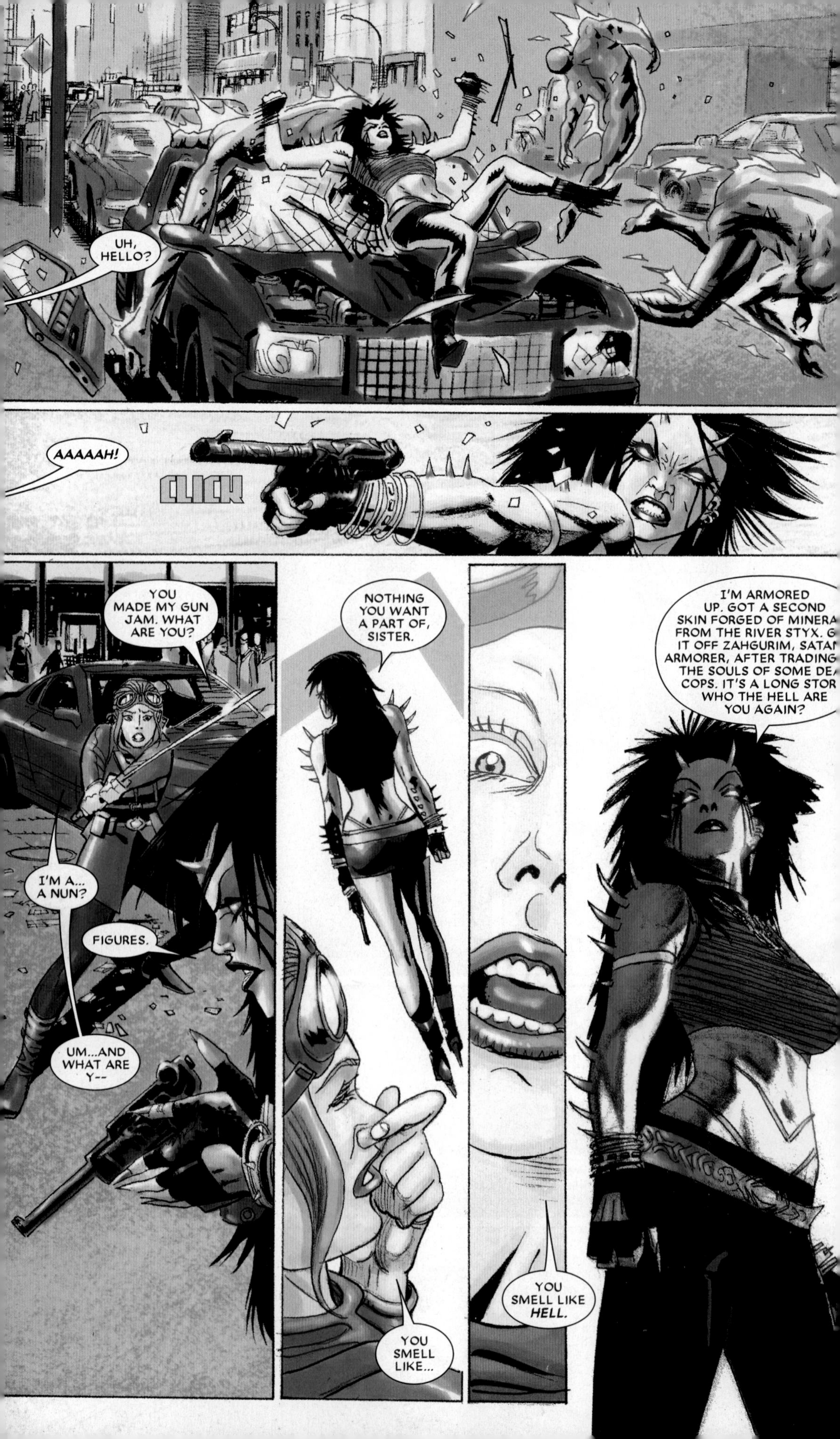
UH, HELLO?
AAAAAH!
CLICK
YOU MADE MY GUN JAM. WHAT ARE YOU?
I'M A... A NUN?
FIGURES.
UM...AND WHAT ARE Y--
NOTHING YOU WANT A PART OF, SISTER.
YOU SMELL LIKE...
YOU SMELL LIKE HELL.
I'M ARMORED UP. GOT A SECOND SKIN FORGED OF MINERA FROM THE RIVER STYX. G IT OFF ZAHGURIM, SATAN ARMORER, AFTER TRADING THE SOULS OF SOME DEA COPS. IT'S A LONG STOR WHO THE HELL ARE YOU AGAIN?

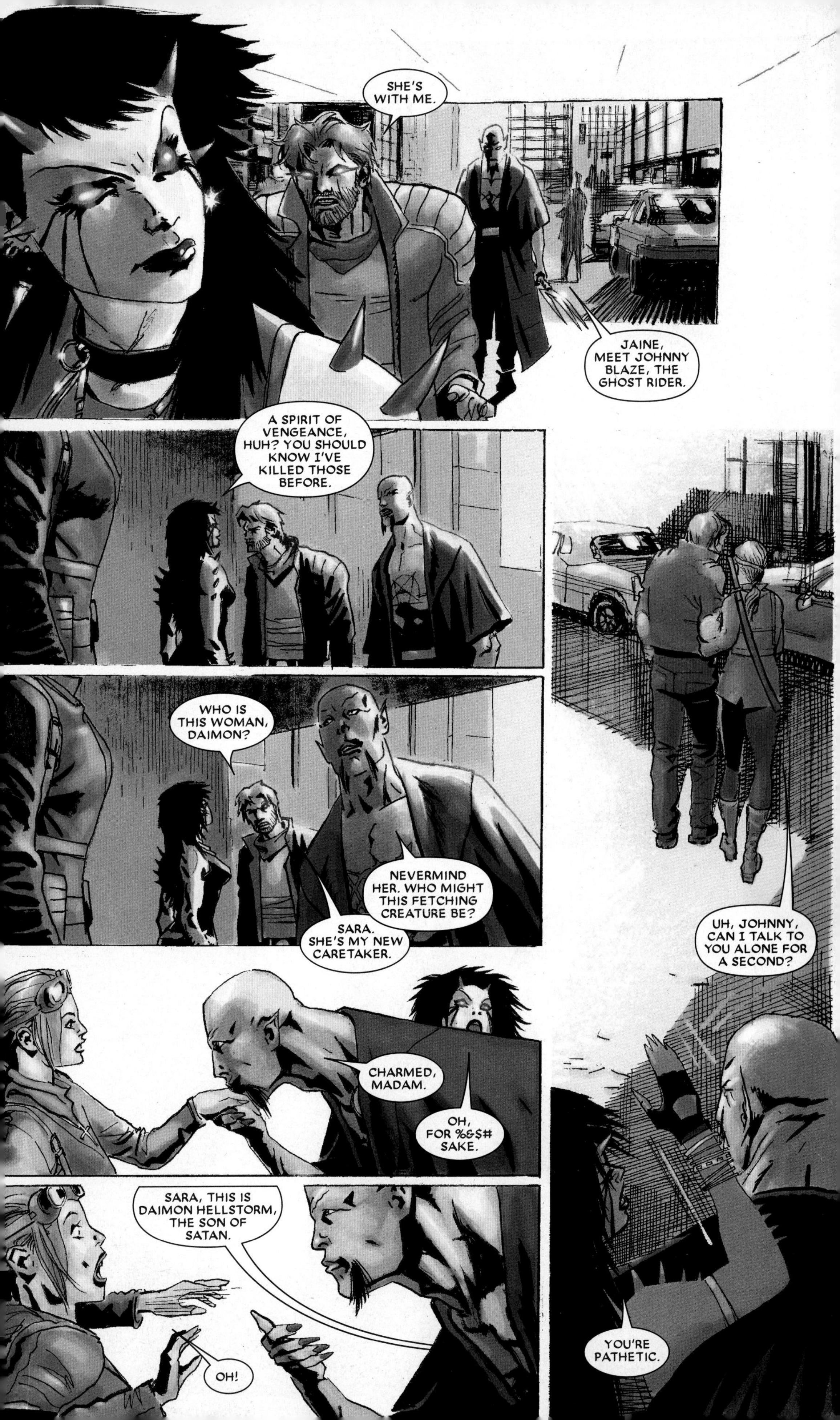

SHE'S WITH ME.
JAINE, MEET JOHNNY BLAZE, THE GHOST RIDER.
A SPIRIT OF VENGEANCE, HUH? YOU SHOULD KNOW I'VE KILLED THOSE BEFORE.
WHO IS THIS WOMAN, DAIMON?
NEVERMIND HER. WHO MIGHT THIS FETCHING CREATURE BE?
SARA. SHE'S MY NEW CARETAKER.
CHARMED, MADAM.
OH, FOR %&$# SAKE.
SARA, THIS IS DAIMON HELLSTORM, THE SON OF SATAN.
OH!
UH, JOHNNY, CAN I TALK TO YOU ALONE FOR A SECOND?
YOU'RE PATHETIC.

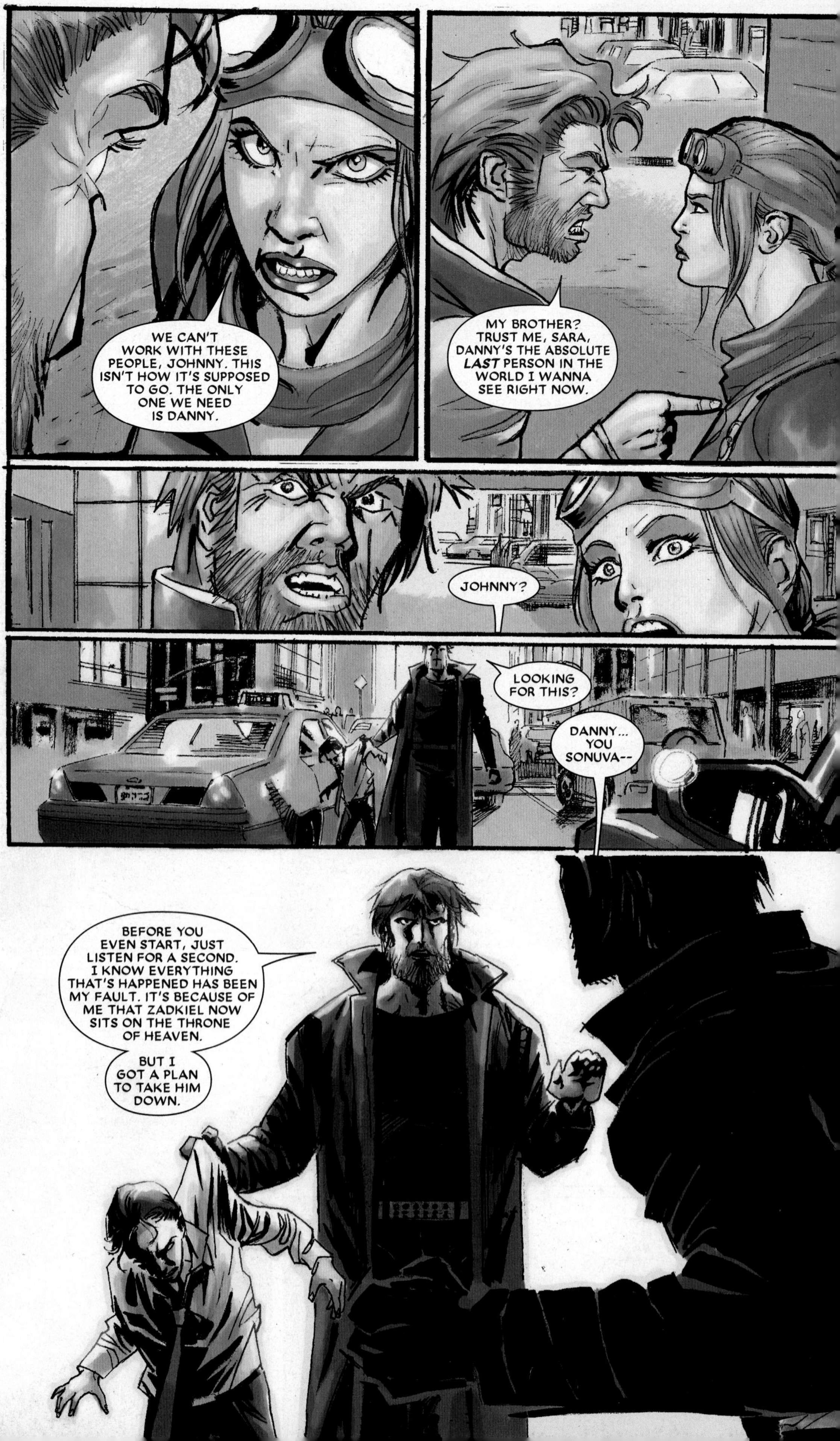
WE CAN'T WORK WITH THESE PEOPLE, JOHNNY. THIS ISN'T HOW IT'S SUPPOSED TO GO. THE ONLY ONE WE NEED IS DANNY.
MY BROTHER? TRUST ME, SARA, DANNY'S THE ABSOLUTE *LAST* PERSON IN THE WORLD I WANNA SEE RIGHT NOW.
JOHNNY?
LOOKING FOR THIS?
DANNY... YOU SONUVA--
BEFORE YOU EVEN START, JUST LISTEN FOR A SECOND. I KNOW EVERYTHING THAT'S HAPPENED HAS BEEN MY FAULT. IT'S BECAUSE OF ME THAT ZADKIEL NOW SITS ON THE THRONE OF HEAVEN.
BUT I GOT A PLAN TO TAKE HIM DOWN.

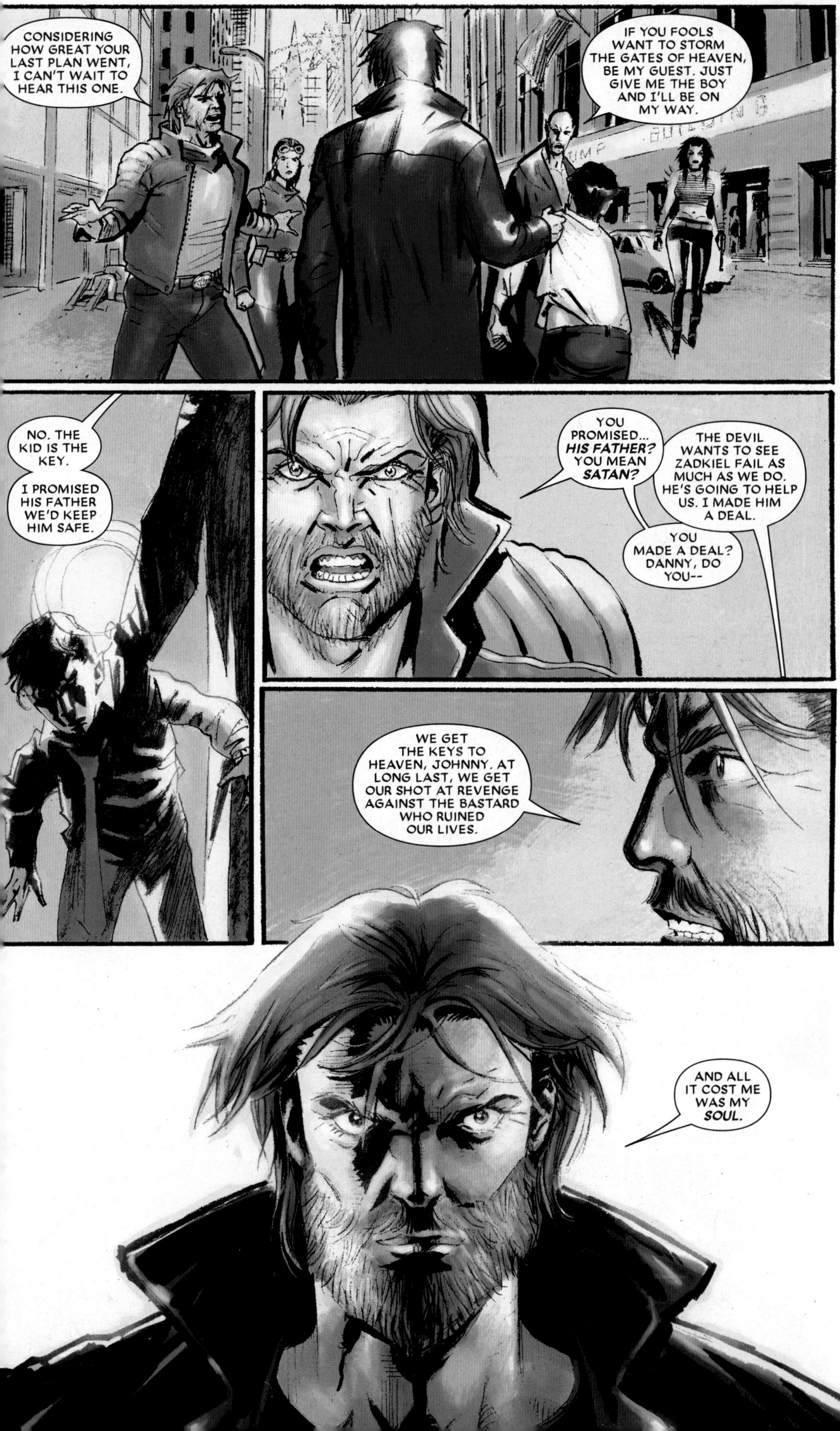
CONSIDERING HOW GREAT YOUR LAST PLAN WENT, I CAN'T WAIT TO HEAR THIS ONE.
IF YOU FOOLS WANT TO STORM THE GATES OF HEAVEN, BE MY GUEST. JUST GIVE ME THE BOY AND I'LL BE ON MY WAY.
NO. THE KID IS THE KEY.
I PROMISED HIS FATHER WE'D KEEP HIM SAFE.
YOU PROMISED... *HIS FATHER?* YOU MEAN *SATAN?*
THE DEVIL WANTS TO SEE ZADKIEL FAIL AS MUCH AS WE DO. HE'S GOING TO HELP US. I MADE HIM A DEAL.
YOU MADE A DEAL? DANNY, DO YOU--
WE GET THE KEYS TO HEAVEN, JOHNNY. AT LONG LAST, WE GET OUR SHOT AT REVENGE AGAINST THE BASTARD WHO RUINED OUR LIVES.
AND ALL IT COST ME WAS MY *SOUL.*

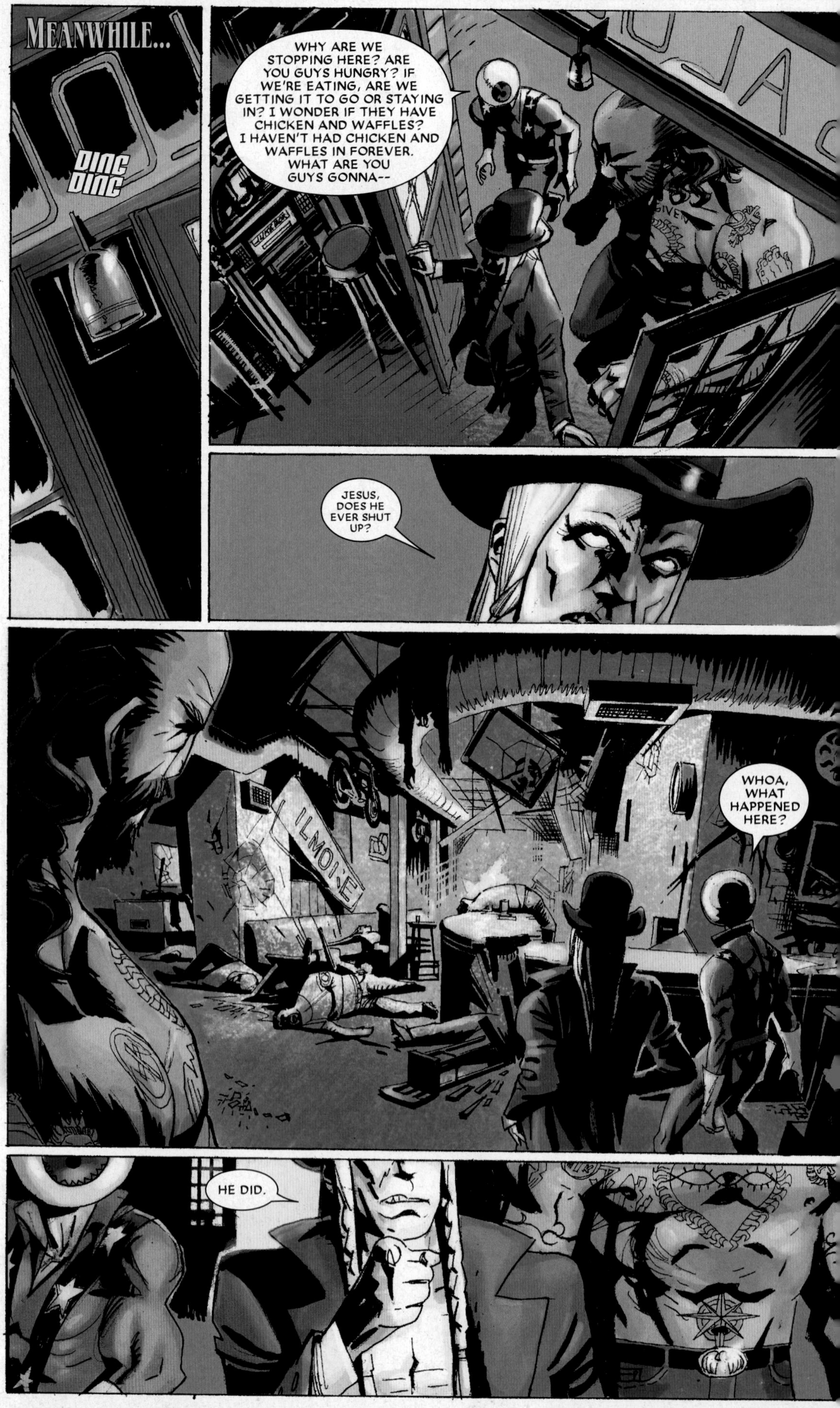
MEANWHILE...
DING DING
WHY ARE WE STOPPING HERE? ARE YOU GUYS HUNGRY? IF WE'RE EATING, ARE WE GETTING IT TO GO OR STAYING IN? I WONDER IF THEY HAVE CHICKEN AND WAFFLES? I HAVEN'T HAD CHICKEN AND WAFFLES IN FOREVER. WHAT ARE YOU GUYS GONNA--
JESUS, DOES HE EVER SHUT UP?
WHOA, WHAT HAPPENED HERE?
HE DID.

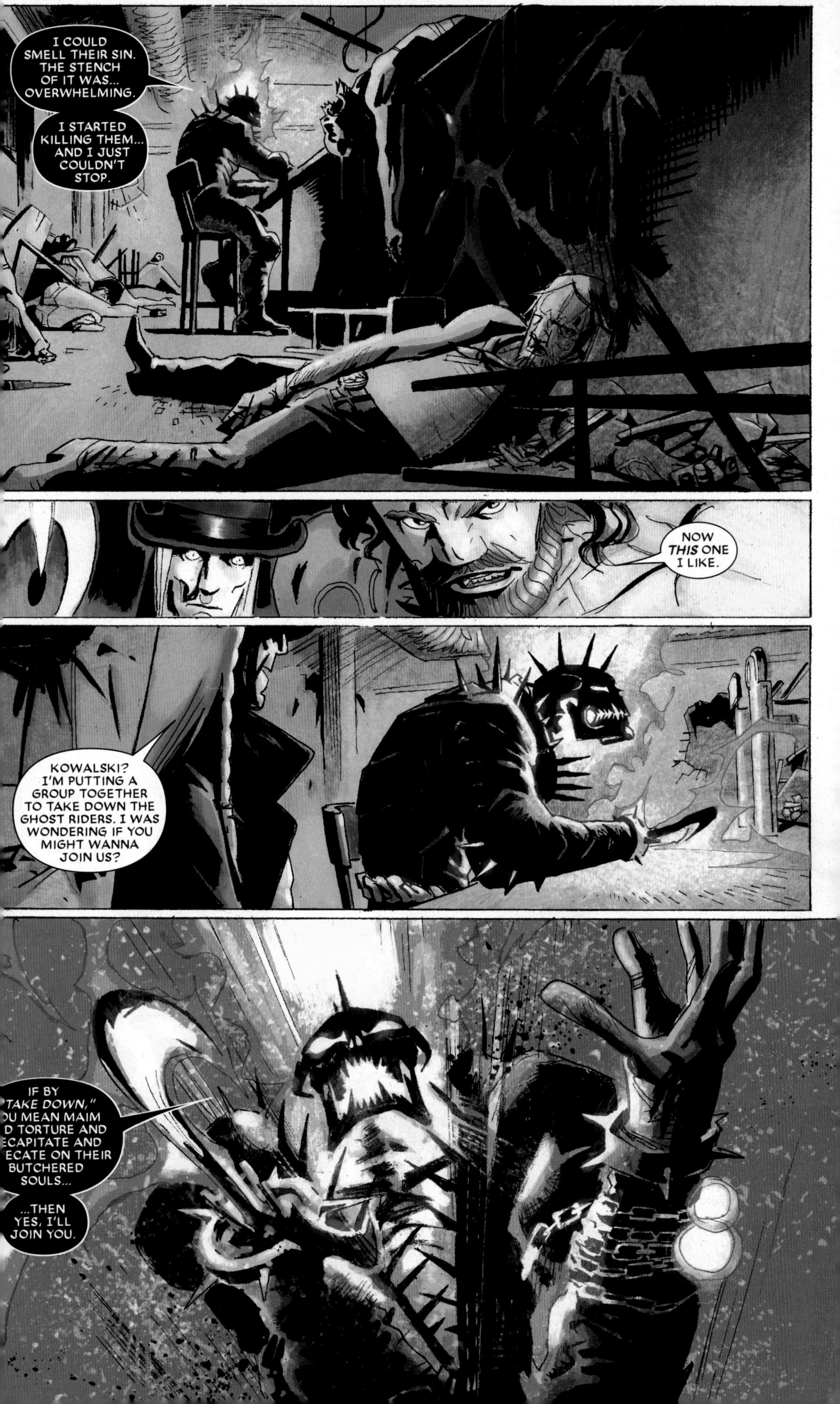
I COULD SMELL THEIR SIN. THE STENCH OF IT WAS... OVERWHELMING.
I STARTED KILLING THEM... AND I JUST COULDN'T STOP.
NOW *THIS* ONE I LIKE.
KOWALSKI? I'M PUTTING A GROUP TOGETHER TO TAKE DOWN THE GHOST RIDERS. I WAS WONDERING IF YOU MIGHT WANNA JOIN US?
IF BY "*TAKE DOWN,*" OU MEAN MAIM D TORTURE AND ECAPITATE AND ECATE ON THEIR BUTCHERED SOULS...
...THEN YES, I'LL JOIN YOU.

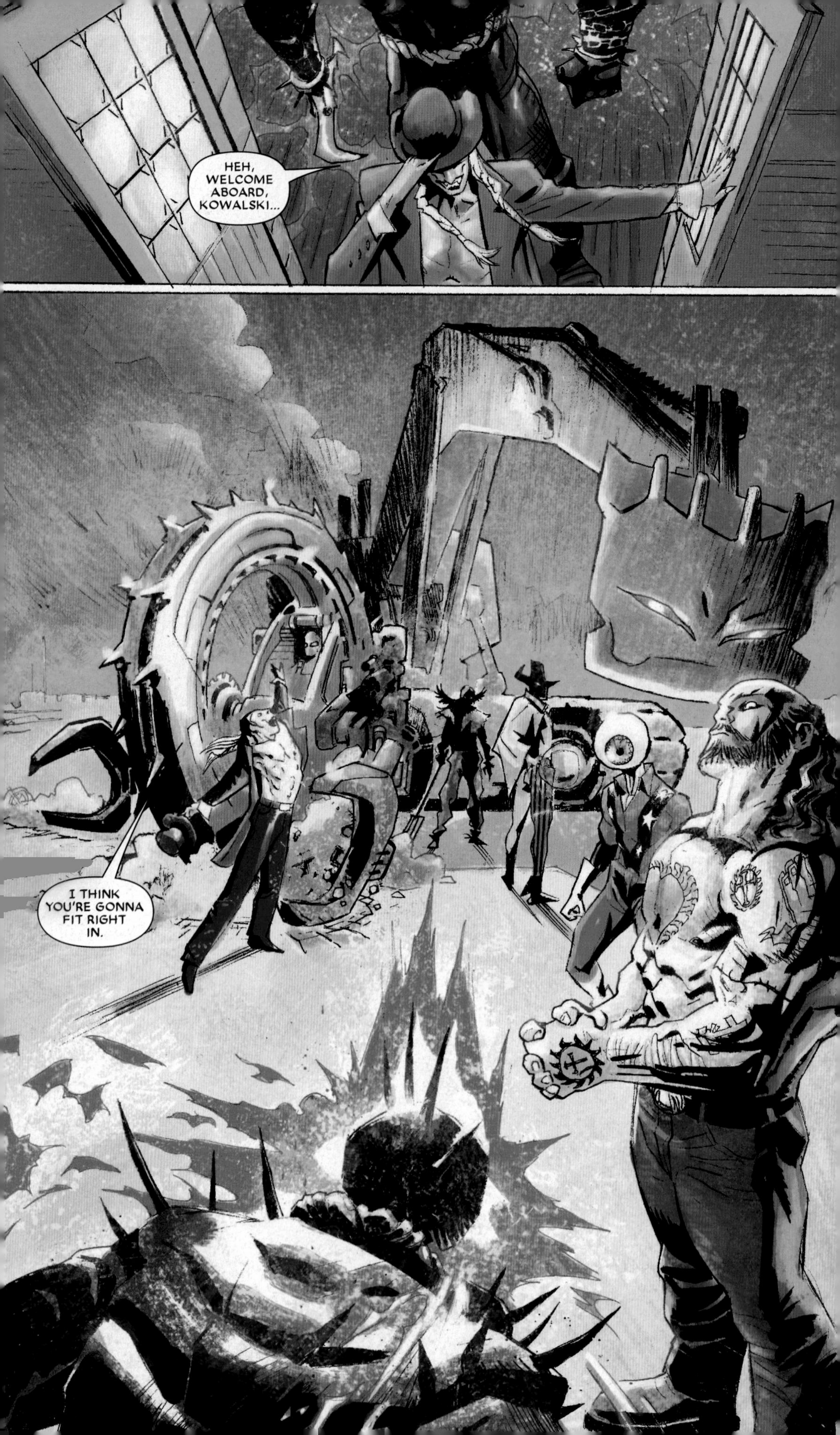
HEH, WELCOME ABOARD, KOWALSKI...
I THINK YOU'RE GONNA FIT RIGHT IN.

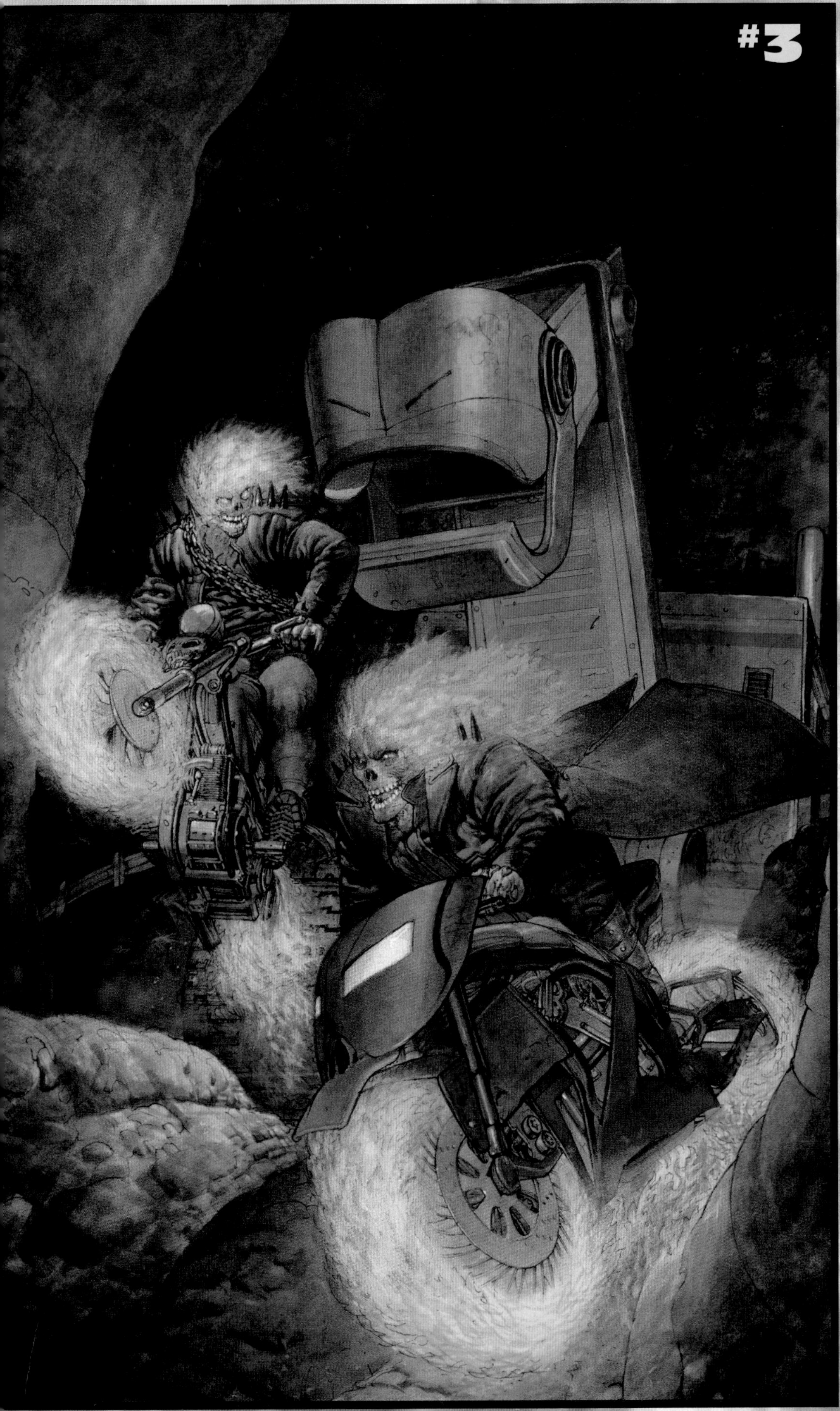
#3

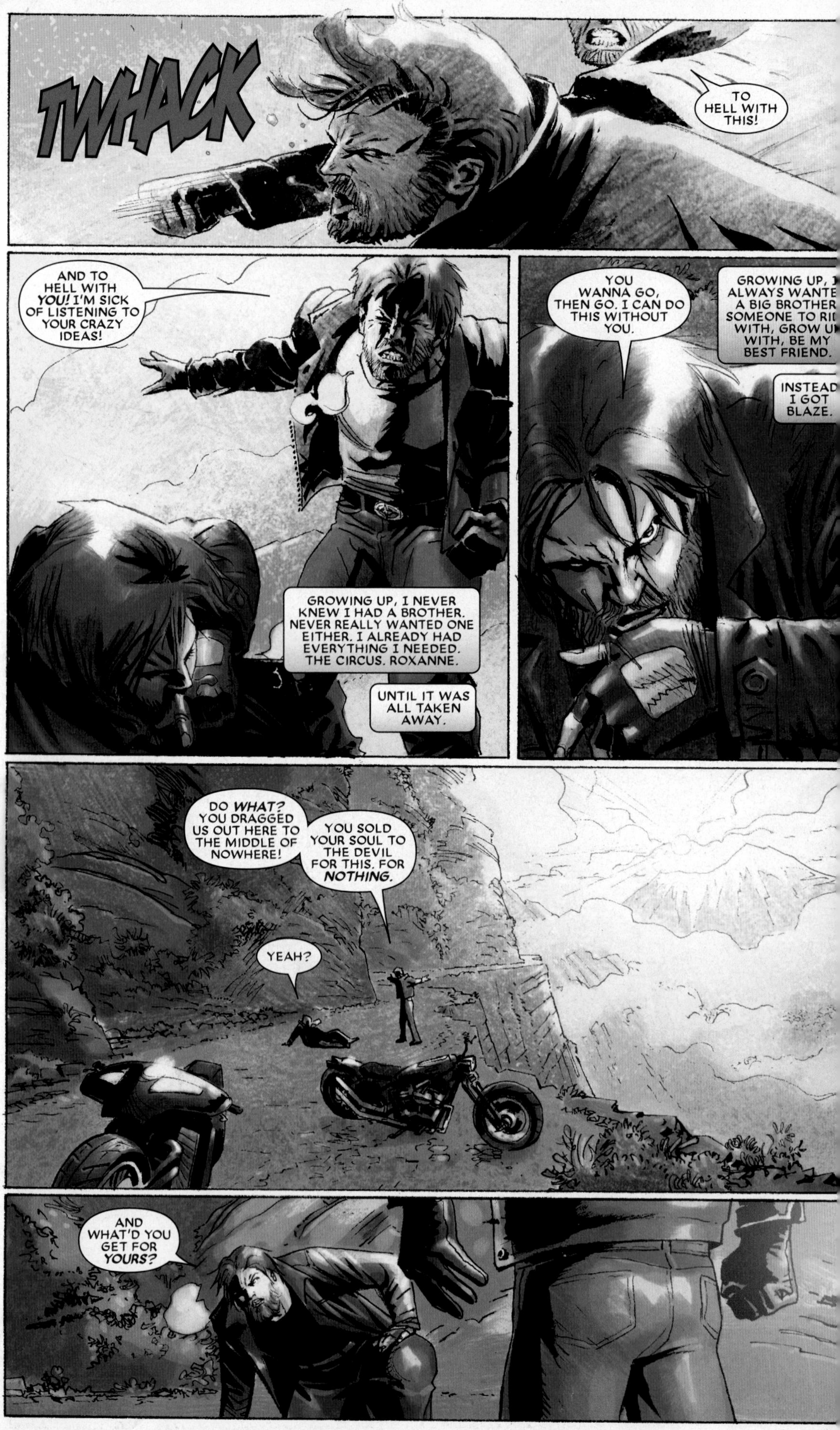

TWHACK
TO HELL WITH THIS!
AND TO HELL WITH YOU! I'M SICK OF LISTENING TO YOUR CRAZY IDEAS!
GROWING UP, I NEVER KNEW I HAD A BROTHER. NEVER REALLY WANTED ONE EITHER. I ALREADY HAD EVERYTHING I NEEDED. THE CIRCUS. ROXANNE.
UNTIL IT WAS ALL TAKEN AWAY.
YOU WANNA GO, THEN GO. I CAN DO THIS WITHOUT YOU.
DO WHAT? YOU DRAGGED US OUT HERE TO THE MIDDLE OF NOWHERE!
YOU SOLD YOUR SOUL TO THE DEVIL FOR THIS. FOR NOTHING.
YEAH?
AND WHAT'D YOU GET FOR YOURS?

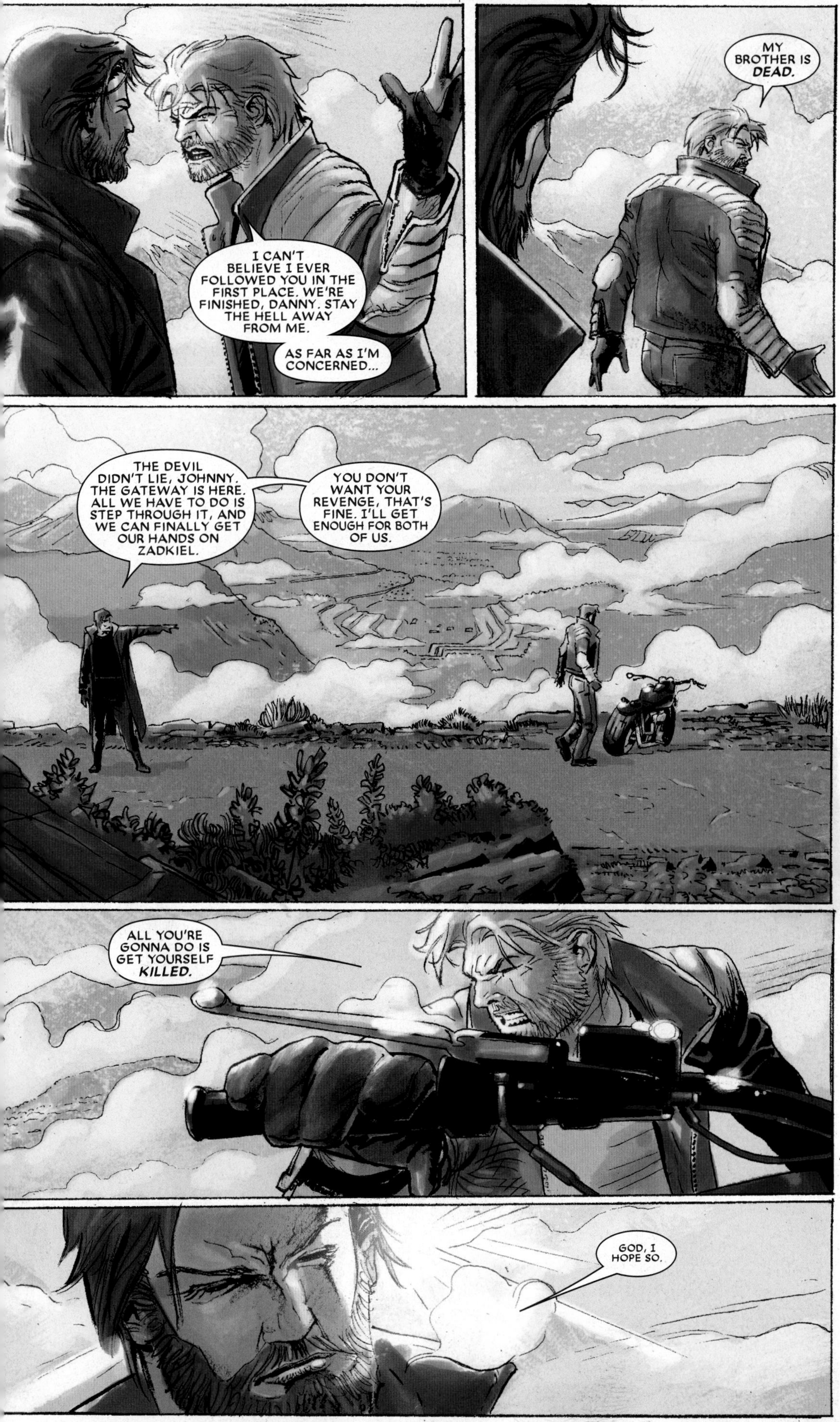
I CAN'T BELIEVE I EVER FOLLOWED YOU IN THE FIRST PLACE. WE'RE FINISHED, DANNY. STAY THE HELL AWAY FROM ME.
AS FAR AS I'M CONCERNED...
MY BROTHER IS *DEAD.*
THE DEVIL DIDN'T LIE, JOHNNY. THE GATEWAY IS HERE. ALL WE HAVE TO DO IS STEP THROUGH IT, AND WE CAN FINALLY GET OUR HANDS ON ZADKIEL.
YOU DON'T WANT YOUR REVENGE, THAT'S FINE. I'LL GET ENOUGH FOR BOTH OF US.
ALL YOU'RE GONNA DO IS GET YOURSELF *KILLED.*
GOD, I HOPE SO.

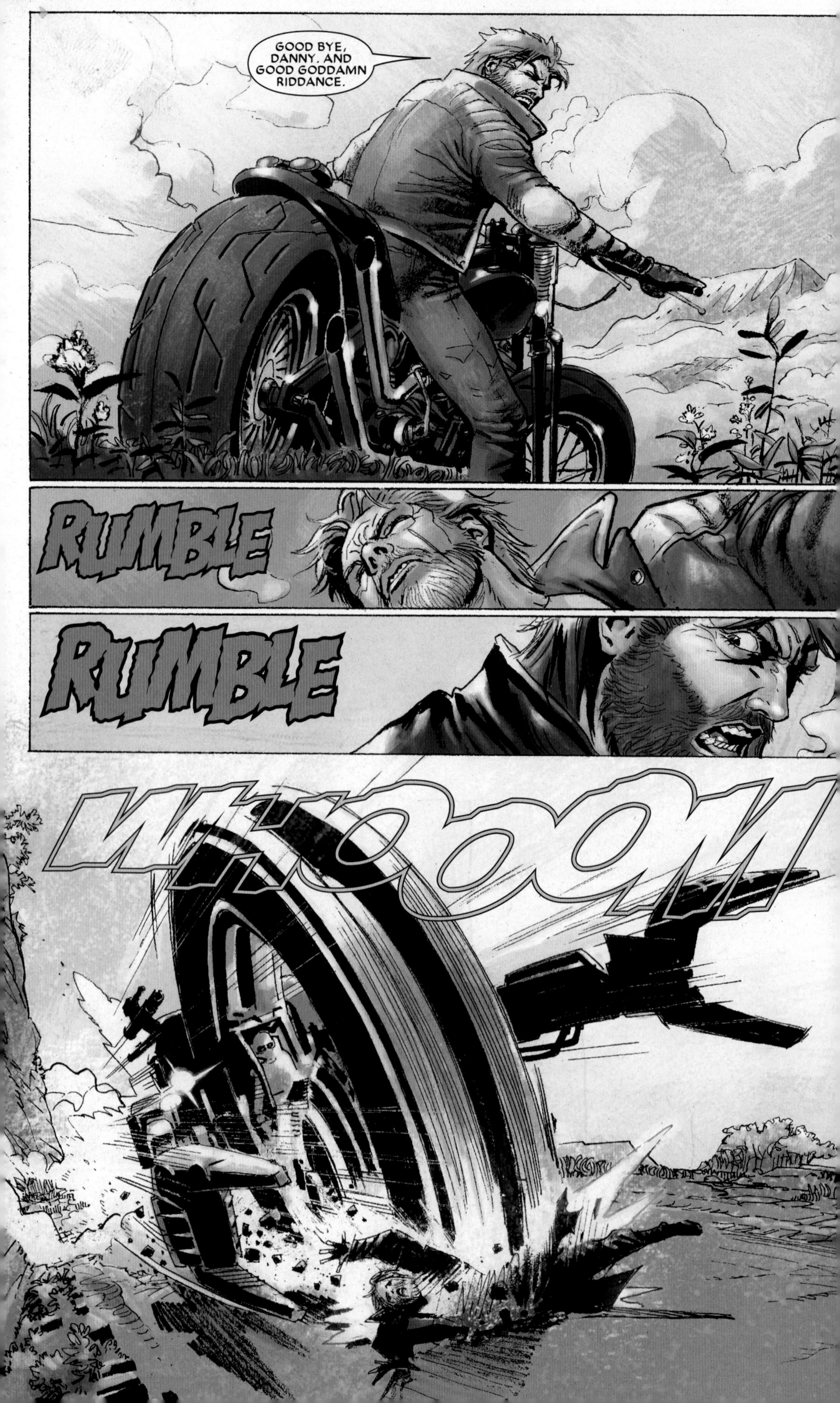
GOOD BYE, DANNY. AND GOOD GODDAMN RIDDANCE.
RUMBLE
RUMBLE
WHOOOM

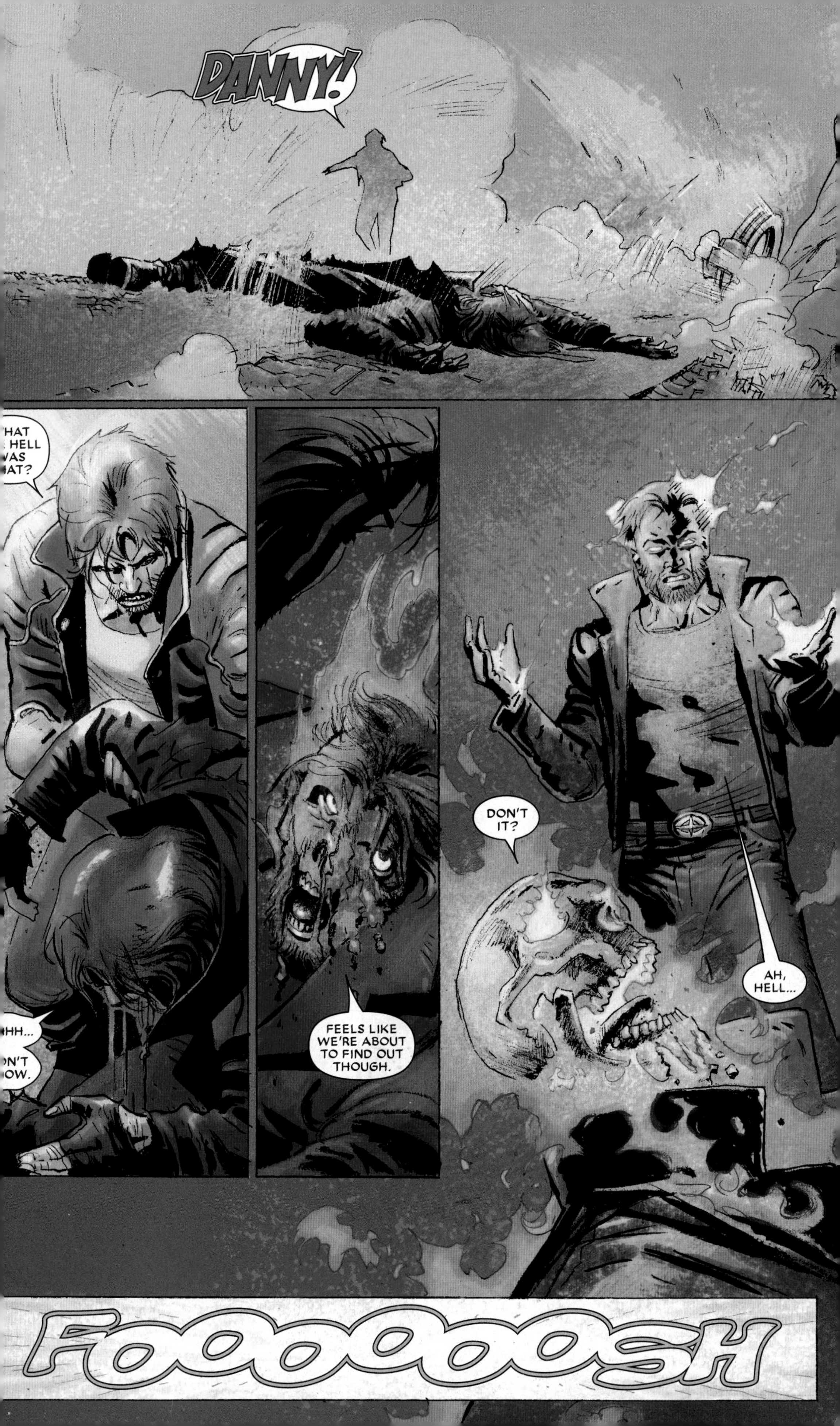
DANNY!
HAT
HELL
VAS
HAT?
HH...
ON'T
OW.
FEELS LIKE WE'RE ABOUT TO FIND OUT THOUGH.
DON'T IT?
AH, HELL...
FOOOOOSH

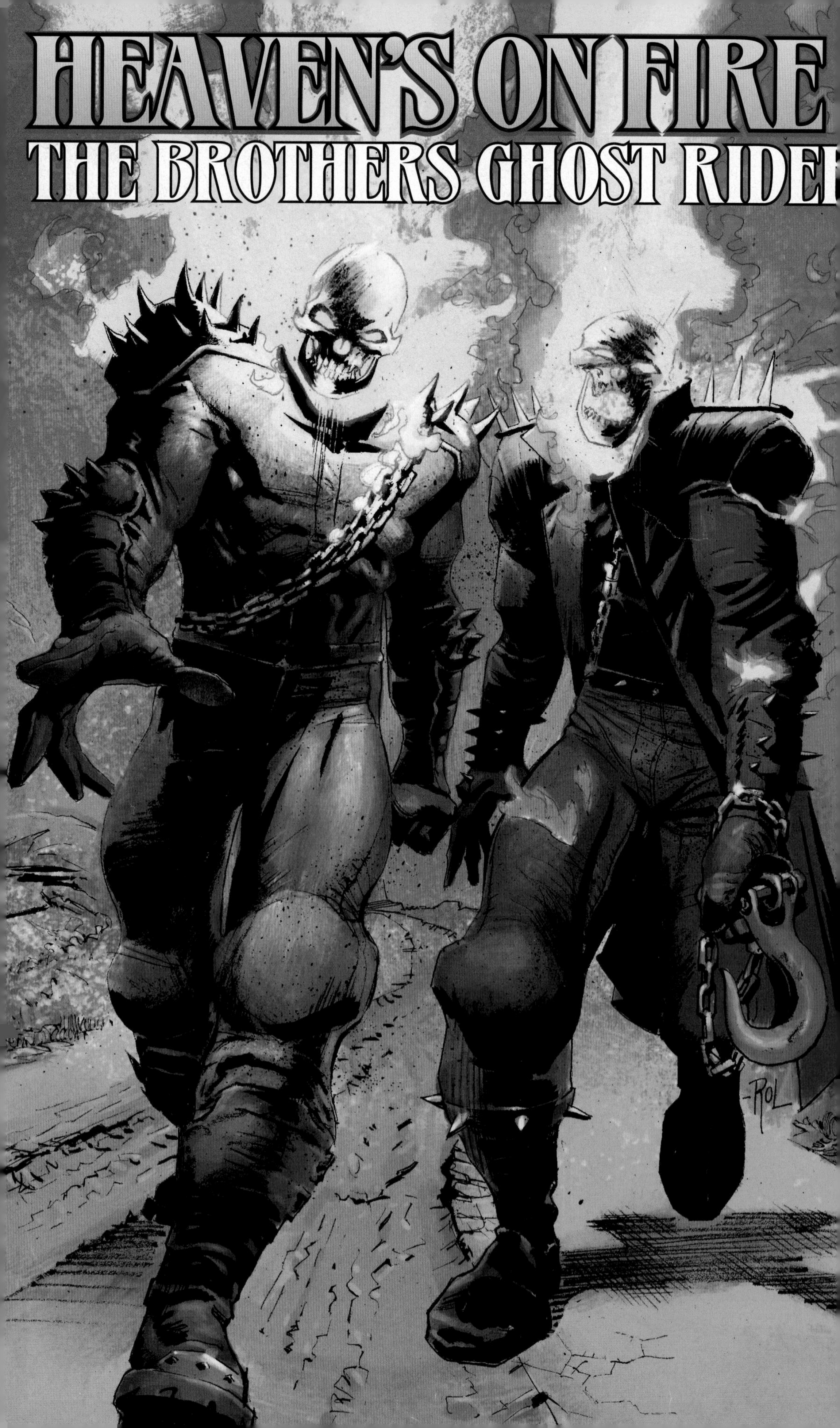
HEAVEN'S ON FIRE
THE BROTHERS GHOST RIDE
-ROL

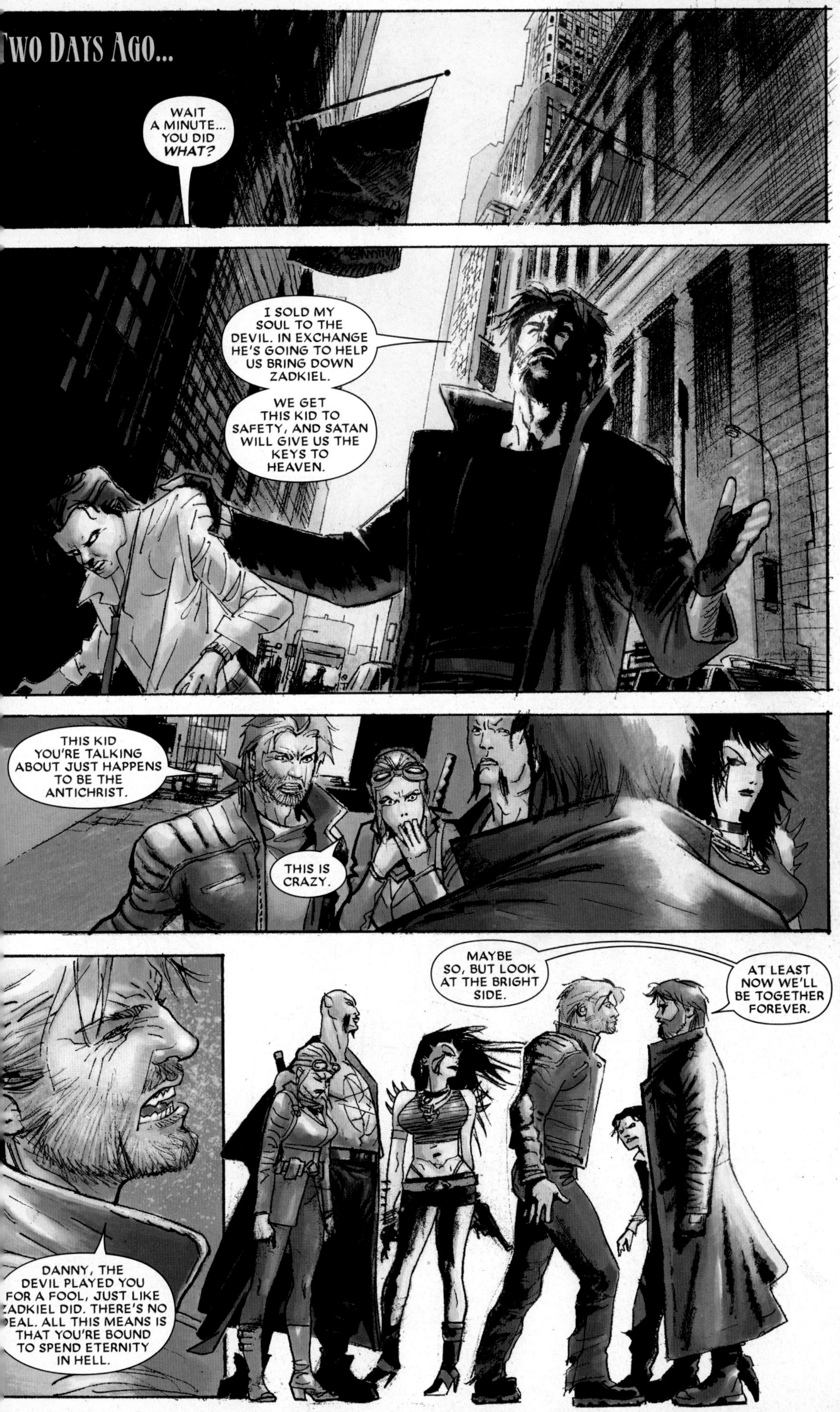
TWO DAYS AGO...
WAIT A MINUTE... YOU DID *WHAT?*
I SOLD MY SOUL TO THE DEVIL. IN EXCHANGE HE'S GOING TO HELP US BRING DOWN ZADKIEL.
WE GET THIS KID TO SAFETY, AND SATAN WILL GIVE US THE KEYS TO HEAVEN.
THIS KID YOU'RE TALKING ABOUT JUST HAPPENS TO BE THE ANTICHRIST.
THIS IS CRAZY.
DANNY, THE DEVIL PLAYED YOU FOR A FOOL, JUST LIKE ZADKIEL DID. THERE'S NO DEAL. ALL THIS MEANS IS THAT YOU'RE BOUND TO SPEND ETERNITY IN HELL.
MAYBE SO, BUT LOOK AT THE BRIGHT SIDE.
AT LEAST NOW WE'LL BE TOGETHER FOREVER.

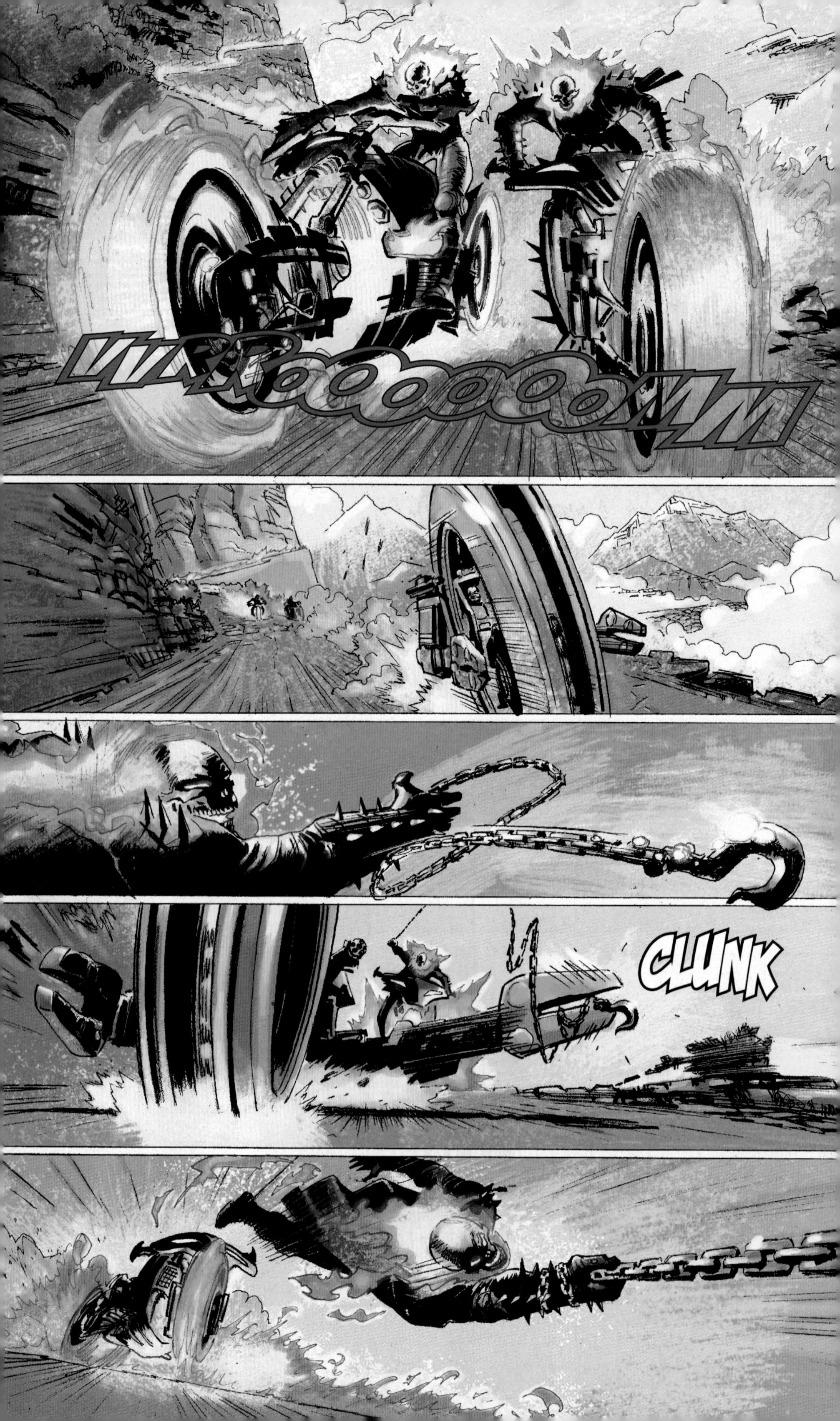
VVRROOOOOOOOOM
CLUNK

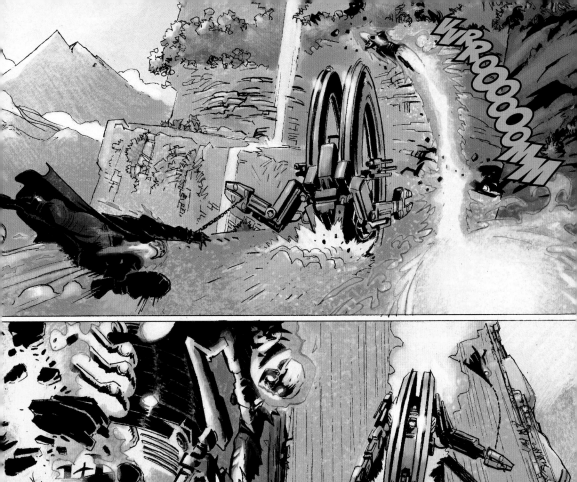

VRROOOOMM

FOOSH

THOOM

CLUNK

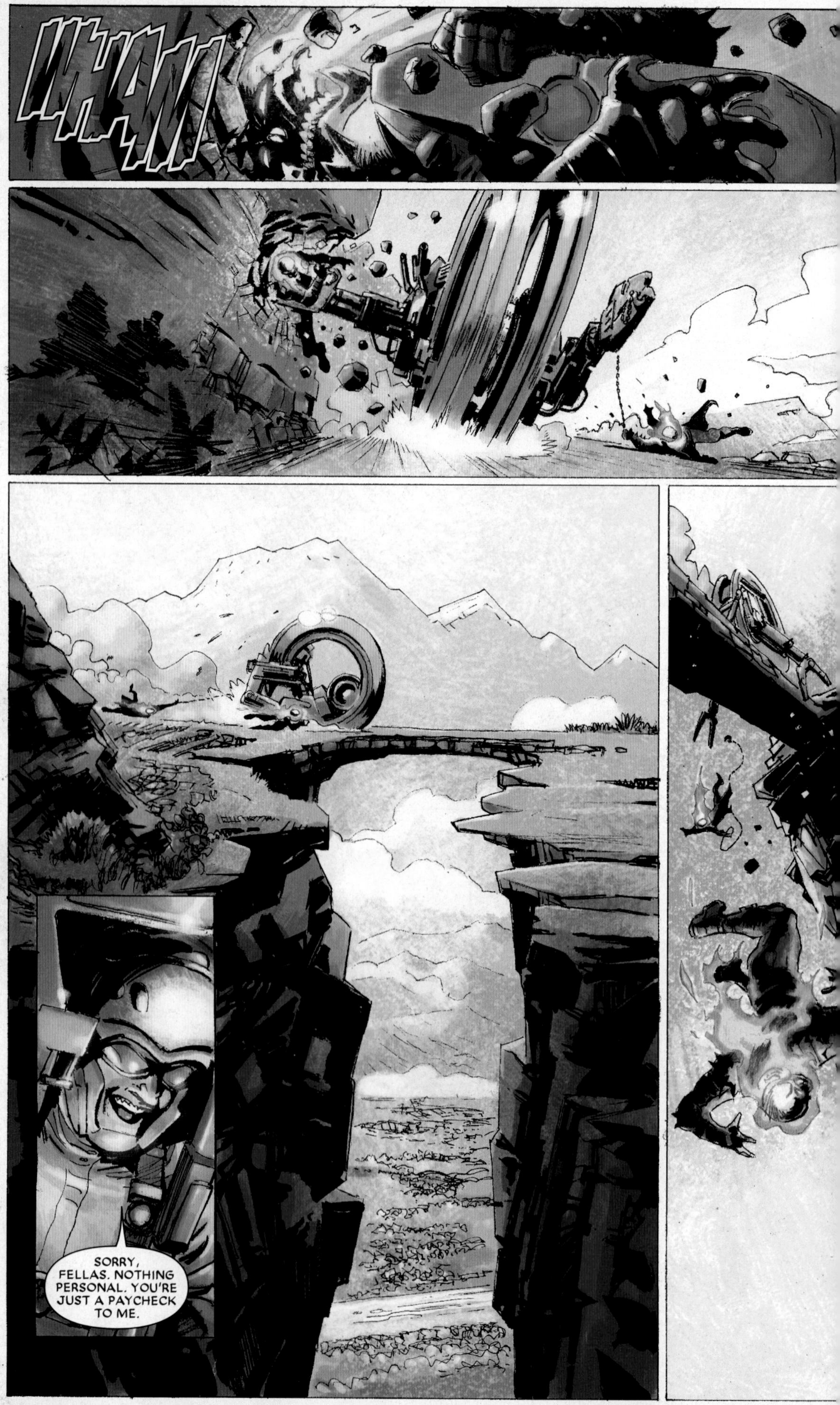
WHAM
SORRY, FELLAS. NOTHING PERSONAL. YOU'RE JUST A PAYCHECK TO ME.

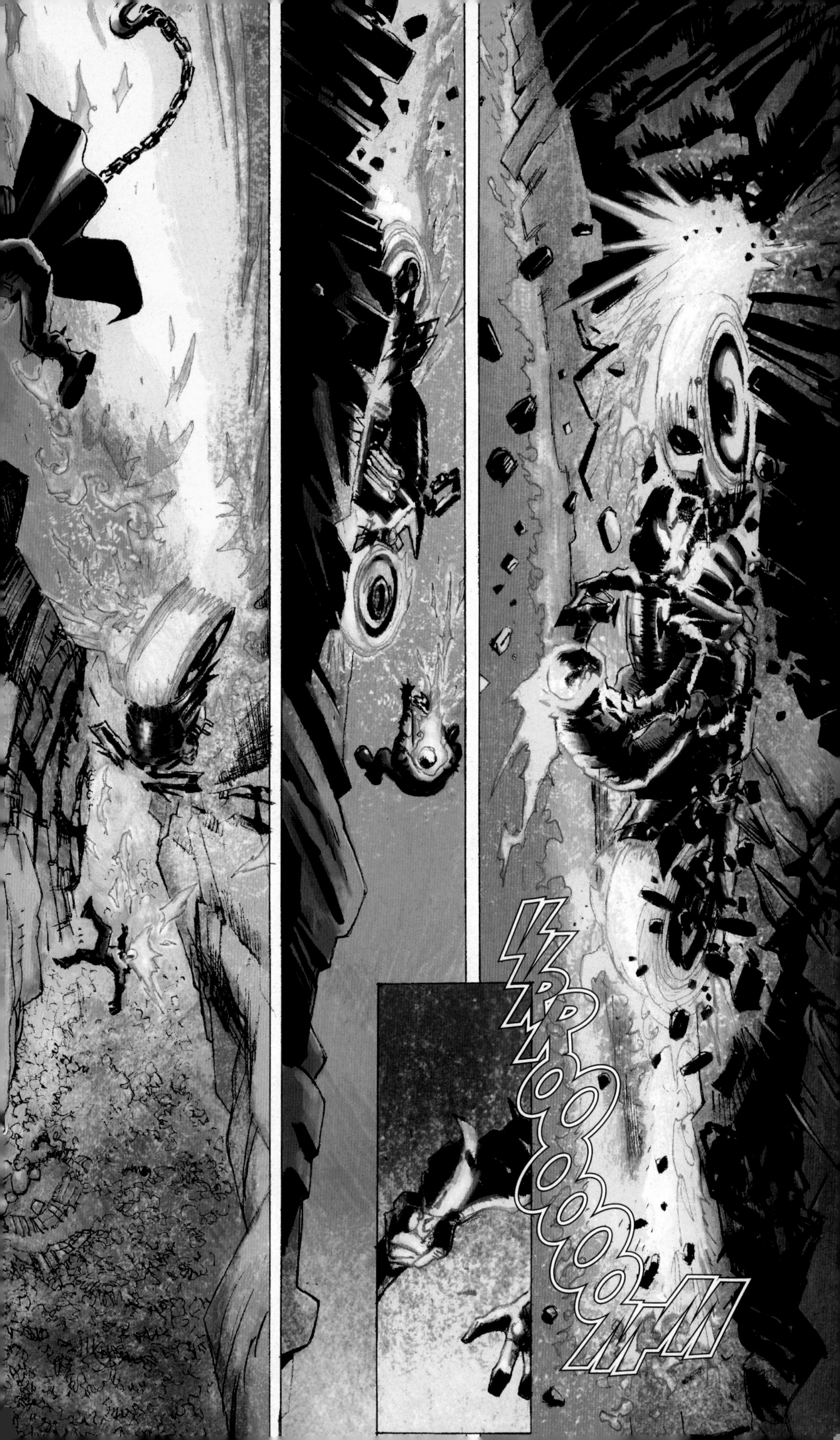
KROOOOOOOM

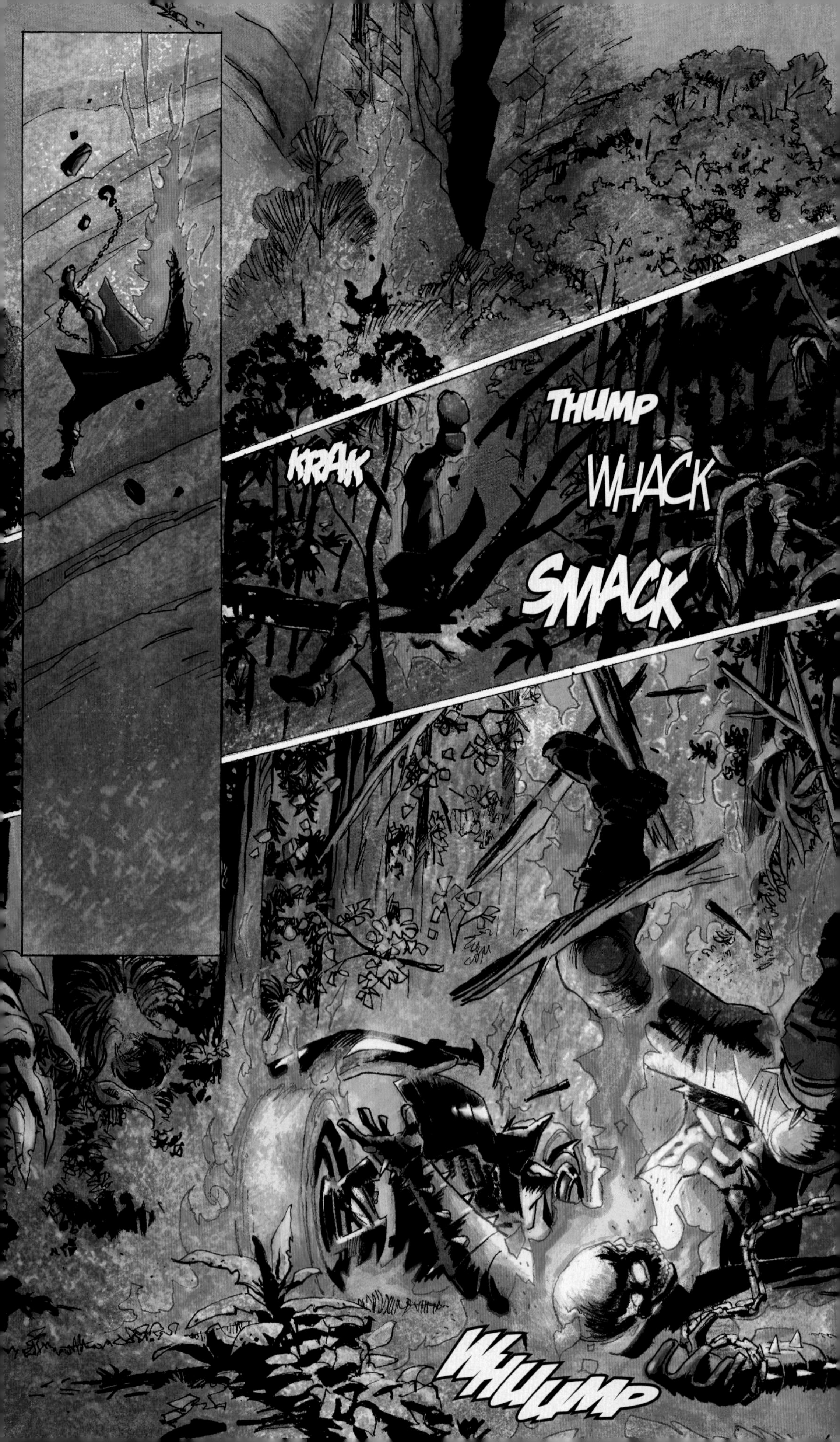
KRAK
THUMP
WHACK
SMACK
WHUMP

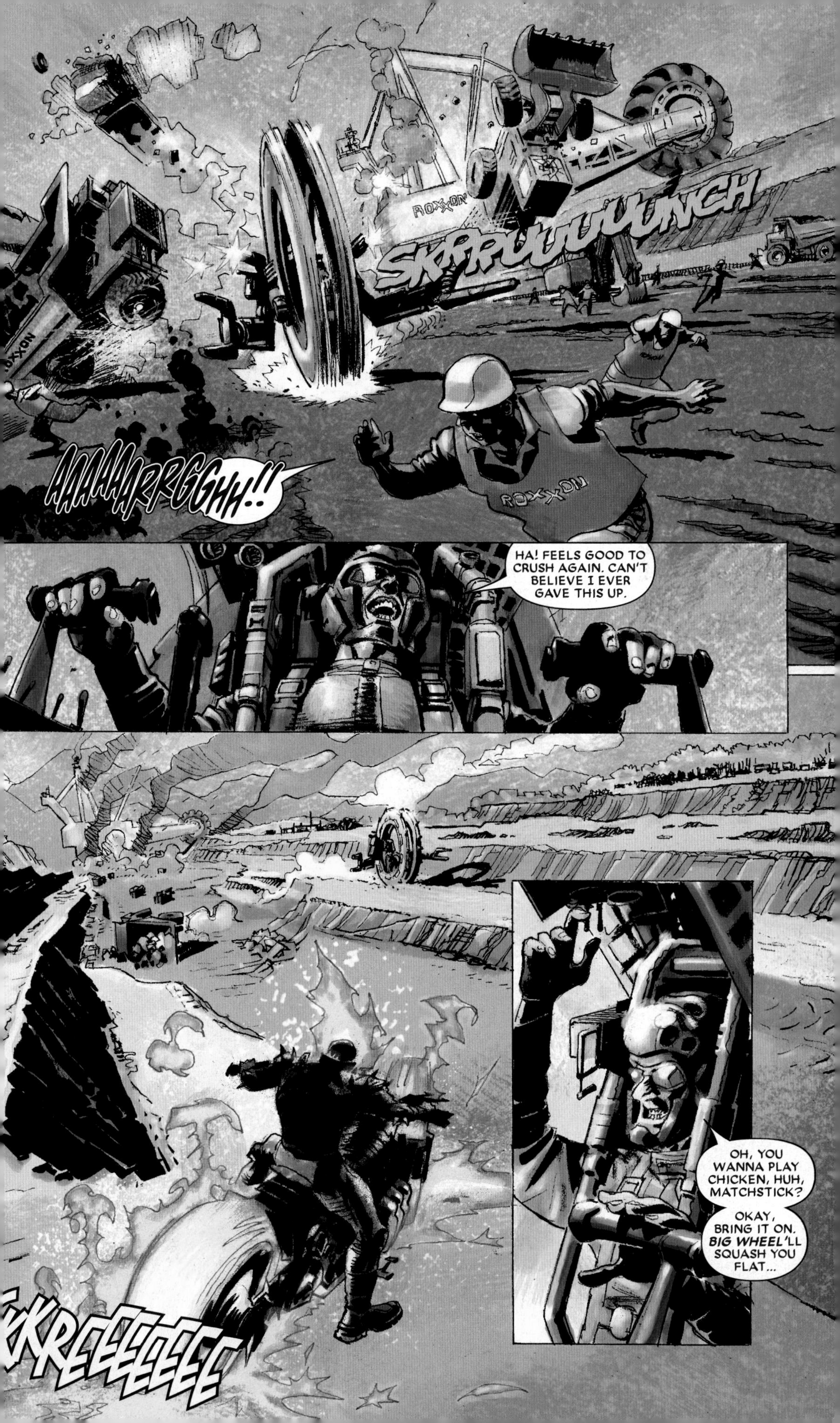
ROXXON
SKRRUUUUUNCH
ROXXON
ROXXON
AAAAAARRRGGHH!!
HA! FEELS GOOD TO CRUSH AGAIN. CAN'T BELIEVE I EVER GAVE THIS UP.
OH, YOU WANNA PLAY CHICKEN, HUH, MATCHSTICK?
OKAY, BRING IT ON. *BIG WHEEL*'LL SQUASH YOU FLAT...
KREEEEEEEE

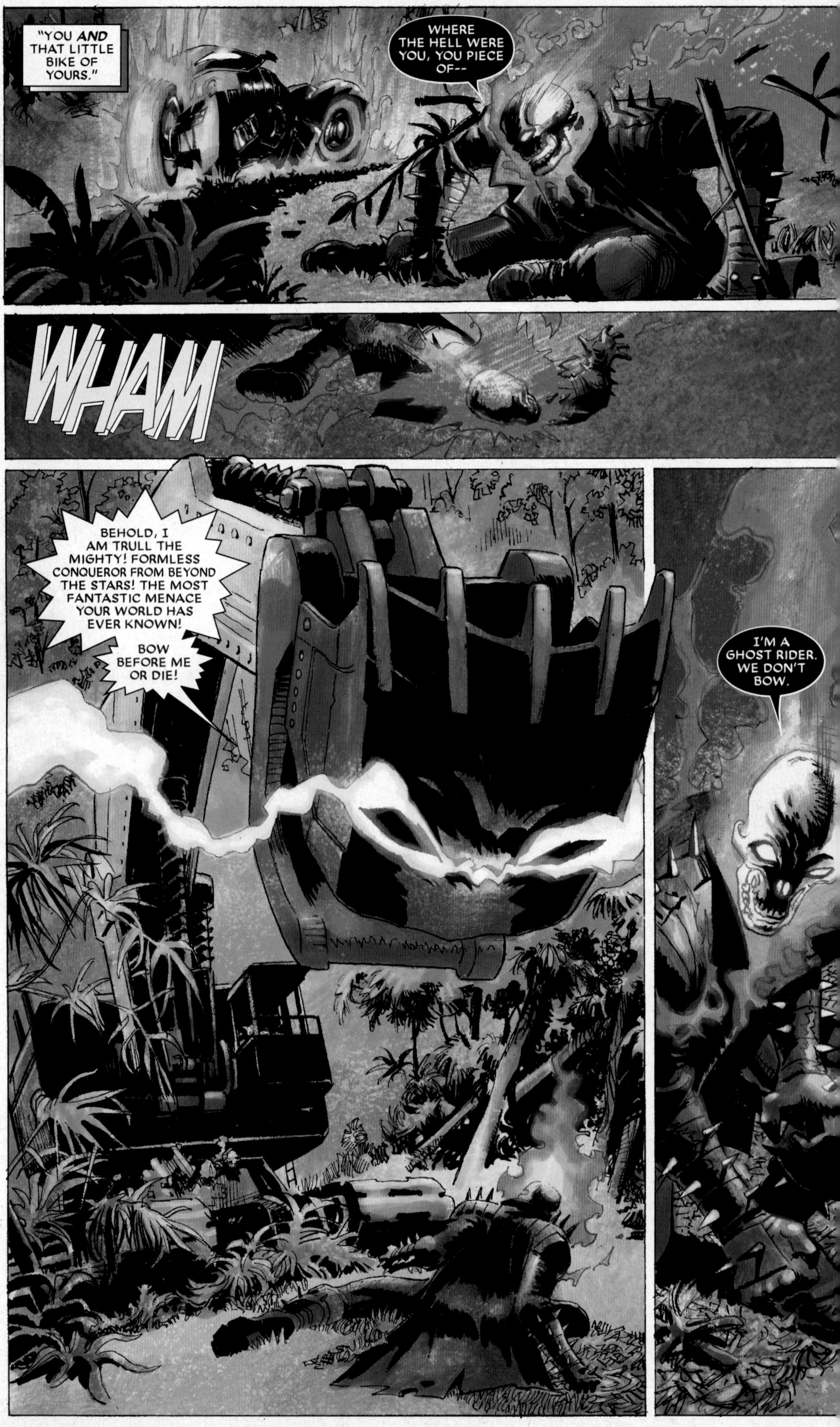
"YOU AND THAT LITTLE BIKE OF YOURS."
WHERE THE HELL WERE YOU, YOU PIECE OF--
WHAM
BEHOLD, I AM TRULL THE MIGHTY! FORMLESS CONQUEROR FROM BEYOND THE STARS! THE MOST FANTASTIC MENACE YOUR WORLD HAS EVER KNOWN!
BOW BEFORE ME OR DIE!
I'M A GHOST RIDER. WE DON'T BOW.

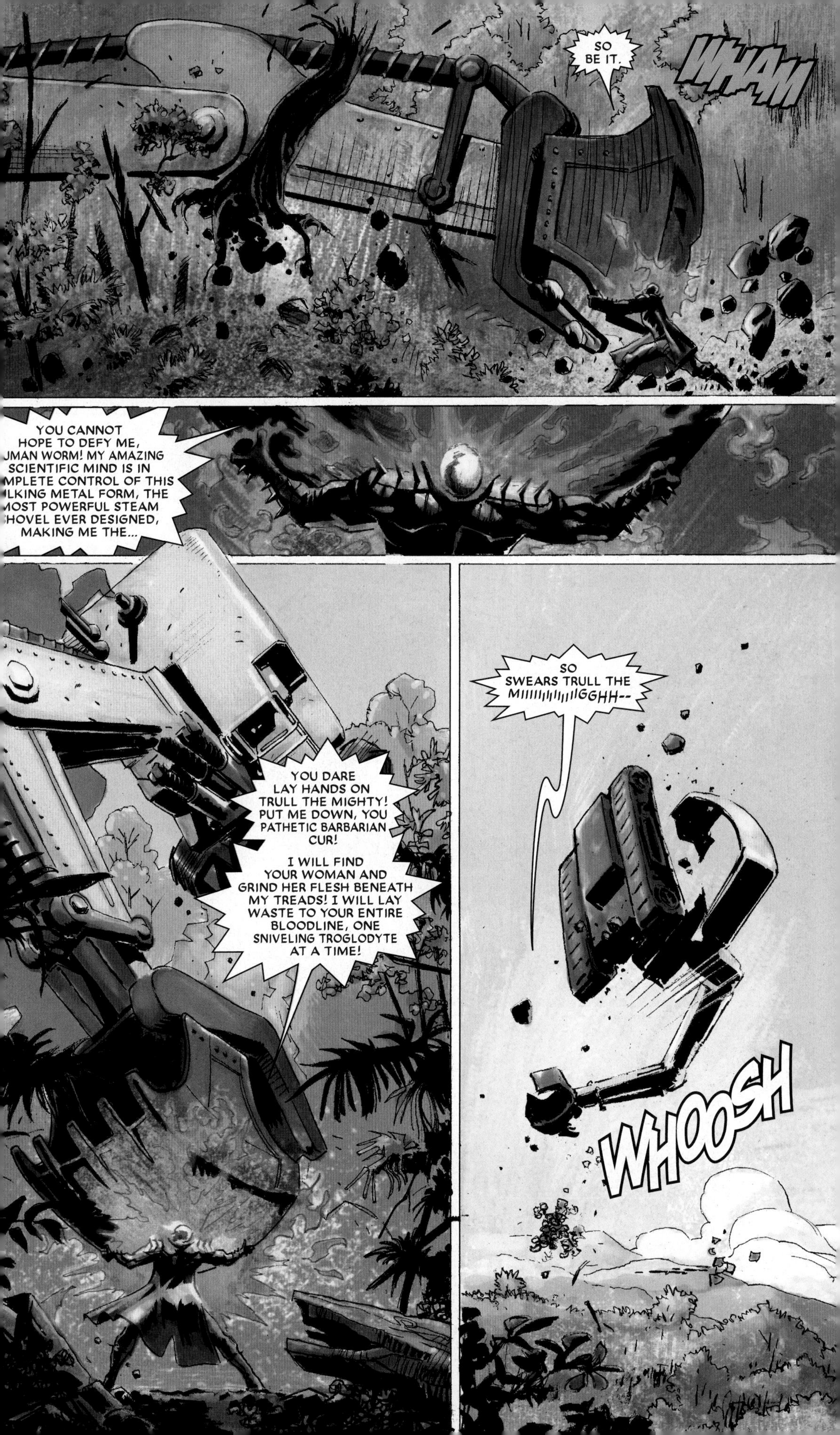
SO BE IT.
WHAM
YOU CANNOT HOPE TO DEFY ME, UMAN WORM! MY AMAZING SCIENTIFIC MIND IS IN MPLETE CONTROL OF THIS ILKING METAL FORM, THE MOST POWERFUL STEAM HOVEL EVER DESIGNED, MAKING ME THE...
YOU DARE LAY HANDS ON TRULL THE MIGHTY! PUT ME DOWN, YOU PATHETIC BARBARIAN CUR!
I WILL FIND YOUR WOMAN AND GRIND HER FLESH BENEATH MY TREADS! I WILL LAY WASTE TO YOUR ENTIRE BLOODLINE, ONE SNIVELING TROGLODYTE AT A TIME!
SO SWEARS TRULL THE MIIIIIIIIIIIIGGHH--
WHOOSH

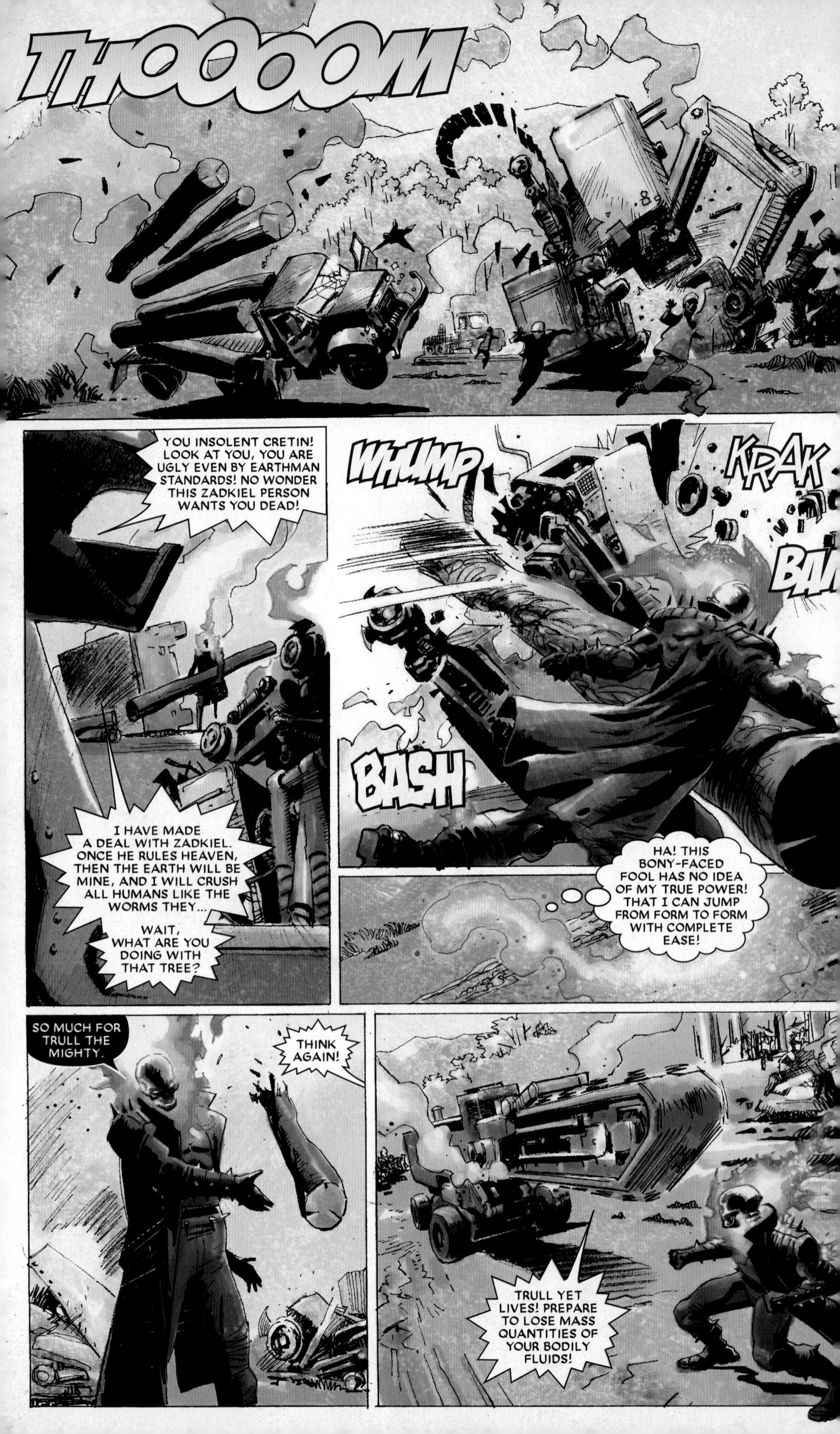
THOOOOM
YOU INSOLENT CRETIN! LOOK AT YOU, YOU ARE UGLY EVEN BY EARTHMAN STANDARDS! NO WONDER THIS ZADKIEL PERSON WANTS YOU DEAD!
I HAVE MADE A DEAL WITH ZADKIEL. ONCE HE RULES HEAVEN, THEN THE EARTH WILL BE MINE, AND I WILL CRUSH ALL HUMANS LIKE THE WORMS THEY...
WAIT, WHAT ARE YOU DOING WITH THAT TREE?
WHUMP
KRAK
BASH
HA! THIS BONY-FACED FOOL HAS NO IDEA OF MY TRUE POWER! THAT I CAN JUMP FROM FORM TO FORM WITH COMPLETE EASE!
SO MUCH FOR TRULL THE MIGHTY.
THINK AGAIN!
TRULL YET LIVES! PREPARE TO LOSE MASS QUANTITIES OF YOUR BODILY FLUIDS!

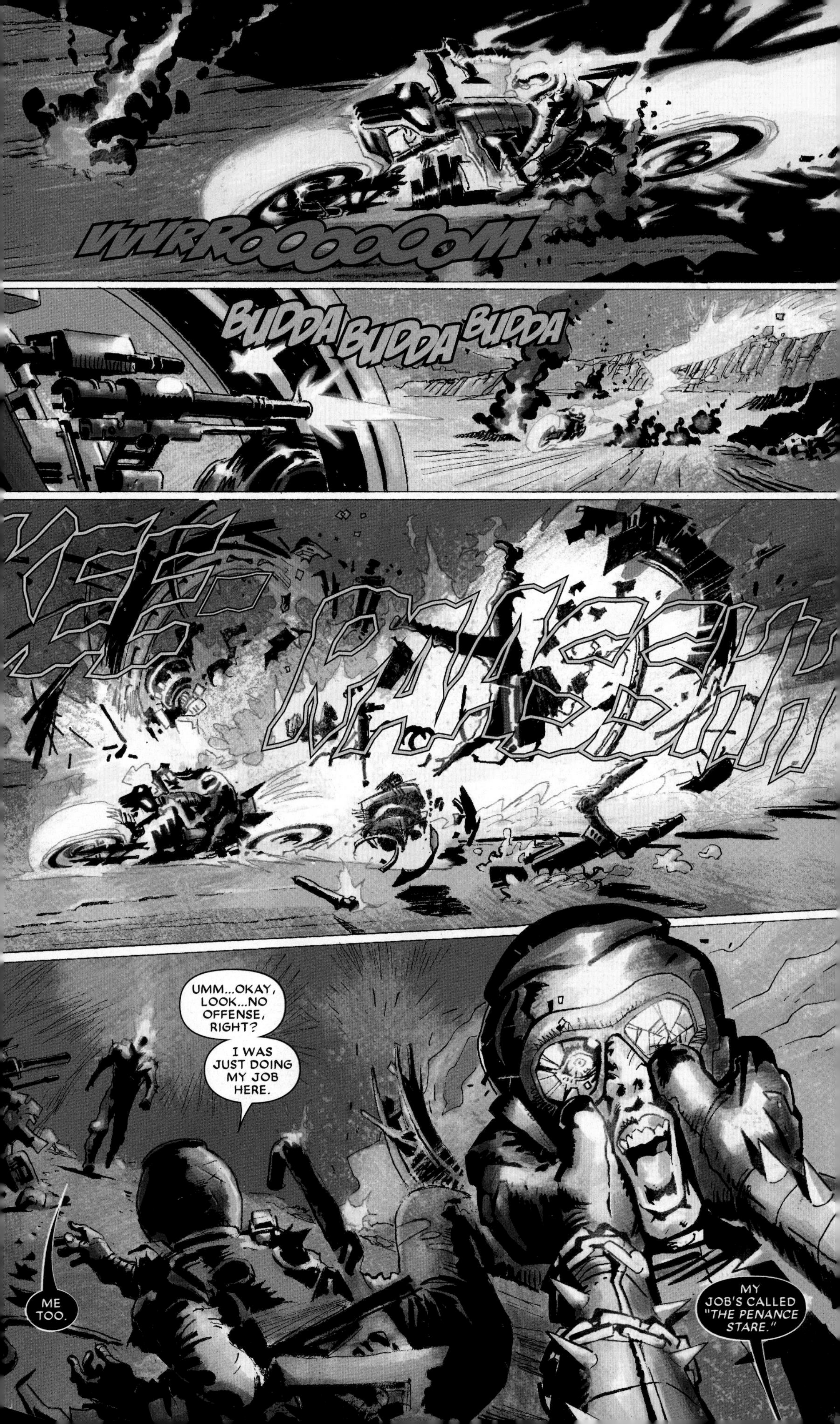
VVVRROOOOOOM
BUDDA BUDDA BUDDA
UMM...OKAY, LOOK...NO OFFENSE, RIGHT?
I WAS JUST DOING MY JOB HERE.
ME TOO.
MY JOB'S CALLED *"THE PENANCE STARE."*

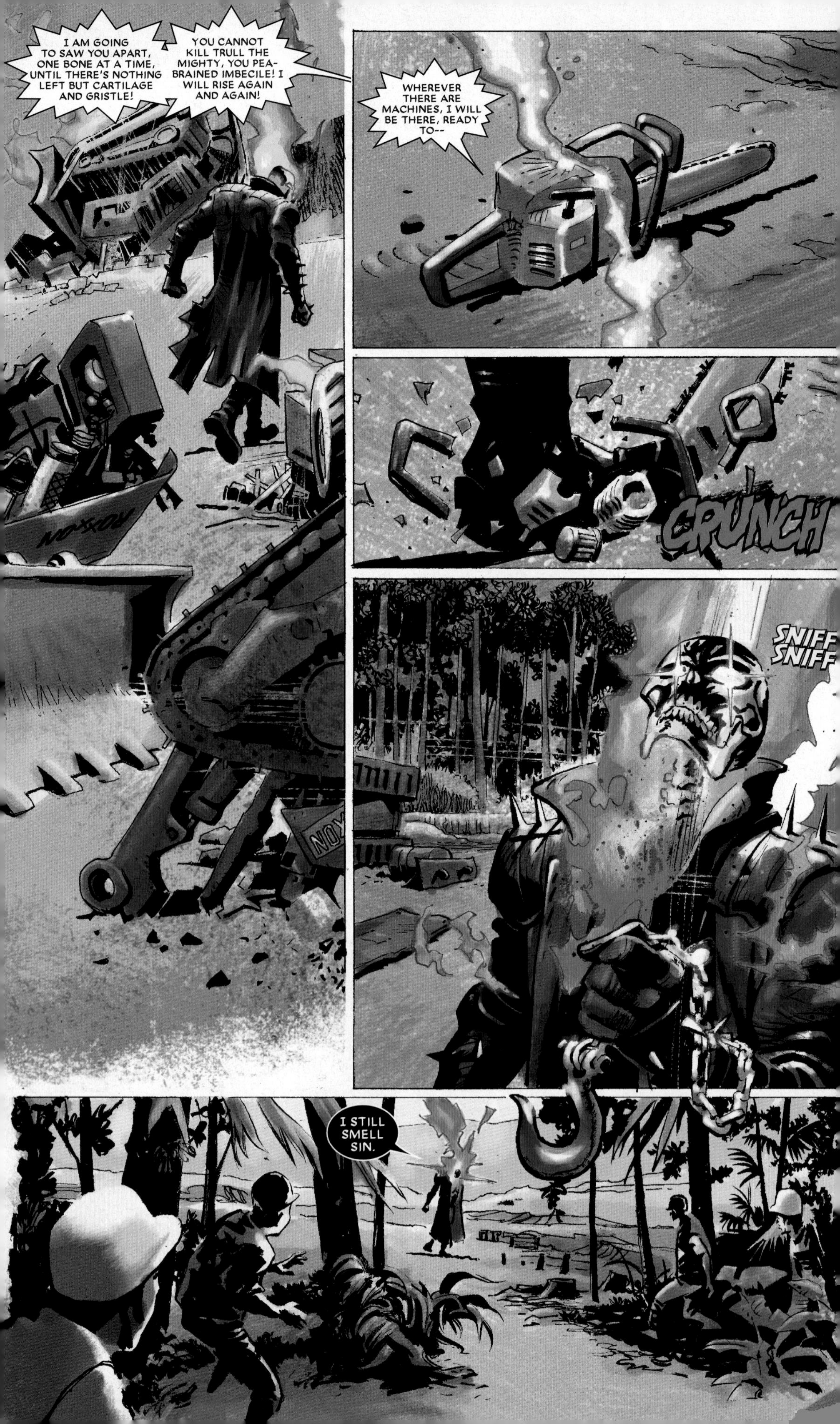
I AM GOING TO SAW YOU APART, ONE BONE AT A TIME, UNTIL THERE'S NOTHING LEFT BUT CARTILAGE AND GRISTLE!
YOU CANNOT KILL TRULL THE MIGHTY, YOU PEA-BRAINED IMBECILE! I WILL RISE AGAIN AND AGAIN!
WHEREVER THERE ARE MACHINES, I WILL BE THERE, READY TO--
ROXXON
CRUNCH
SNIFF SNIFF
I STILL SMELL SIN.

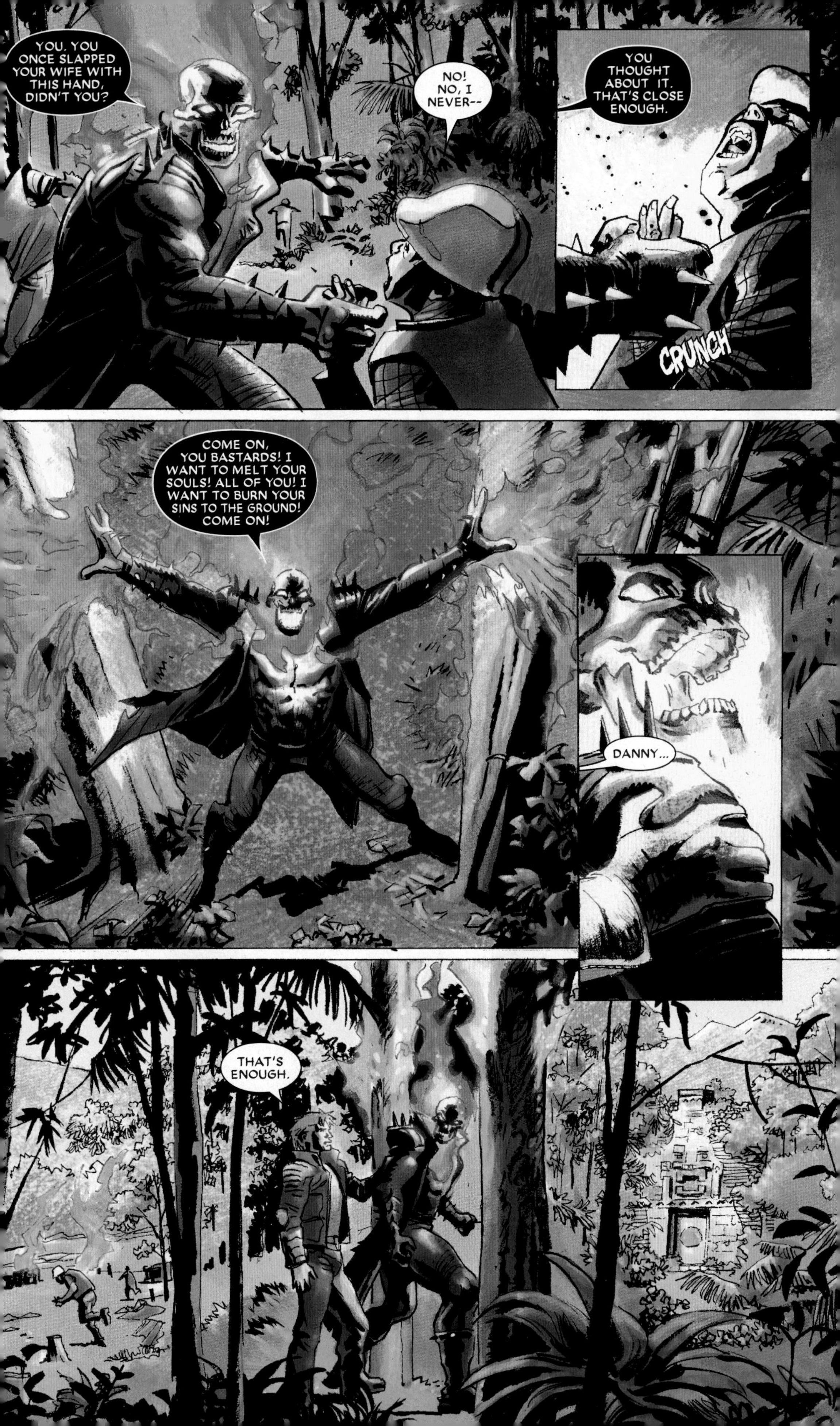
YOU. YOU ONCE SLAPPED YOUR WIFE WITH THIS HAND, DIDN'T YOU?
NO! NO, I NEVER--
YOU THOUGHT ABOUT IT. THAT'S CLOSE ENOUGH.
CRUNCH
COME ON, YOU BASTARDS! I WANT TO MELT YOUR SOULS! ALL OF YOU! I WANT TO BURN YOUR SINS TO THE GROUND! COME ON!
DANNY...
THAT'S ENOUGH.

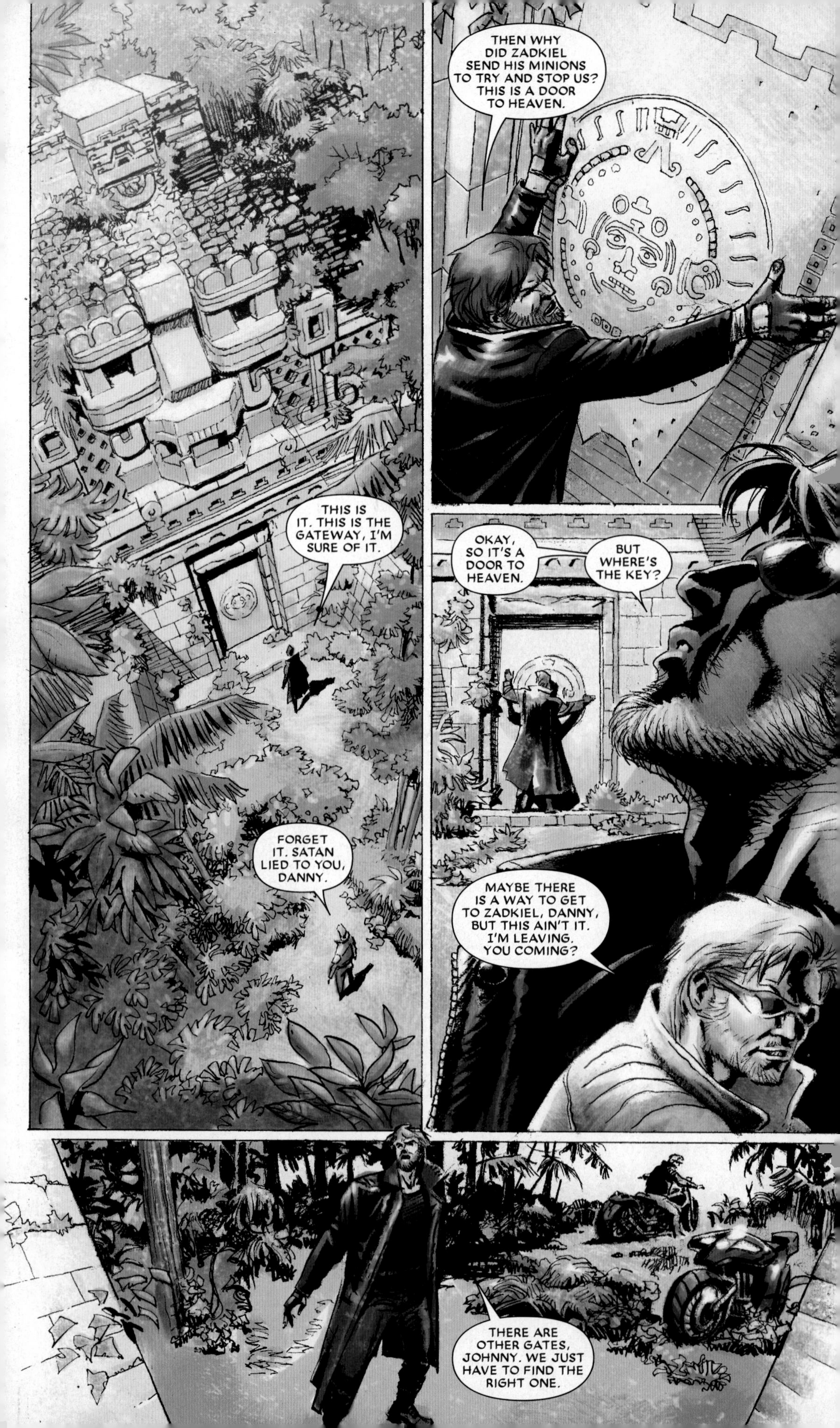
THIS IS IT. THIS IS THE GATEWAY, I'M SURE OF IT.
FORGET IT. SATAN LIED TO YOU, DANNY.
THEN WHY DID ZADKIEL SEND HIS MINIONS TO TRY AND STOP US? THIS IS A DOOR TO HEAVEN.
OKAY, SO IT'S A DOOR TO HEAVEN.
BUT WHERE'S THE KEY?
MAYBE THERE IS A WAY TO GET TO ZADKIEL, DANNY, BUT THIS AIN'T IT. I'M LEAVING. YOU COMING?
THERE ARE OTHER GATES, JOHNNY. WE JUST HAVE TO FIND THE RIGHT ONE.

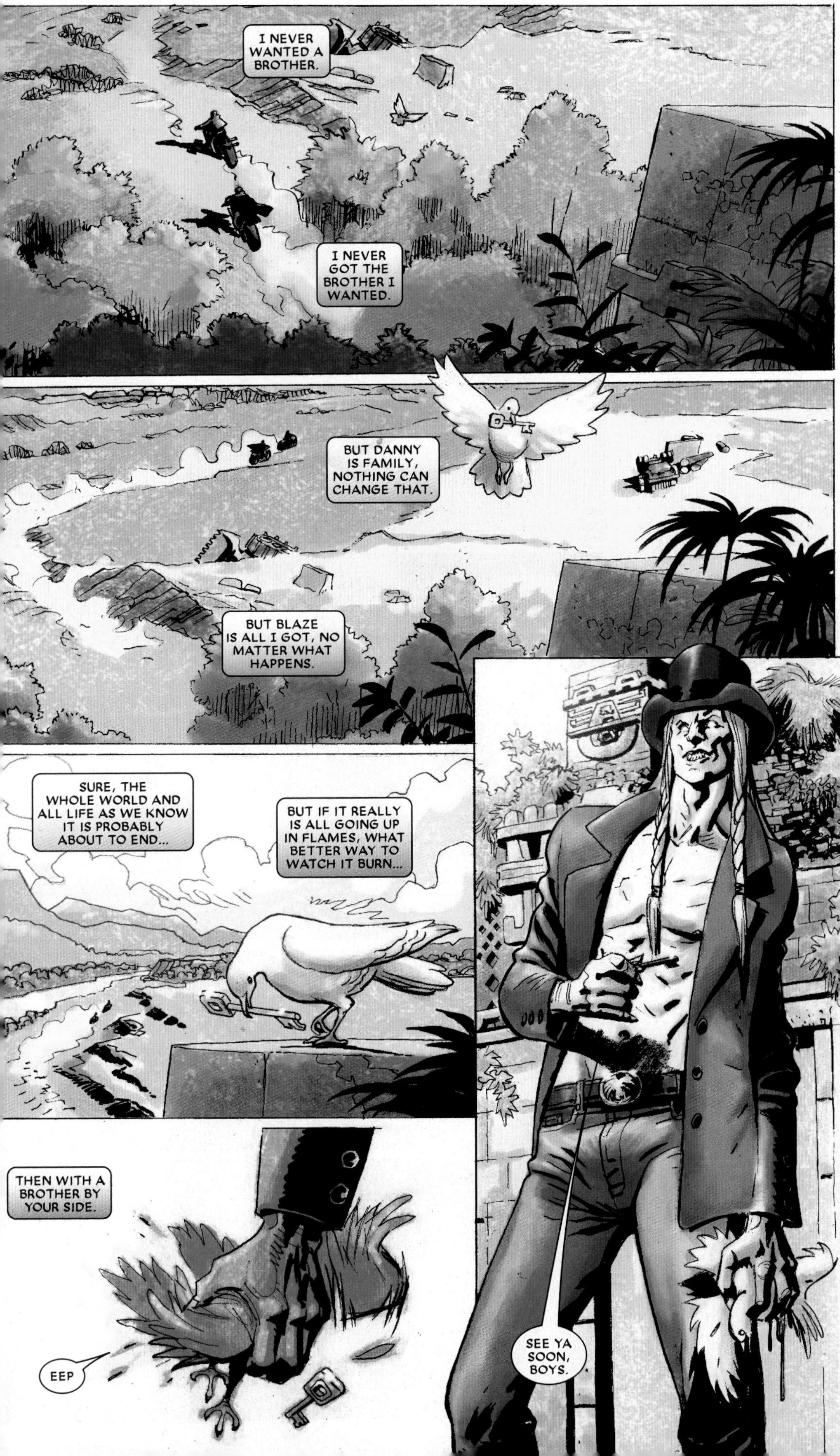

I NEVER WANTED A BROTHER.
I NEVER GOT THE BROTHER I WANTED.
BUT DANNY IS FAMILY, NOTHING CAN CHANGE THAT.
BUT BLAZE IS ALL I GOT, NO MATTER WHAT HAPPENS.
SURE, THE WHOLE WORLD AND ALL LIFE AS WE KNOW IT IS PROBABLY ABOUT TO END...
BUT IF IT REALLY IS ALL GOING UP IN FLAMES, WHAT BETTER WAY TO WATCH IT BURN...
THEN WITH A BROTHER BY YOUR SIDE.
EEP
SEE YA SOON, BOYS.

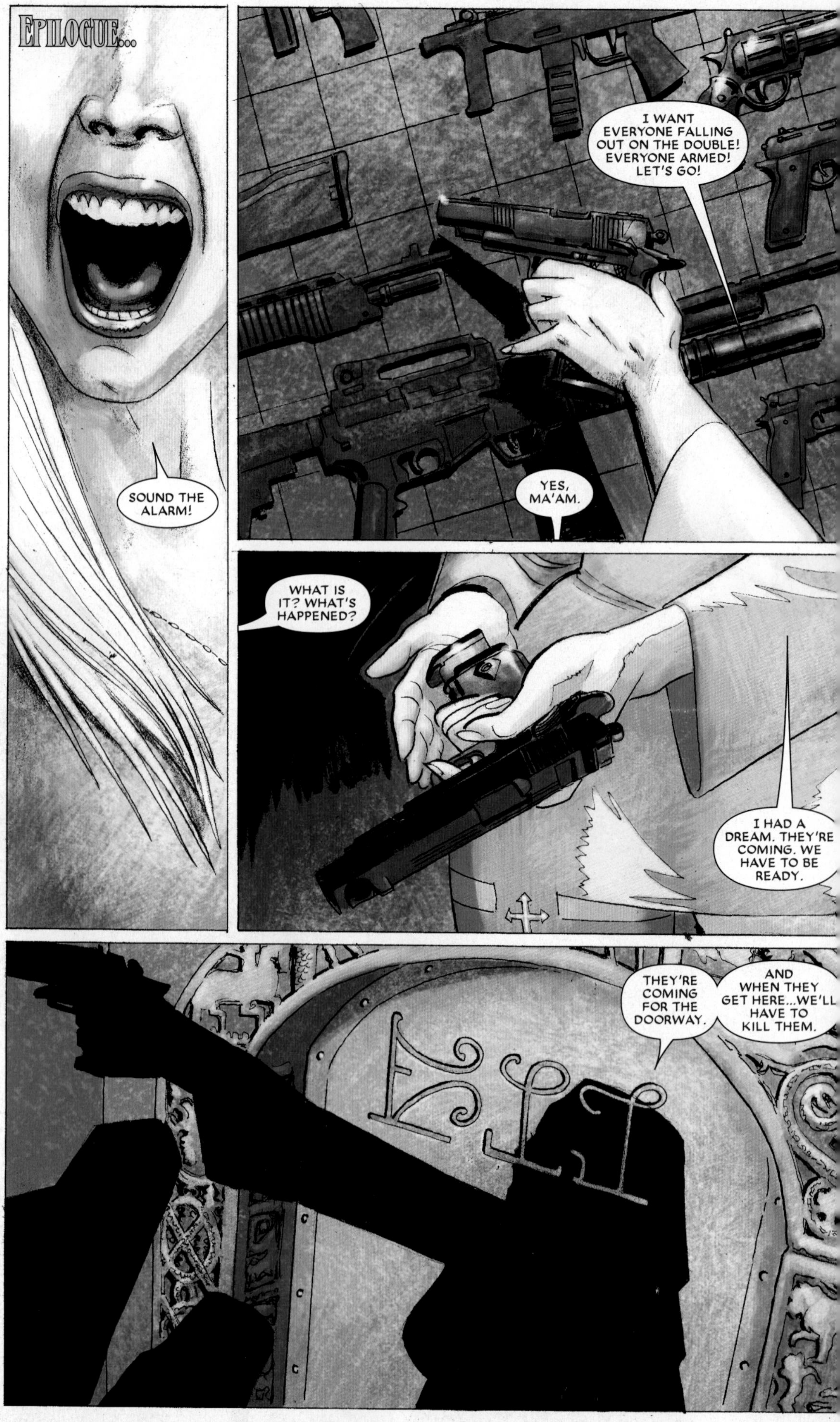
EPILOGUE...
SOUND THE ALARM!
I WANT EVERYONE FALLING OUT ON THE DOUBLE! EVERYONE ARMED! LET'S GO!
YES, MA'AM.
WHAT IS IT? WHAT'S HAPPENED?
I HAD A DREAM. THEY'RE COMING. WE HAVE TO BE READY.
THEY'RE COMING FOR THE DOORWAY.
AND WHEN THEY GET HERE...WE'LL HAVE TO KILL THEM.

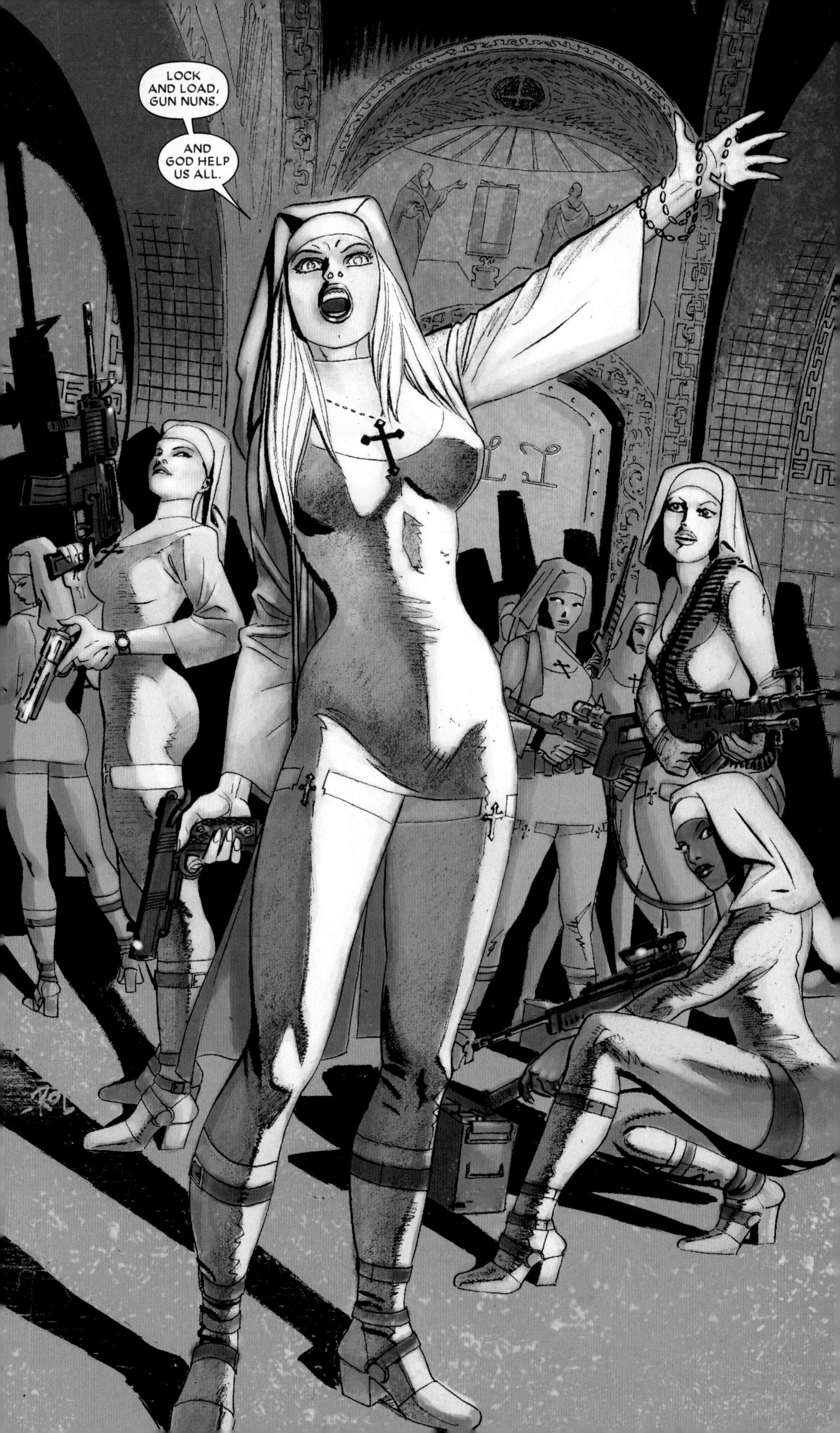
LOCK AND LOAD, GUN NUNS.
AND GOD HELP US ALL.

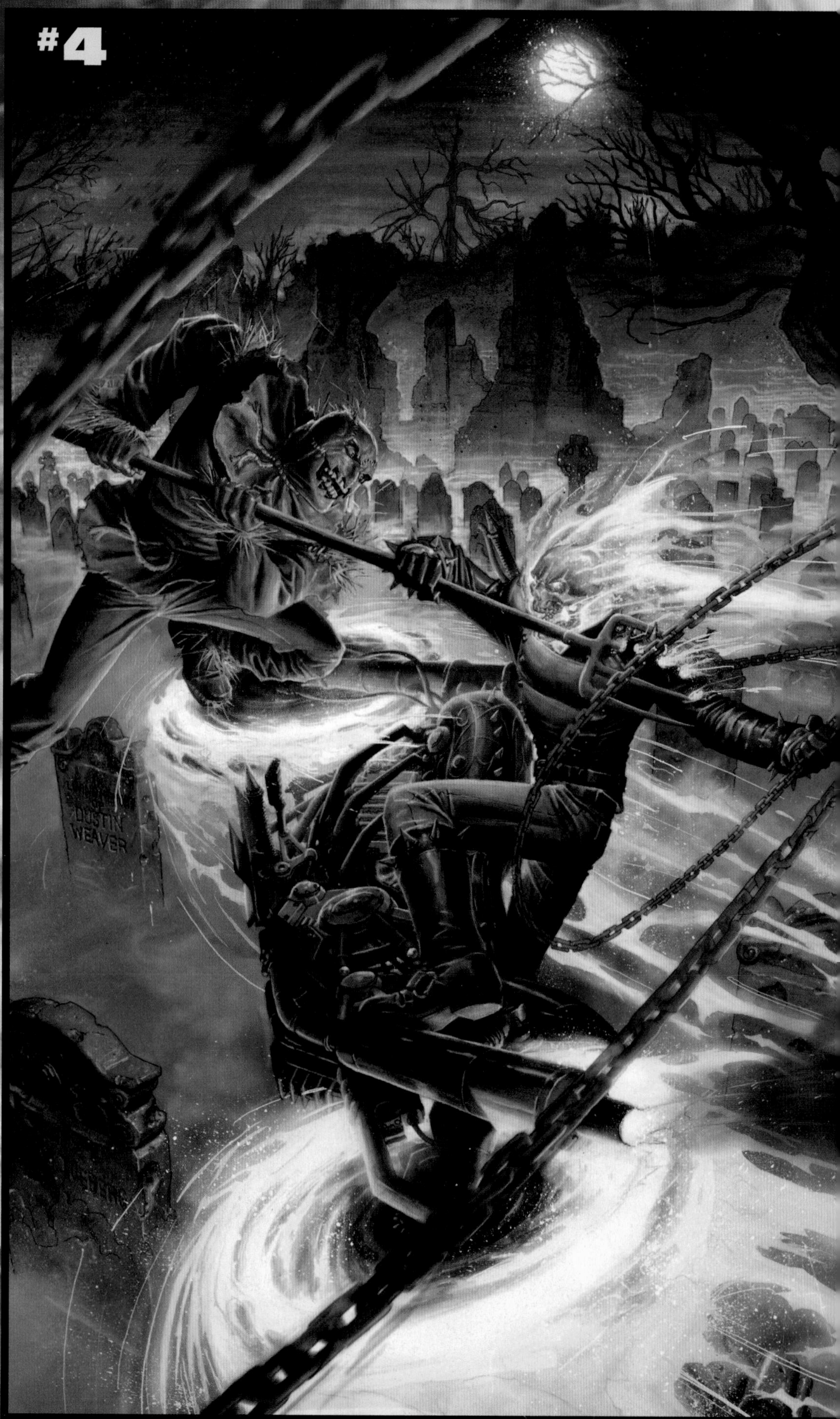
#4
DUSTIN
WEAVER

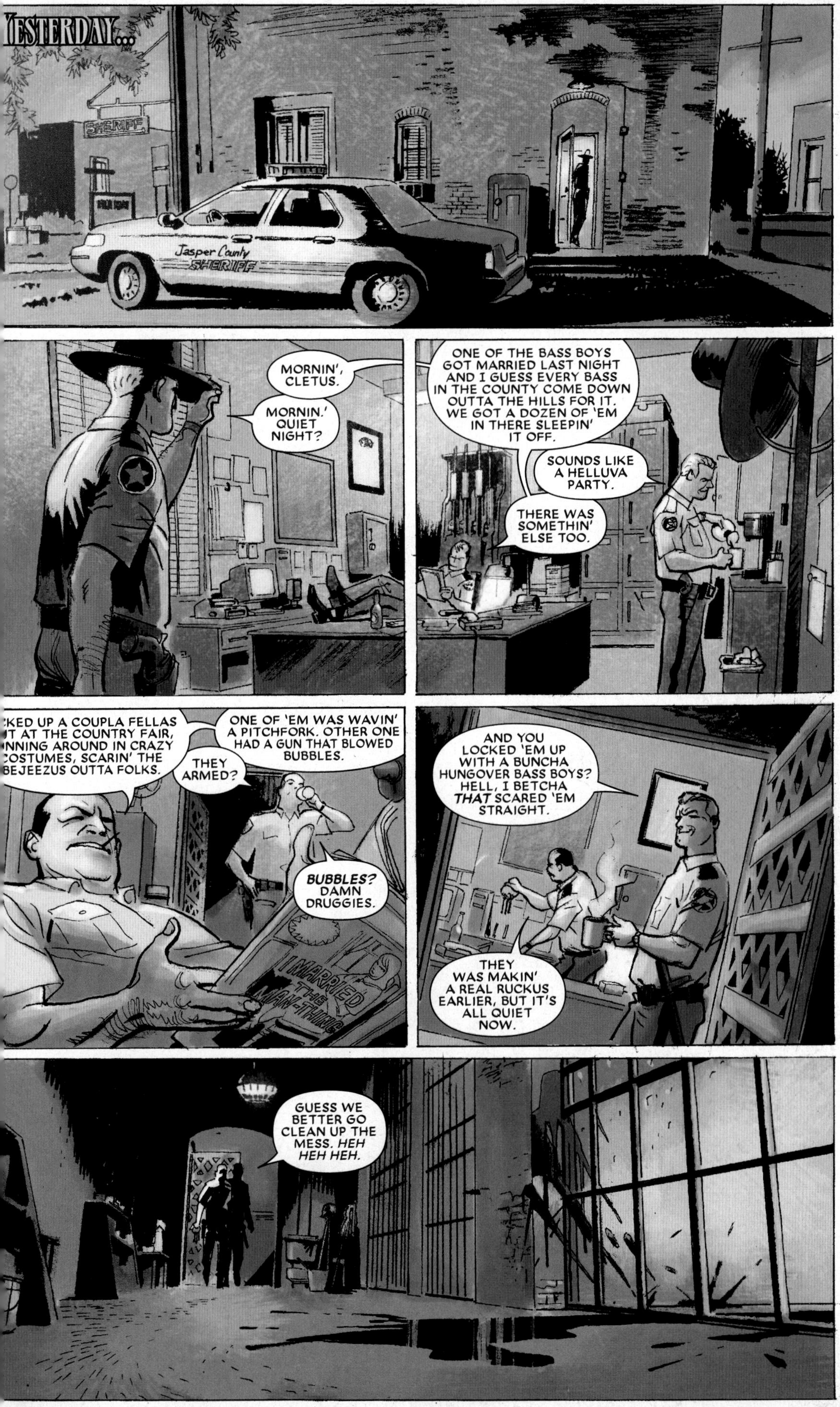
YESTERDAY...
SHERIFF
Jasper County
SHERIFF
MORNIN', CLETUS.
MORNIN.' QUIET NIGHT?
ONE OF THE BASS BOYS GOT MARRIED LAST NIGHT AND I GUESS EVERY BASS IN THE COUNTY COME DOWN OUTTA THE HILLS FOR IT. WE GOT A DOZEN OF 'EM IN THERE SLEEPIN' IT OFF.
SOUNDS LIKE A HELLUVA PARTY.
THERE WAS SOMETHIN' ELSE TOO.
CKED UP A COUPLA FELLAS T AT THE COUNTRY FAIR, NNING AROUND IN CRAZY COSTUMES, SCARIN' THE BEJEEZUS OUTTA FOLKS.
THEY ARMED?
ONE OF 'EM WAS WAVIN' A PITCHFORK. OTHER ONE HAD A GUN THAT BLOWED BUBBLES.
BUBBLES? DAMN DRUGGIES.
I MARRIED THE MAN-THING
AND YOU LOCKED 'EM UP WITH A BUNCHA HUNGOVER BASS BOYS? HELL, I BETCHA THAT SCARED 'EM STRAIGHT.
THEY WAS MAKIN' A REAL RUCKUS EARLIER, BUT IT'S ALL QUIET NOW.
GUESS WE BETTER GO CLEAN UP THE MESS. HEH HEH HEH.

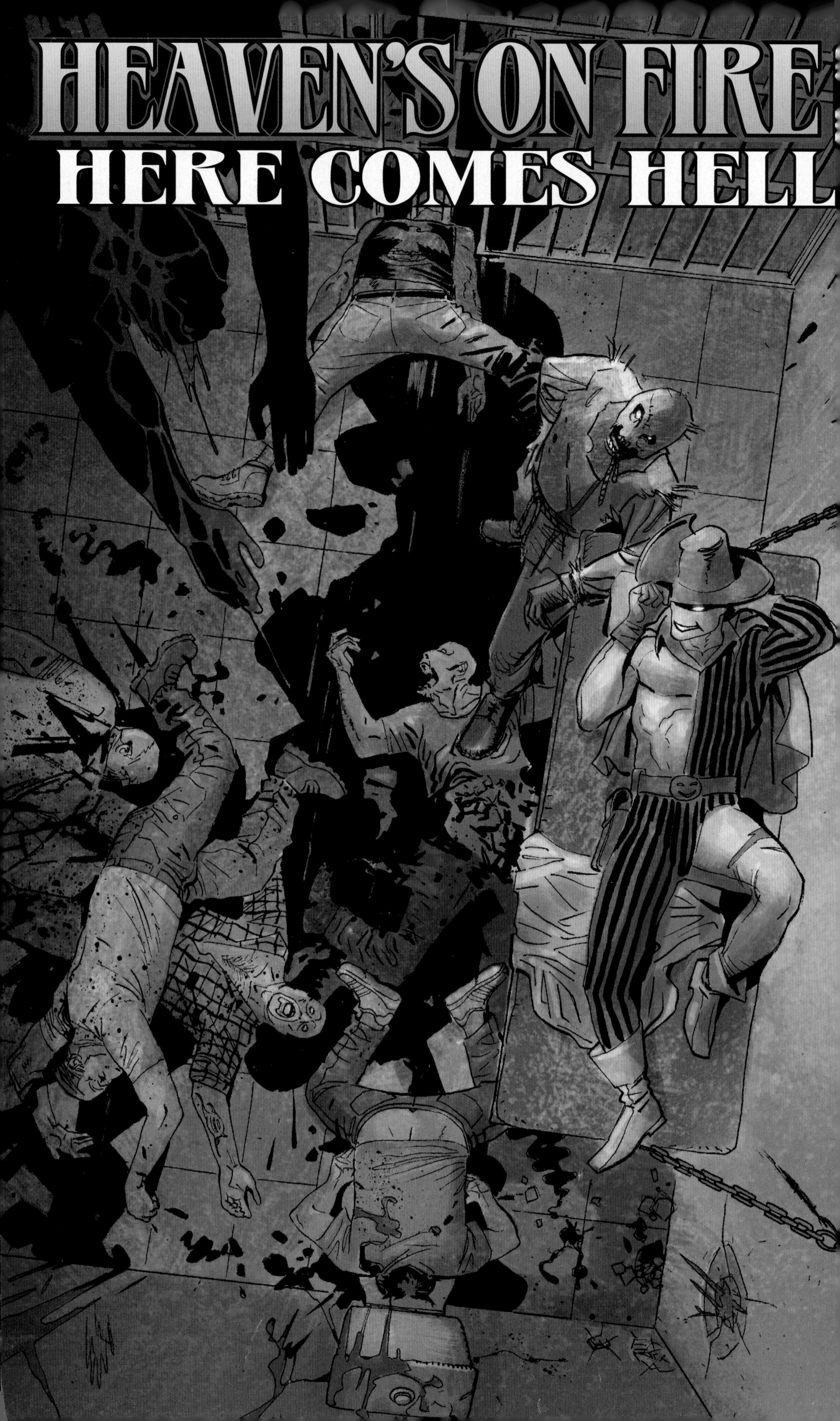
HEAVEN'S ON FIRE
HERE COMES HELL

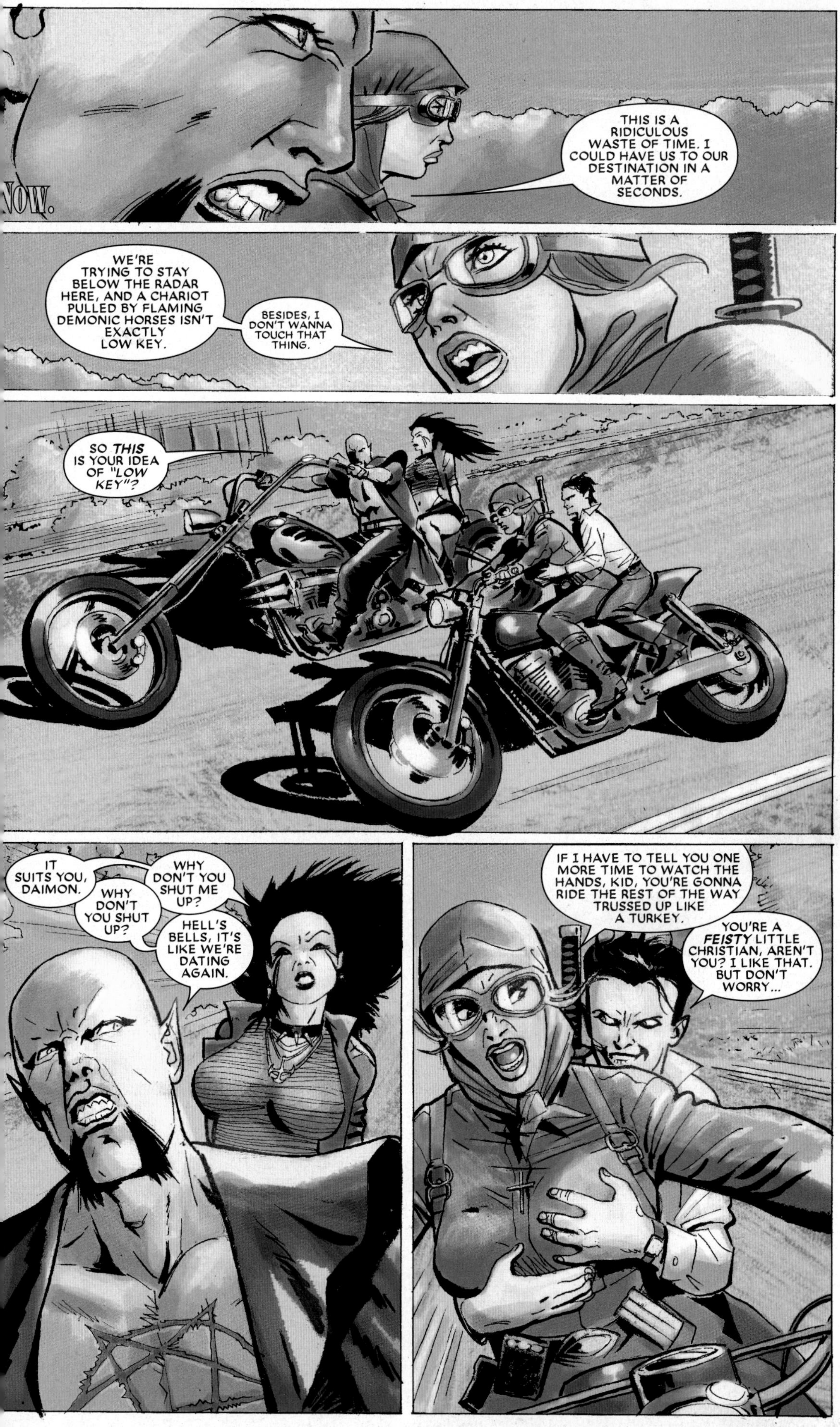
NOW.
THIS IS A RIDICULOUS WASTE OF TIME. I COULD HAVE US TO OUR DESTINATION IN A MATTER OF SECONDS.
WE'RE TRYING TO STAY BELOW THE RADAR HERE, AND A CHARIOT PULLED BY FLAMING DEMONIC HORSES ISN'T EXACTLY LOW KEY.
BESIDES, I DON'T WANNA TOUCH THAT THING.
SO THIS IS YOUR IDEA OF "LOW KEY"?
IT SUITS YOU, DAIMON.
WHY DON'T YOU SHUT ME UP?
WHY DON'T YOU SHUT UP?
HELL'S BELLS, IT'S LIKE WE'RE DATING AGAIN.
IF I HAVE TO TELL YOU ONE MORE TIME TO WATCH THE HANDS, KID, YOU'RE GONNA RIDE THE REST OF THE WAY TRUSSED UP LIKE A TURKEY.
YOU'RE A FEISTY LITTLE CHRISTIAN, AREN'T YOU? I LIKE THAT. BUT DON'T WORRY...

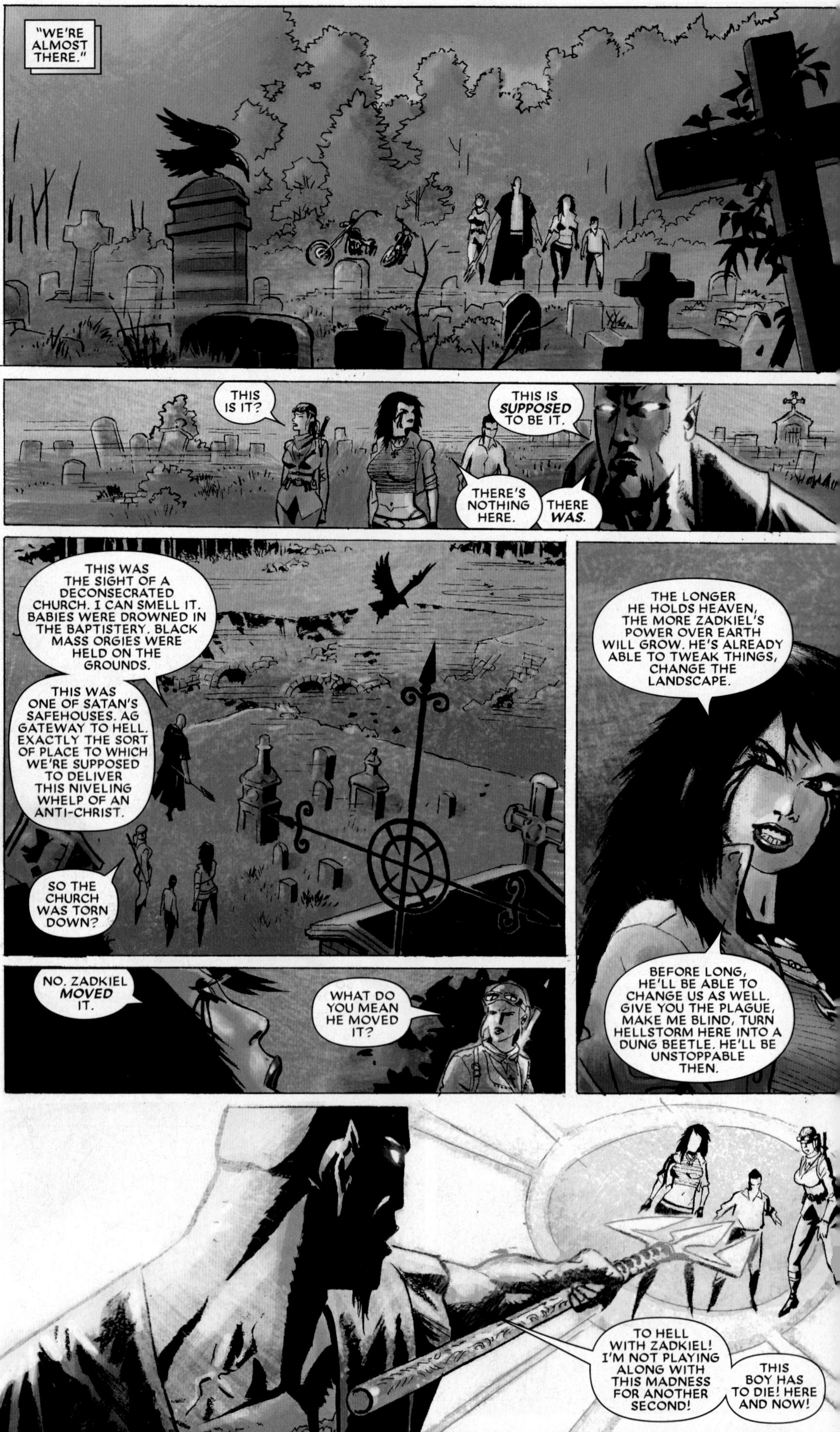
"WE'RE ALMOST THERE."
THIS IS IT?
THIS IS SUPPOSED TO BE IT.
THERE'S NOTHING HERE.
THERE WAS.
THIS WAS THE SIGHT OF A DECONSECRATED CHURCH. I CAN SMELL IT. BABIES WERE DROWNED IN THE BAPTISTERY. BLACK MASS ORGIES WERE HELD ON THE GROUNDS.
THIS WAS ONE OF SATAN'S SAFEHOUSES. AG GATEWAY TO HELL. EXACTLY THE SORT OF PLACE TO WHICH WE'RE SUPPOSED TO DELIVER THIS NIVELING WHELP OF AN ANTI-CHRIST.
SO THE CHURCH WAS TORN DOWN?
NO. ZADKIEL MOVED IT.
WHAT DO YOU MEAN HE MOVED IT?
THE LONGER HE HOLDS HEAVEN, THE MORE ZADKIEL'S POWER OVER EARTH WILL GROW. HE'S ALREADY ABLE TO TWEAK THINGS, CHANGE THE LANDSCAPE.
BEFORE LONG, HE'LL BE ABLE TO CHANGE US AS WELL. GIVE YOU THE PLAGUE, MAKE ME BLIND, TURN HELLSTORM HERE INTO A DUNG BEETLE. HE'LL BE UNSTOPPABLE THEN.
TO HELL WITH ZADKIEL! I'M NOT PLAYING ALONG WITH THIS MADNESS FOR ANOTHER SECOND!
THIS BOY HAS TO DIE! HERE AND NOW!

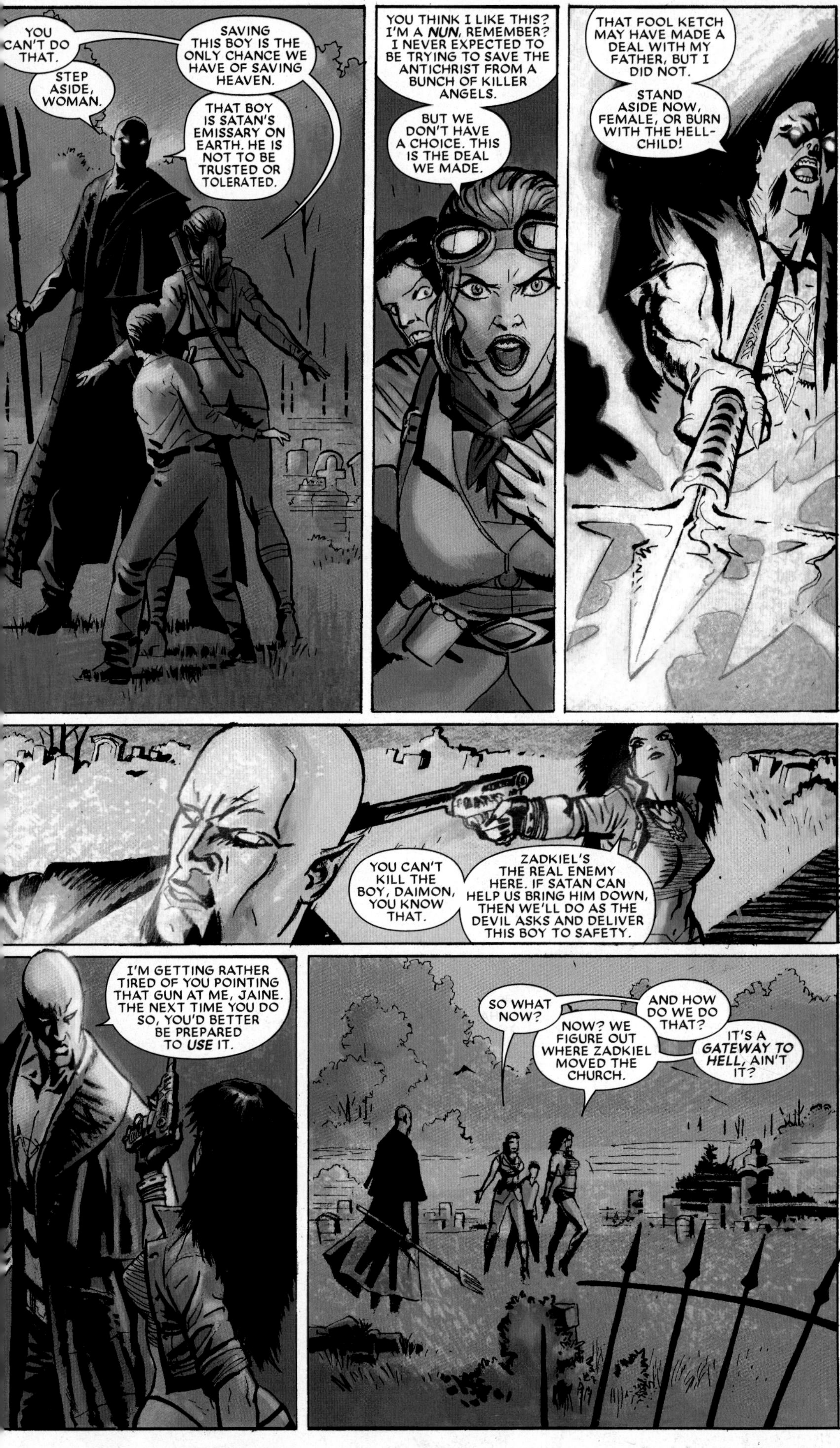
YOU CAN'T DO THAT.
SAVING THIS BOY IS THE ONLY CHANCE WE HAVE OF SAVING HEAVEN.
STEP ASIDE, WOMAN.
THAT BOY IS SATAN'S EMISSARY ON EARTH. HE IS NOT TO BE TRUSTED OR TOLERATED.
YOU THINK I LIKE THIS? I'M A NUN, REMEMBER? I NEVER EXPECTED TO BE TRYING TO SAVE THE ANTICHRIST FROM A BUNCH OF KILLER ANGELS.
BUT WE DON'T HAVE A CHOICE. THIS IS THE DEAL WE MADE.
THAT FOOL KETCH MAY HAVE MADE A DEAL WITH MY FATHER, BUT I DID NOT.
STAND ASIDE NOW, FEMALE, OR BURN WITH THE HELL-CHILD!
YOU CAN'T KILL THE BOY, DAIMON, YOU KNOW THAT.
ZADKIEL'S THE REAL ENEMY HERE. IF SATAN CAN HELP US BRING HIM DOWN, THEN WE'LL DO AS THE DEVIL ASKS AND DELIVER THIS BOY TO SAFETY.
I'M GETTING RATHER TIRED OF YOU POINTING THAT GUN AT ME, JAINE. THE NEXT TIME YOU DO SO, YOU'D BETTER BE PREPARED TO USE IT.
SO WHAT NOW?
NOW? WE FIGURE OUT WHERE ZADKIEL MOVED THE CHURCH.
AND HOW DO WE DO THAT?
IT'S A GATEWAY TO HELL, AIN'T IT?

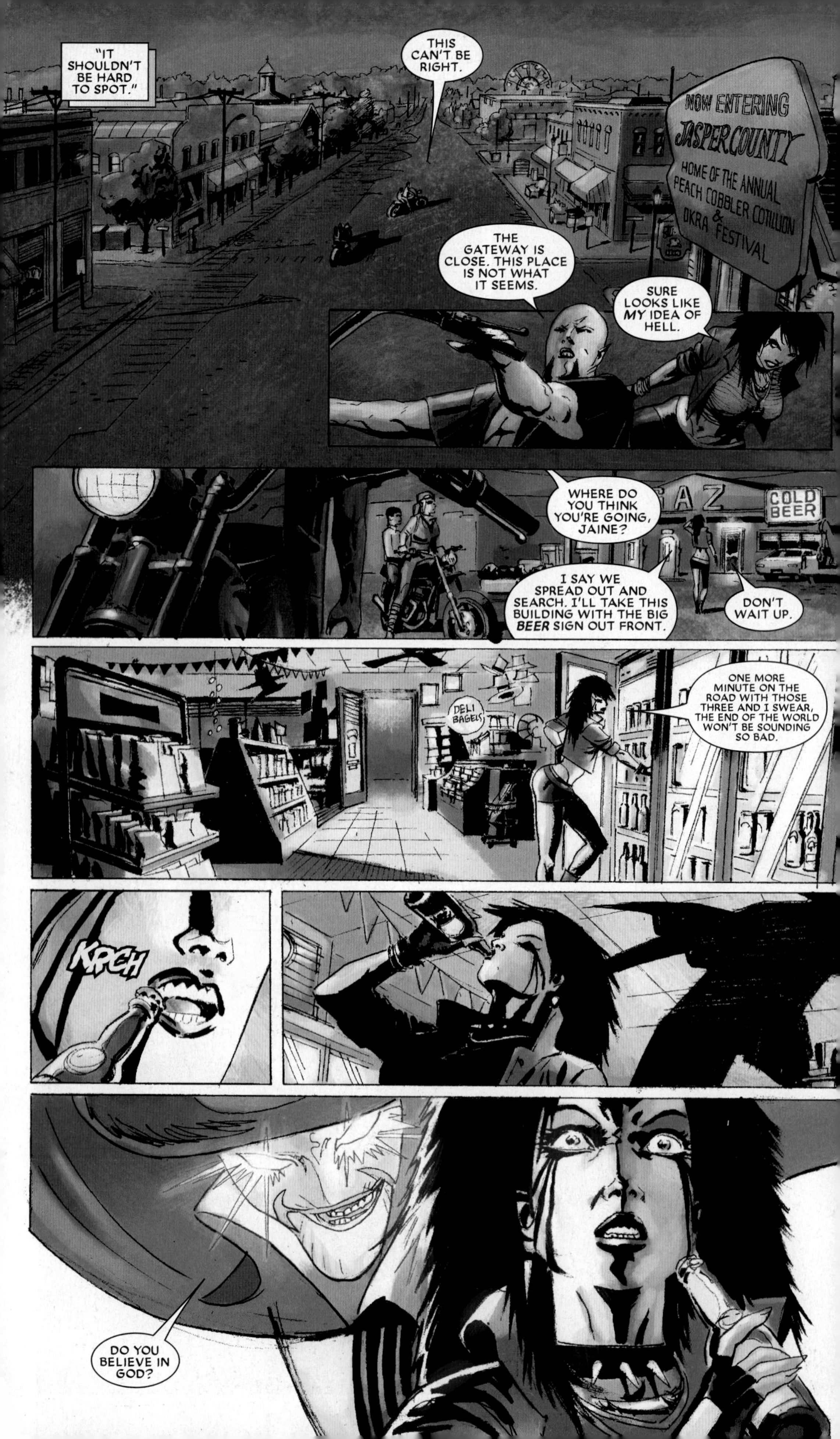
"IT SHOULDN'T BE HARD TO SPOT."
THIS CAN'T BE RIGHT.
NOW ENTERING JASPER COUNTY HOME OF THE ANNUAL PEACH COBBLER COTILLION & OKRA FESTIVAL
THE GATEWAY IS CLOSE. THIS PLACE IS NOT WHAT IT SEEMS.
SURE LOOKS LIKE MY IDEA OF HELL.
WHERE DO YOU THINK YOU'RE GOING, JAINE?
COLD BEER
I SAY WE SPREAD OUT AND SEARCH. I'LL TAKE THIS BUILDING WITH THE BIG BEER SIGN OUT FRONT.
DON'T WAIT UP.
DELI BAGELS
ONE MORE MINUTE ON THE ROAD WITH THOSE THREE AND I SWEAR, THE END OF THE WORLD WON'T BE SOUNDING SO BAD.
KRCH
DO YOU BELIEVE IN GOD?

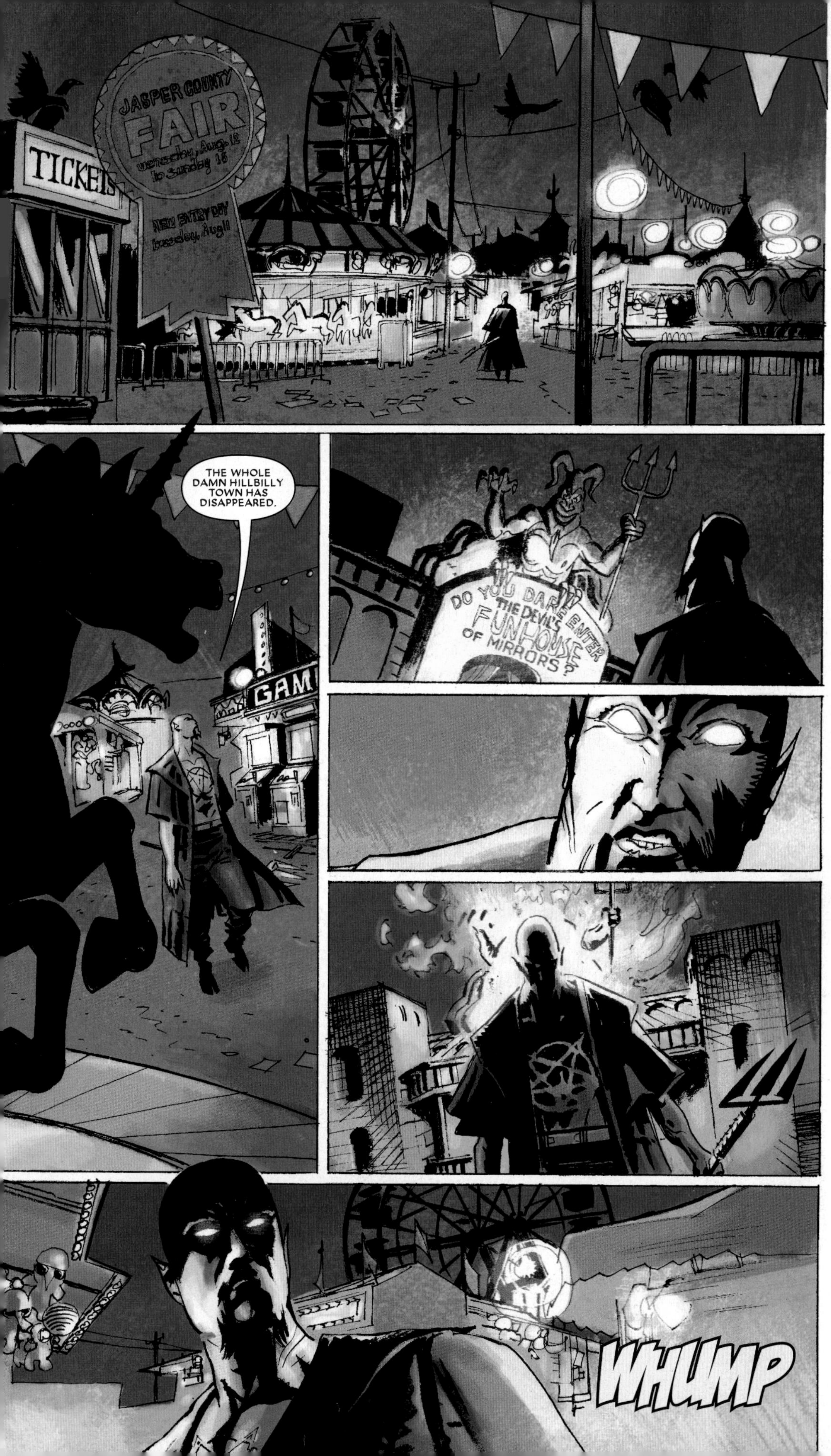

JASPER COUNTY
FAIR
wenesday, Aug. 12
to sunday 16
NEW ENTRY DAY
tuesday, Aug 11
TICKETS
THE WHOLE DAMN HILLBILLY TOWN HAS DISAPPEARED.
GAM
DO YOU DARE ENTER THE DEVIL'S FUNHOUSE OF MIRRORS?
WHUMP

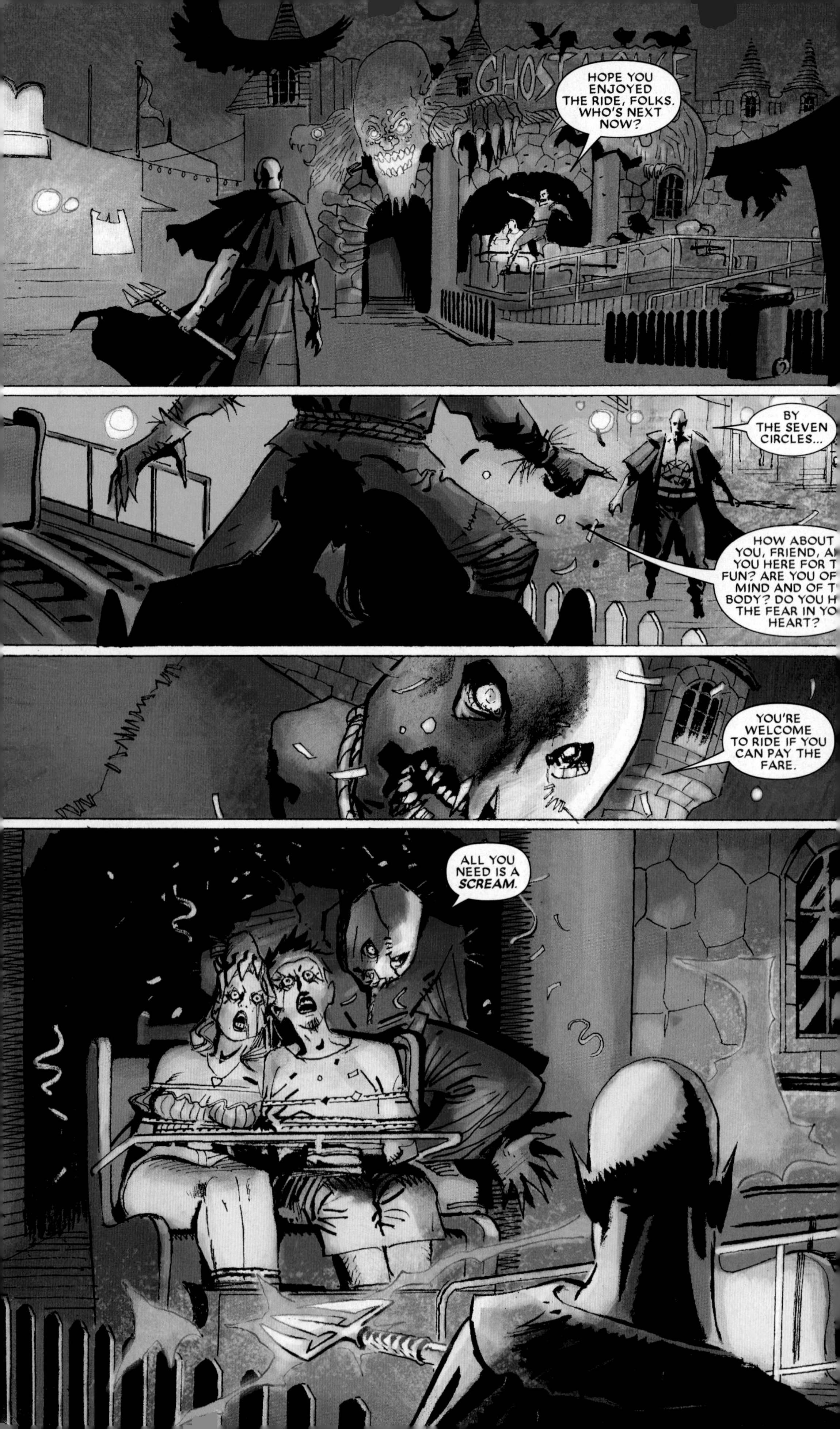
GHOST
HOPE YOU ENJOYED THE RIDE, FOLKS. WHO'S NEXT NOW?
BY THE SEVEN CIRCLES...
HOW ABOUT YOU, FRIEND, A YOU HERE FOR T FUN? ARE YOU OF MIND AND OF T BODY? DO YOU H THE FEAR IN YO HEART?
YOU'RE WELCOME TO RIDE IF YOU CAN PAY THE FARE.
ALL YOU NEED IS A *SCREAM*.

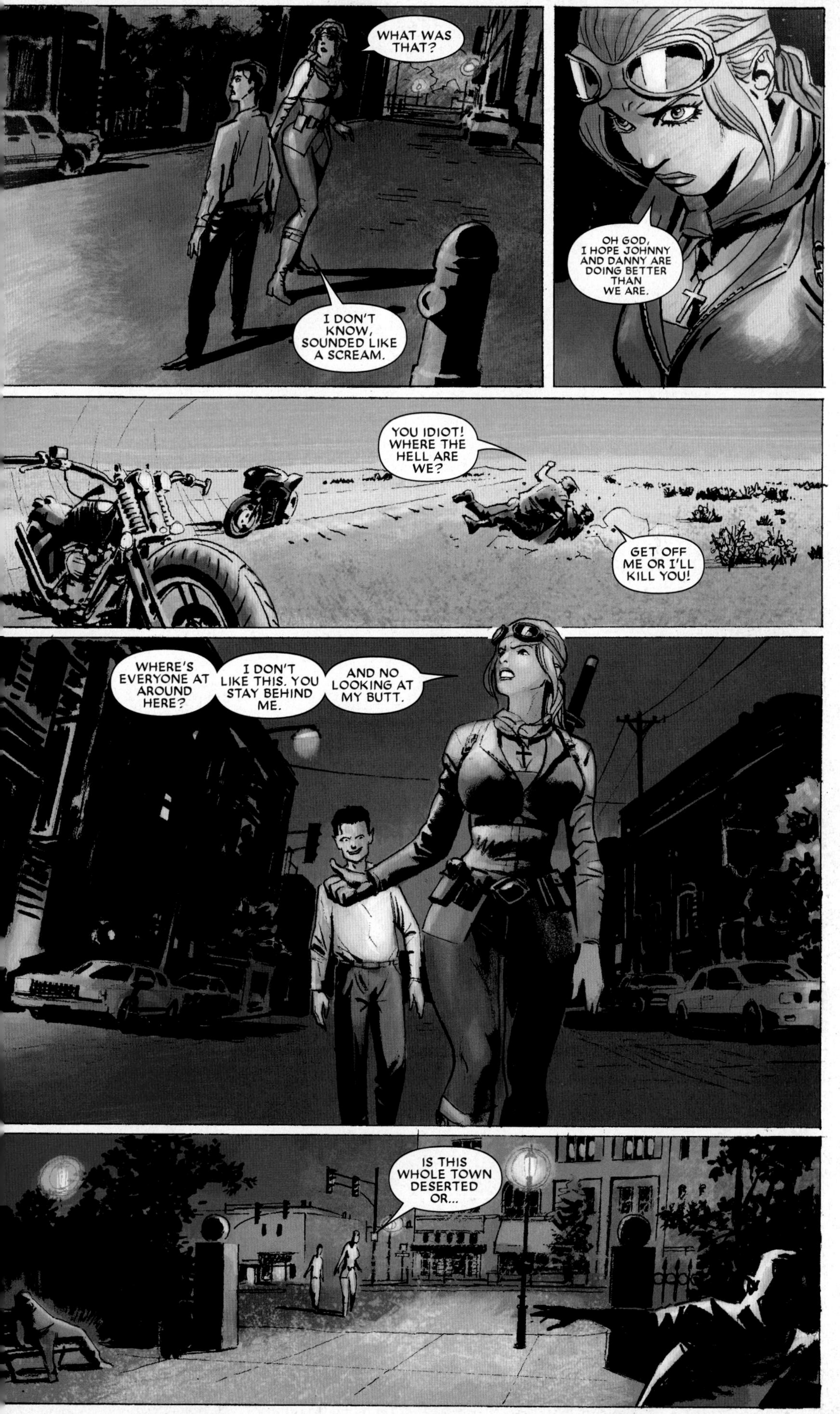
WHAT WAS THAT?
I DON'T KNOW, SOUNDED LIKE A SCREAM.
OH GOD, I HOPE JOHNNY AND DANNY ARE DOING BETTER THAN WE ARE.
YOU IDIOT! WHERE THE HELL ARE WE?
GET OFF ME OR I'LL KILL YOU!
WHERE'S EVERYONE AT AROUND HERE?
I DON'T LIKE THIS. YOU STAY BEHIND ME.
AND NO LOOKING AT MY BUTT.
IS THIS WHOLE TOWN DESERTED OR...

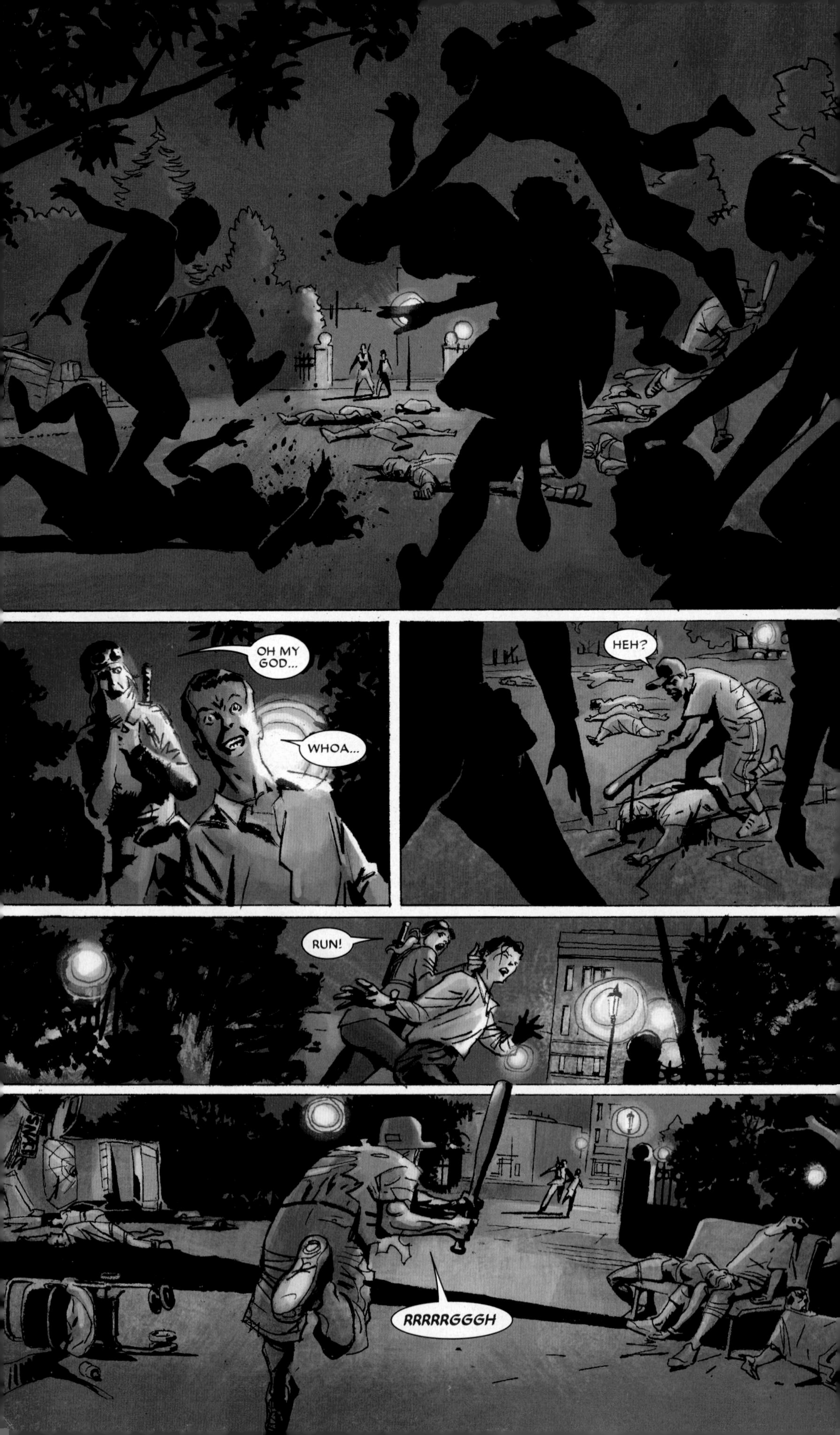
OH MY GOD...
WHOA...
HEH?
RUN!
RRRRRGGGH

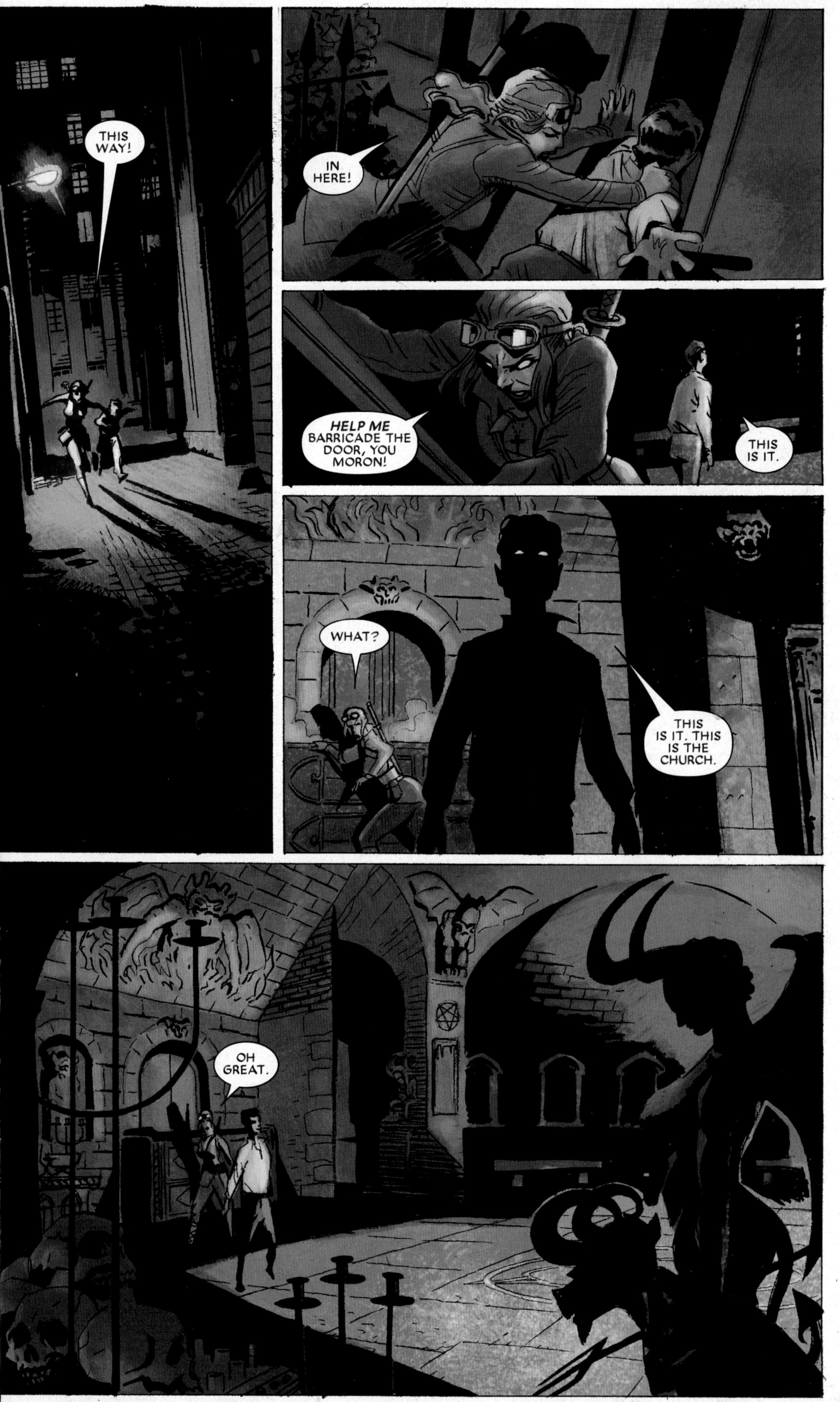
THIS WAY!
IN HERE!
HELP ME BARRICADE THE DOOR, YOU MORON!
THIS IS IT.
WHAT?
THIS IS IT. THIS IS THE CHURCH.
OH GREAT.

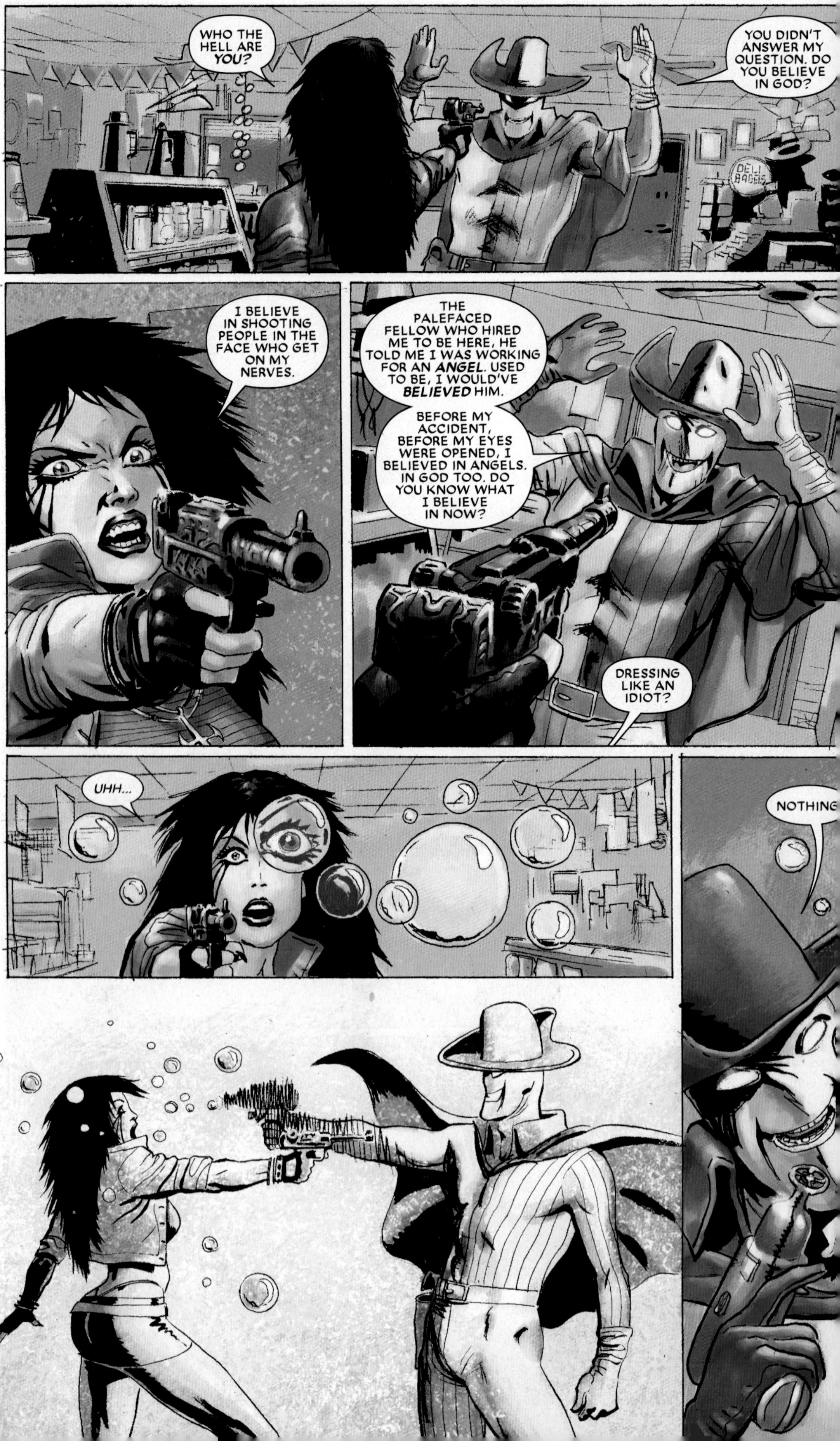
WHO THE HELL ARE *YOU?*
YOU DIDN'T ANSWER MY QUESTION. DO YOU BELIEVE IN GOD?
I BELIEVE IN SHOOTING PEOPLE IN THE FACE WHO GET ON MY NERVES.
THE PALEFACED FELLOW WHO HIRED ME TO BE HERE, HE TOLD ME I WAS WORKING FOR AN *ANGEL*. USED TO BE, I WOULD'VE *BELIEVED* HIM.
BEFORE MY ACCIDENT, BEFORE MY EYES WERE OPENED, I BELIEVED IN ANGELS. IN GOD TOO. DO YOU KNOW WHAT I BELIEVE IN NOW?
DRESSING LIKE AN IDIOT?
UHH...
NOTHING
DELI BAGELS

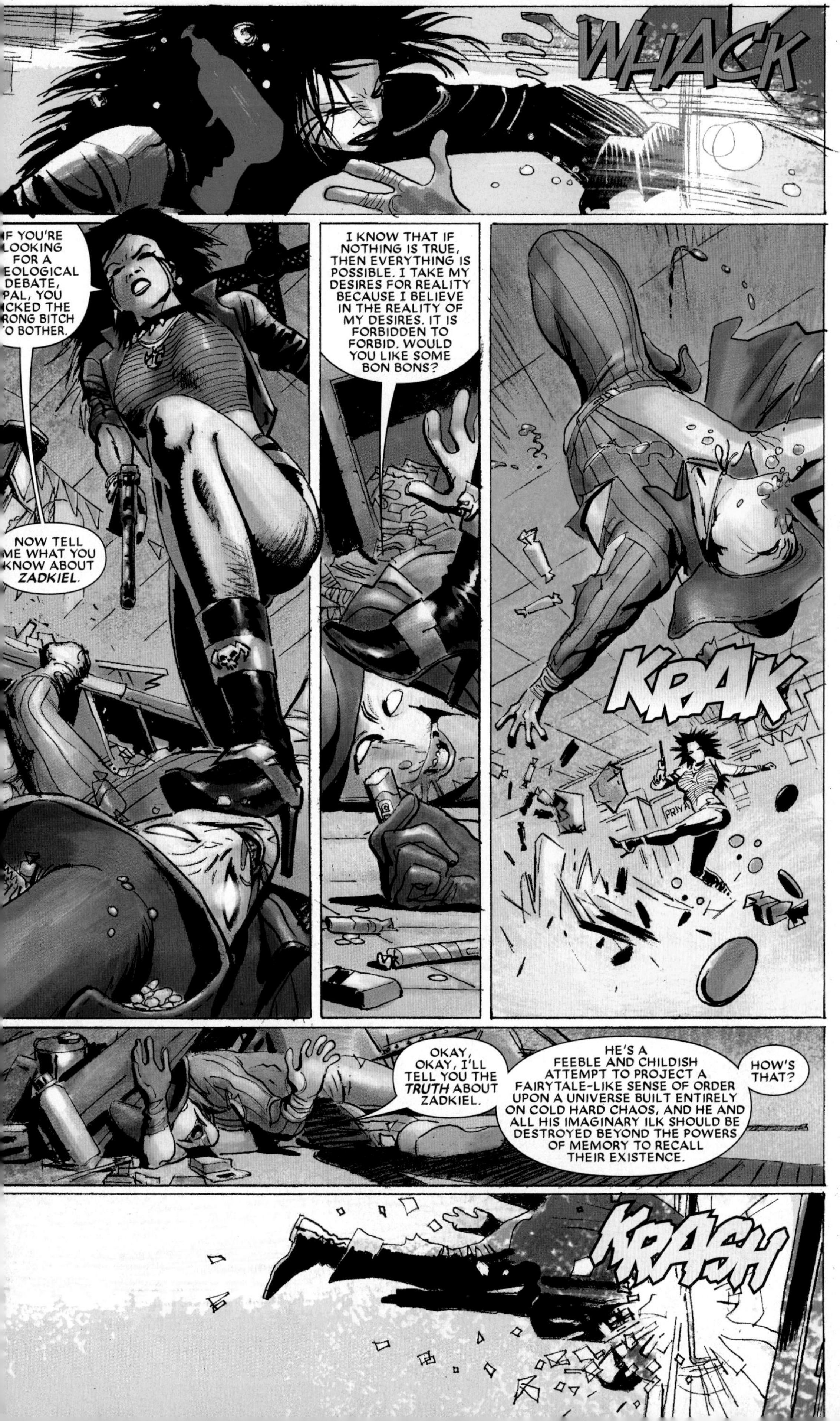
WHACK
IF YOU'RE LOOKING FOR A EOLOGICAL DEBATE, PAL, YOU ICKED THE RONG BITCH TO BOTHER.
NOW TELL ME WHAT YOU KNOW ABOUT *ZADKIEL*.
I KNOW THAT IF NOTHING IS TRUE, THEN EVERYTHING IS POSSIBLE. I TAKE MY DESIRES FOR REALITY BECAUSE I BELIEVE IN THE REALITY OF MY DESIRES. IT IS FORBIDDEN TO FORBID. WOULD YOU LIKE SOME BON BONS?
KRAK
OKAY, OKAY, I'LL TELL YOU THE *TRUTH* ABOUT ZADKIEL.
HE'S A FEEBLE AND CHILDISH ATTEMPT TO PROJECT A FAIRYTALE-LIKE SENSE OF ORDER UPON A UNIVERSE BUILT ENTIRELY ON COLD HARD CHAOS, AND HE AND ALL HIS IMAGINARY ILK SHOULD BE DESTROYED BEYOND THE POWERS OF MEMORY TO RECALL THEIR EXISTENCE.
HOW'S THAT?
KRASH

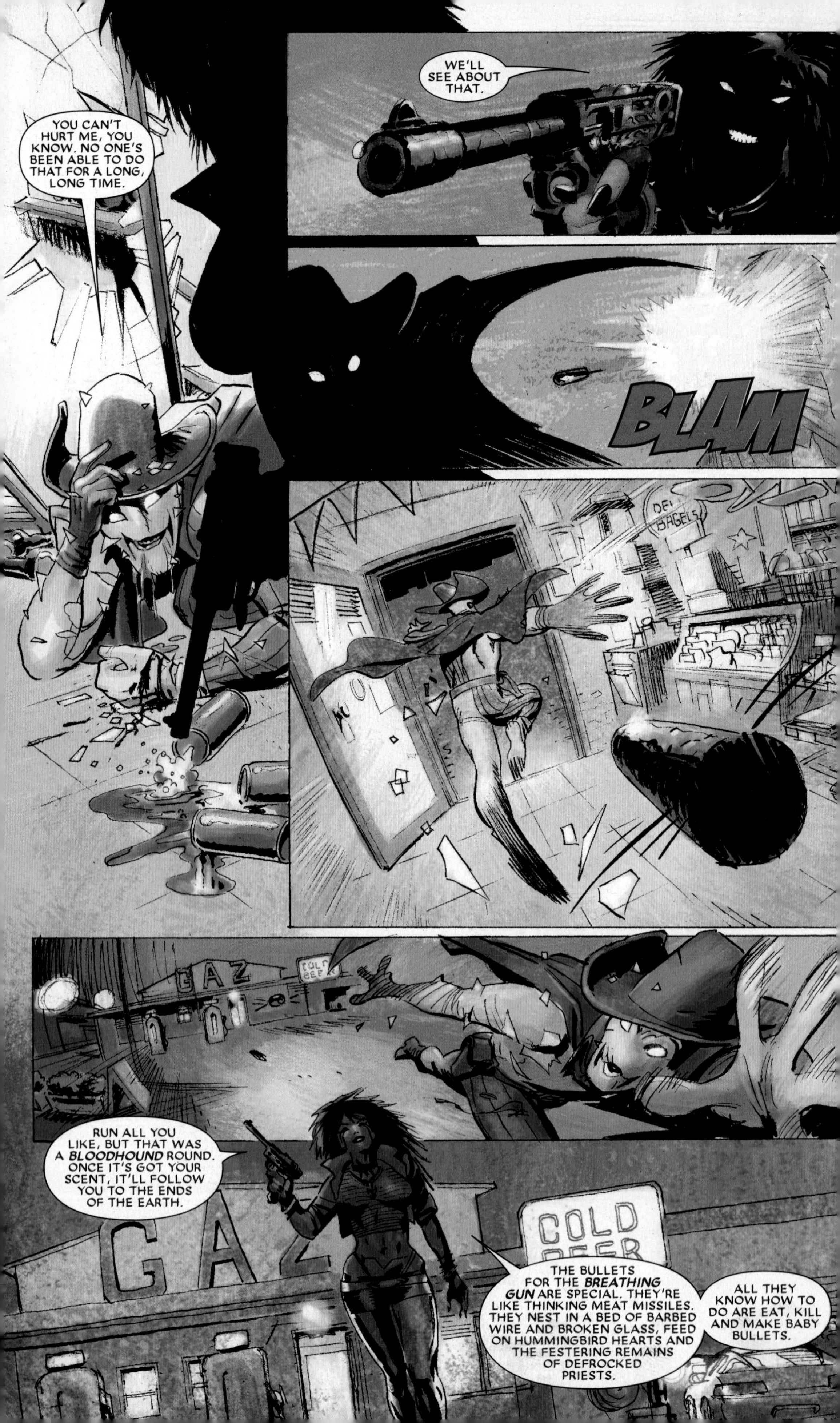
YOU CAN'T HURT ME, YOU KNOW. NO ONE'S BEEN ABLE TO DO THAT FOR A LONG, LONG TIME.
WE'LL SEE ABOUT THAT.
BLAM
DELI BAGELS
GAZ
COLD BEER
RUN ALL YOU LIKE, BUT THAT WAS A *BLOODHOUND* ROUND. ONCE IT'S GOT YOUR SCENT, IT'LL FOLLOW YOU TO THE ENDS OF THE EARTH.
GAZ
COLD BEER
THE BULLETS FOR THE *BREATHING GUN* ARE SPECIAL. THEY'RE LIKE THINKING MEAT MISSILES. THEY NEST IN A BED OF BARBED WIRE AND BROKEN GLASS, FEED ON HUMMINGBIRD HEARTS AND THE FESTERING REMAINS OF DEFROCKED PRIESTS.
ALL THEY KNOW HOW TO DO ARE EAT, KILL AND MAKE BABY BULLETS.

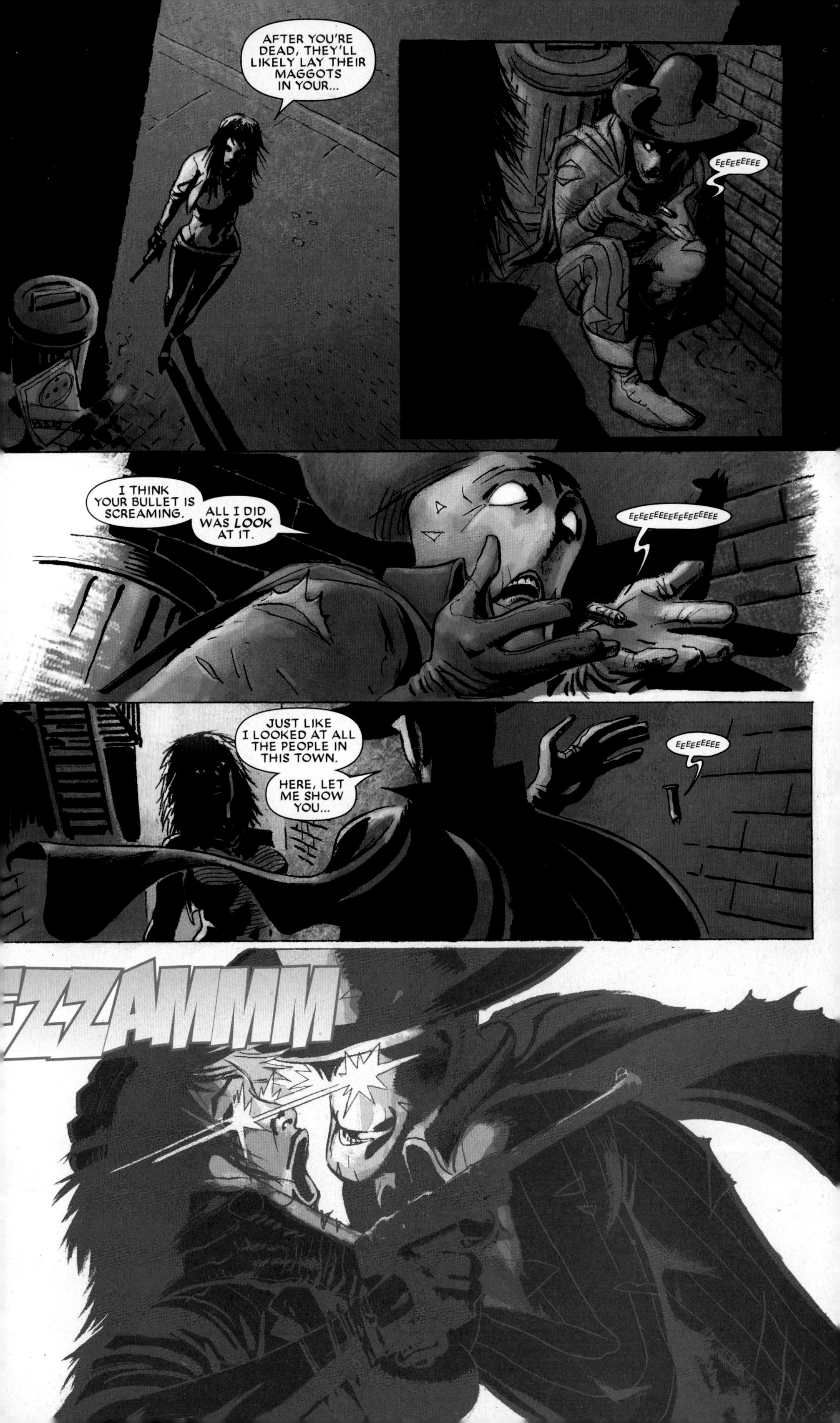
AFTER YOU'RE DEAD, THEY'LL LIKELY LAY THEIR MAGGOTS IN YOUR...
EEEEEEEEE
I THINK YOUR BULLET IS SCREAMING.
ALL I DID WAS LOOK AT IT.
EEEEEEEEEEEEEEEEE
JUST LIKE I LOOKED AT ALL THE PEOPLE IN THIS TOWN.
HERE, LET ME SHOW YOU...
EEEEEEEEE
ZZAMMMM

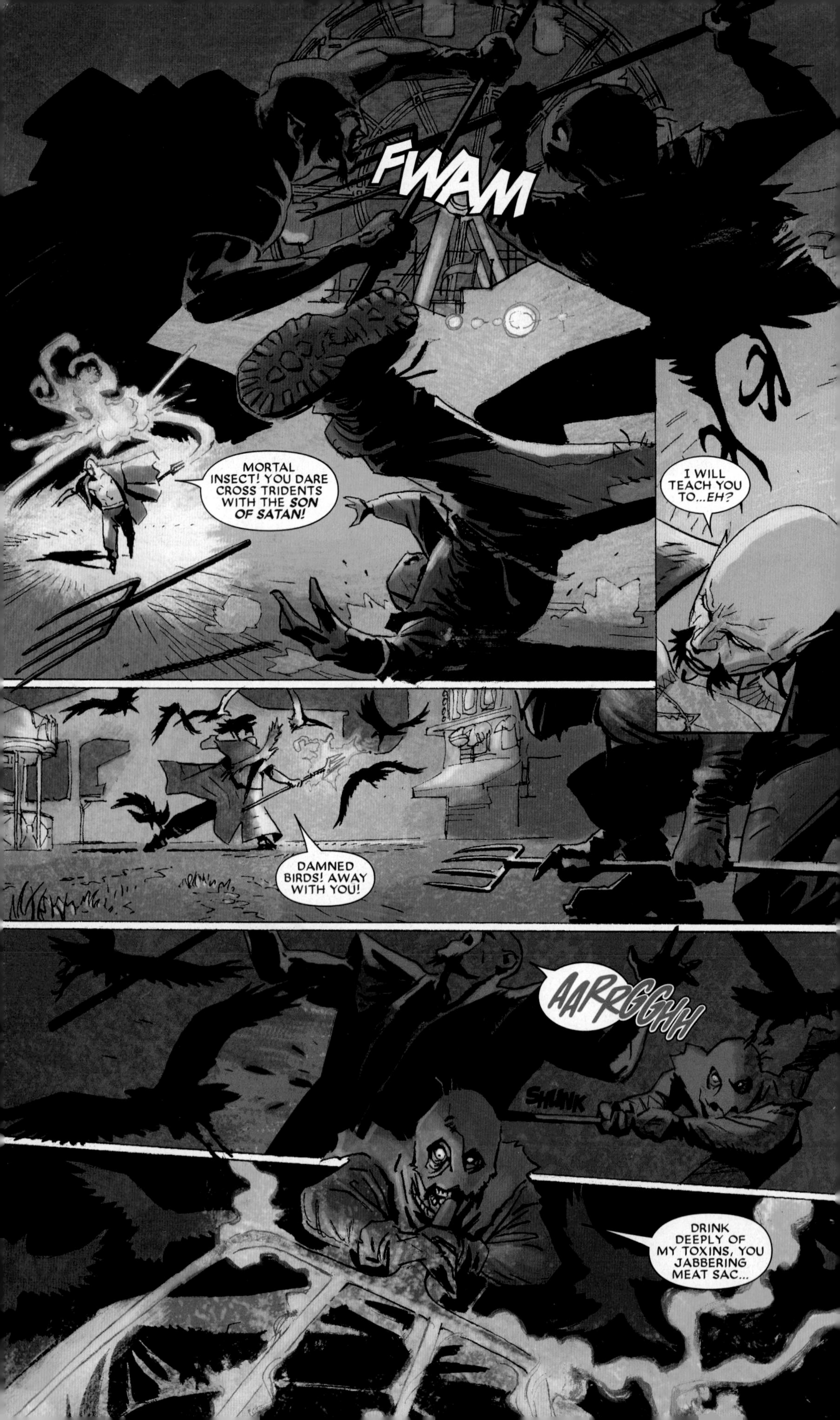
FWAM
MORTAL INSECT! YOU DARE CROSS TRIDENTS WITH THE SON OF SATAN!
I WILL TEACH YOU TO...EH?
DAMNED BIRDS! AWAY WITH YOU!
AARRGGHH
SHUNK
DRINK DEEPLY OF MY TOXINS, YOU JABBERING MEAT SAC...

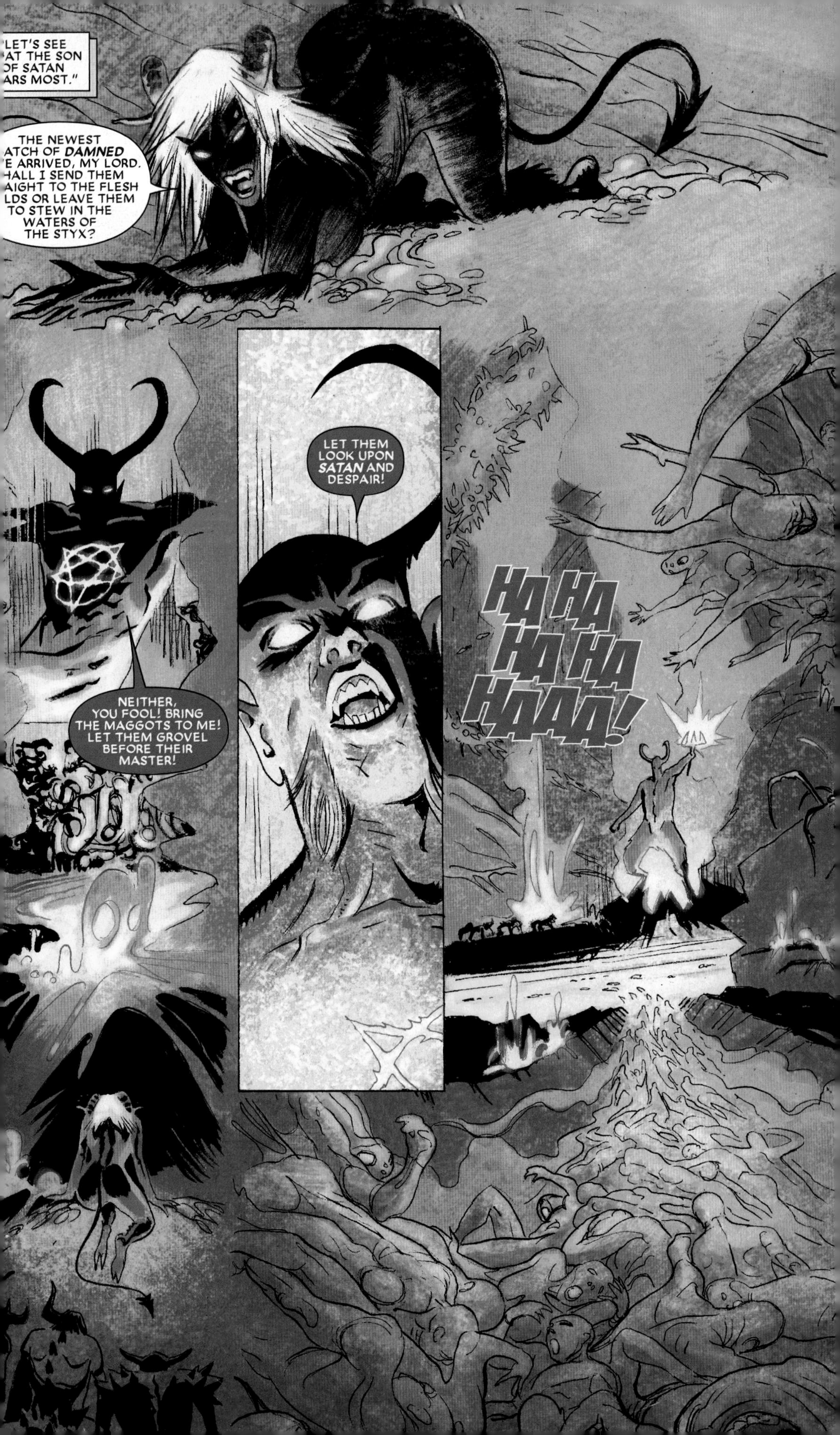
"LET'S SEE
AT THE SON
OF SATAN
ARS MOST."
THE NEWEST
ATCH OF DAMNED
'E ARRIVED, MY LORD.
HALL I SEND THEM
AIGHT TO THE FLESH
LDS OR LEAVE THEM
TO STEW IN THE
WATERS OF
THE STYX?
NEITHER, YOU FOOL! BRING THE MAGGOTS TO ME! LET THEM GROVEL BEFORE THEIR MASTER!
LET THEM LOOK UPON SATAN AND DESPAIR!
HA HA HA HA HAAA!

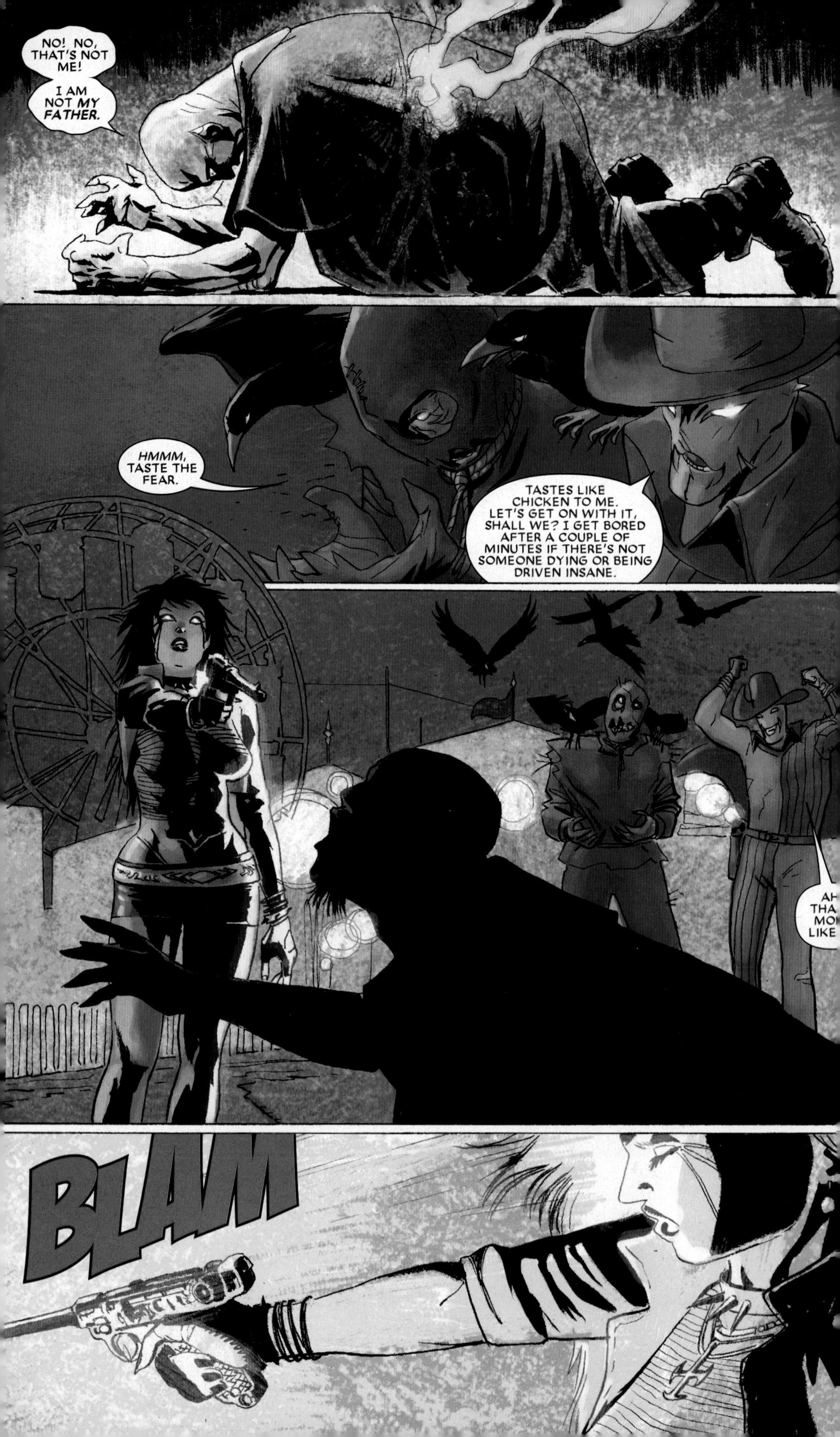

NO! NO, THAT'S NOT ME!
I AM NOT *MY FATHER.*
HMMM, TASTE THE FEAR.
TASTES LIKE CHICKEN TO ME. LET'S GET ON WITH IT, SHALL WE? I GET BORED AFTER A COUPLE OF MINUTES IF THERE'S NOT SOMEONE DYING OR BEING DRIVEN INSANE.
BLAM

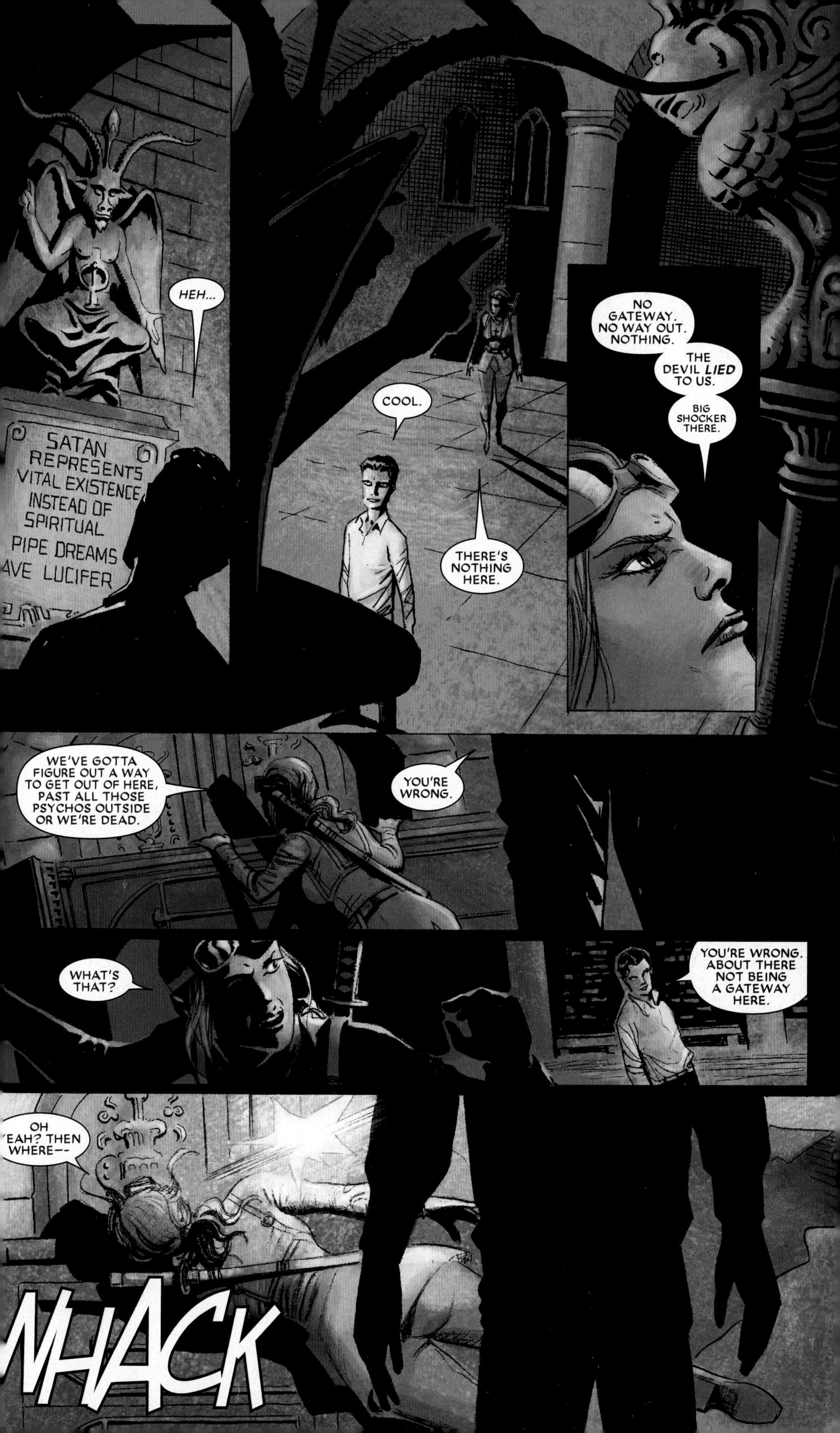
SATAN REPRESENTS VITAL EXISTENCE INSTEAD OF SPIRITUAL PIPE DREAMS
AVE LUCIFER
HEH...
COOL.
THERE'S NOTHING HERE.
NO GATEWAY. NO WAY OUT. NOTHING.
THE DEVIL *LIED* TO US.
BIG SHOCKER THERE.
WE'VE GOTTA FIGURE OUT A WAY TO GET OUT OF HERE, PAST ALL THOSE PSYCHOS OUTSIDE OR WE'RE DEAD.
YOU'RE WRONG.
WHAT'S THAT?
YOU'RE WRONG. ABOUT THERE NOT BEING A GATEWAY HERE.
OH YEAH? THEN WHERE--
WHACK

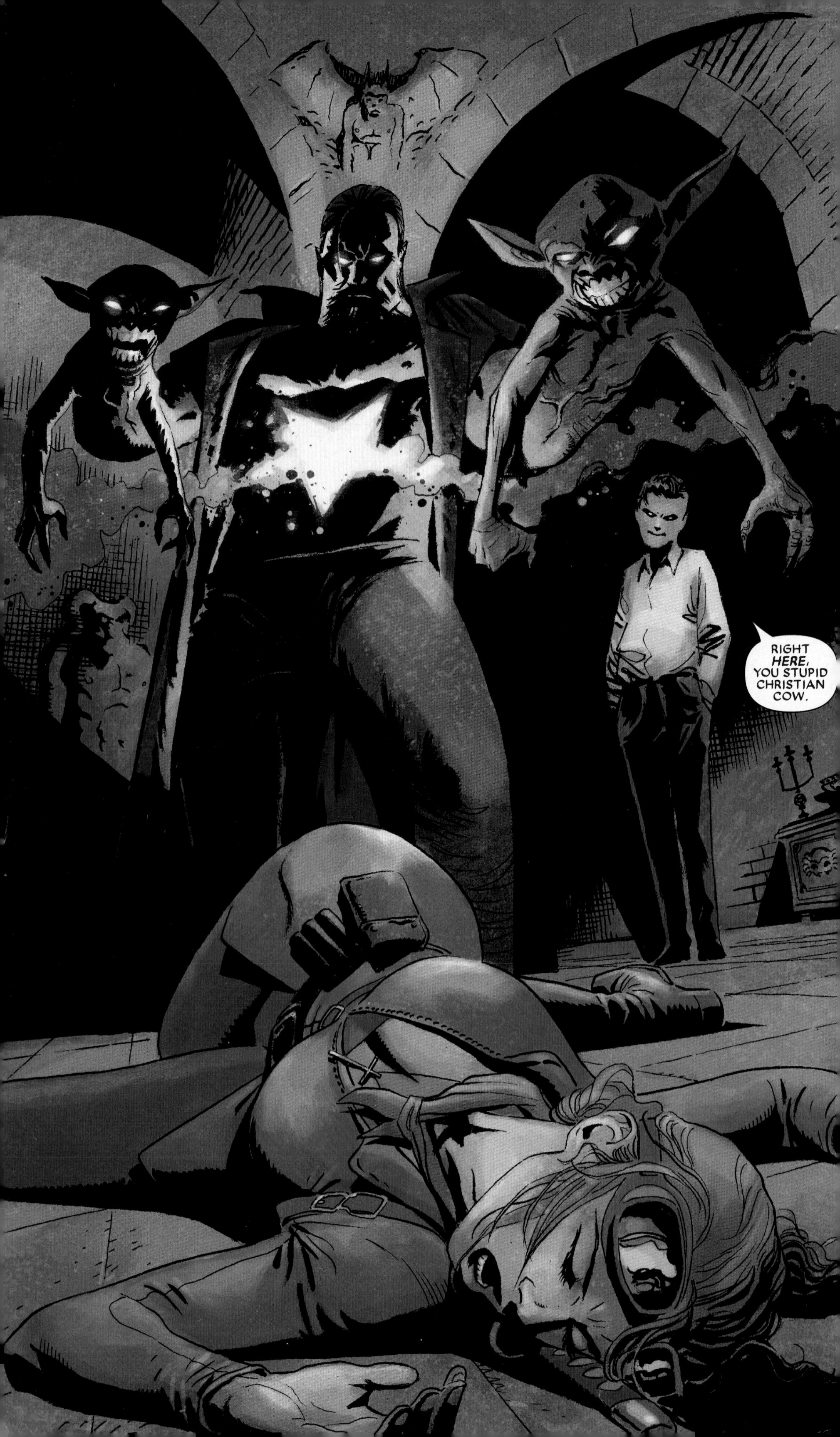
RIGHT HERE, YOU STUPID CHRISTIAN COW.

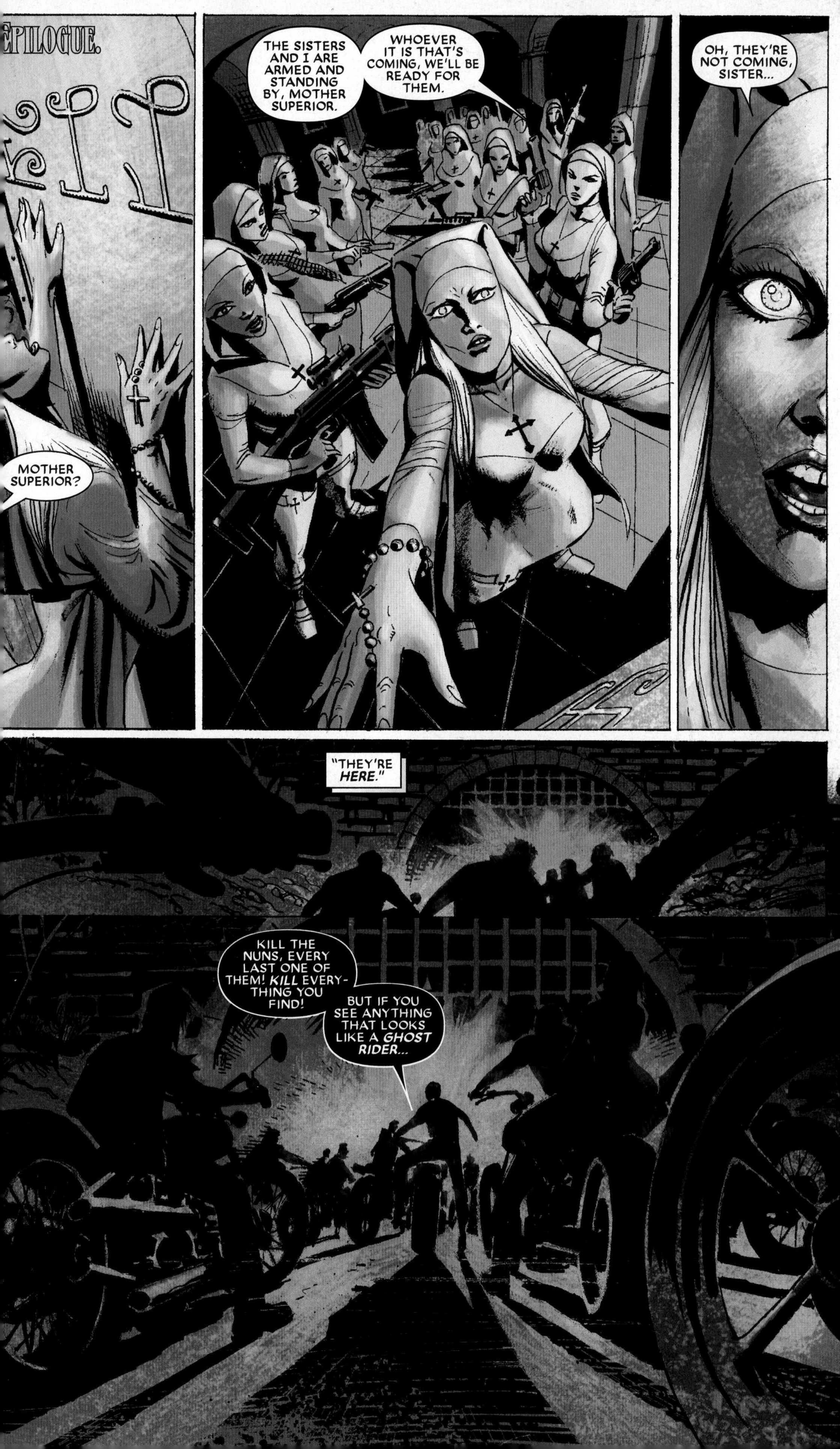
EPILOGUE.
MOTHER SUPERIOR?
THE SISTERS AND I ARE ARMED AND STANDING BY, MOTHER SUPERIOR.
WHOEVER IT IS THAT'S COMING, WE'LL BE READY FOR THEM.
OH, THEY'RE NOT COMING, SISTER...
"THEY'RE HERE."
KILL THE NUNS, EVERY LAST ONE OF THEM! KILL EVERY-THING YOU FIND!
BUT IF YOU SEE ANYTHING THAT LOOKS LIKE A GHOST RIDER...

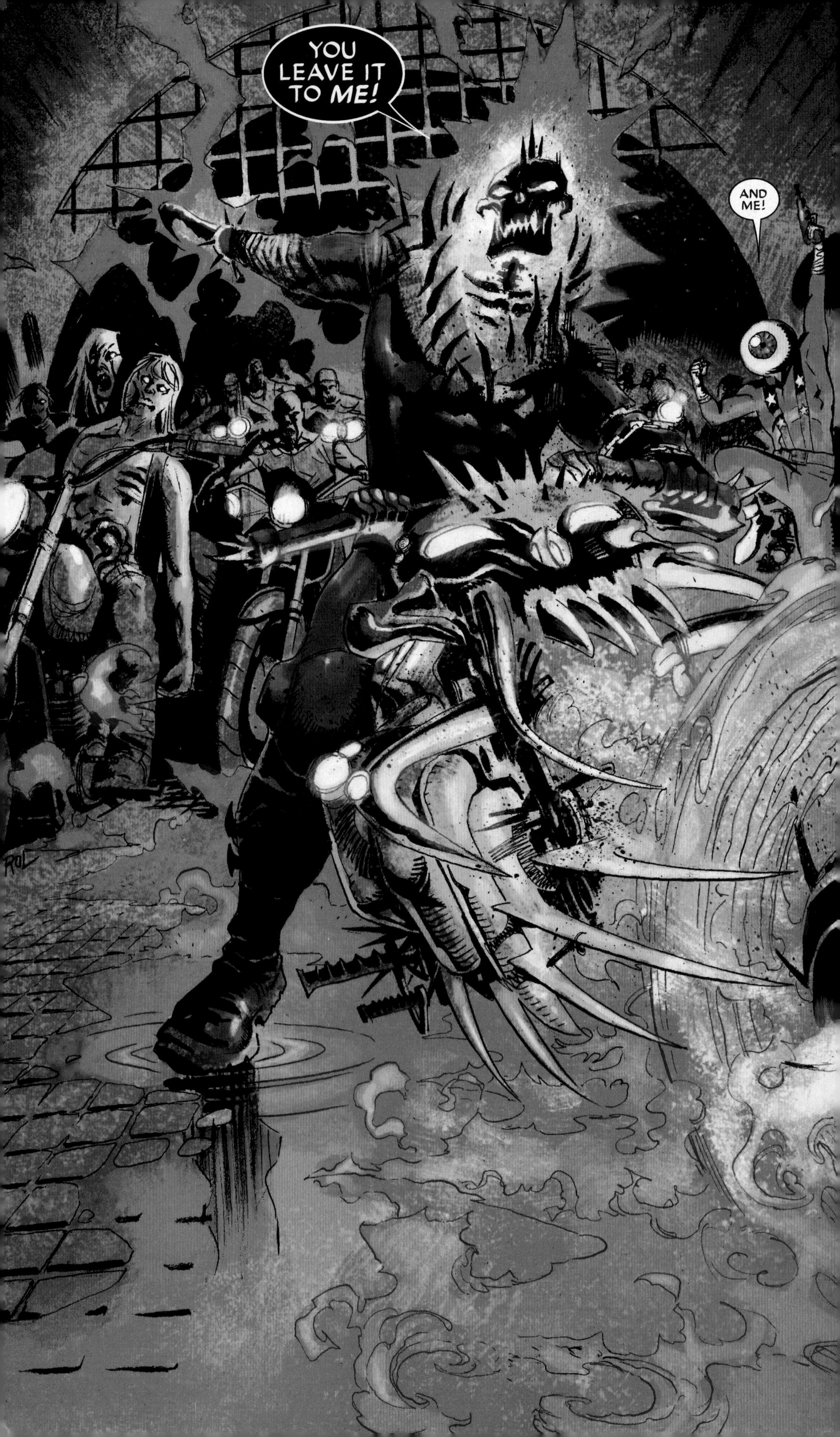
YOU LEAVE IT TO ME!
AND ME!
ROL

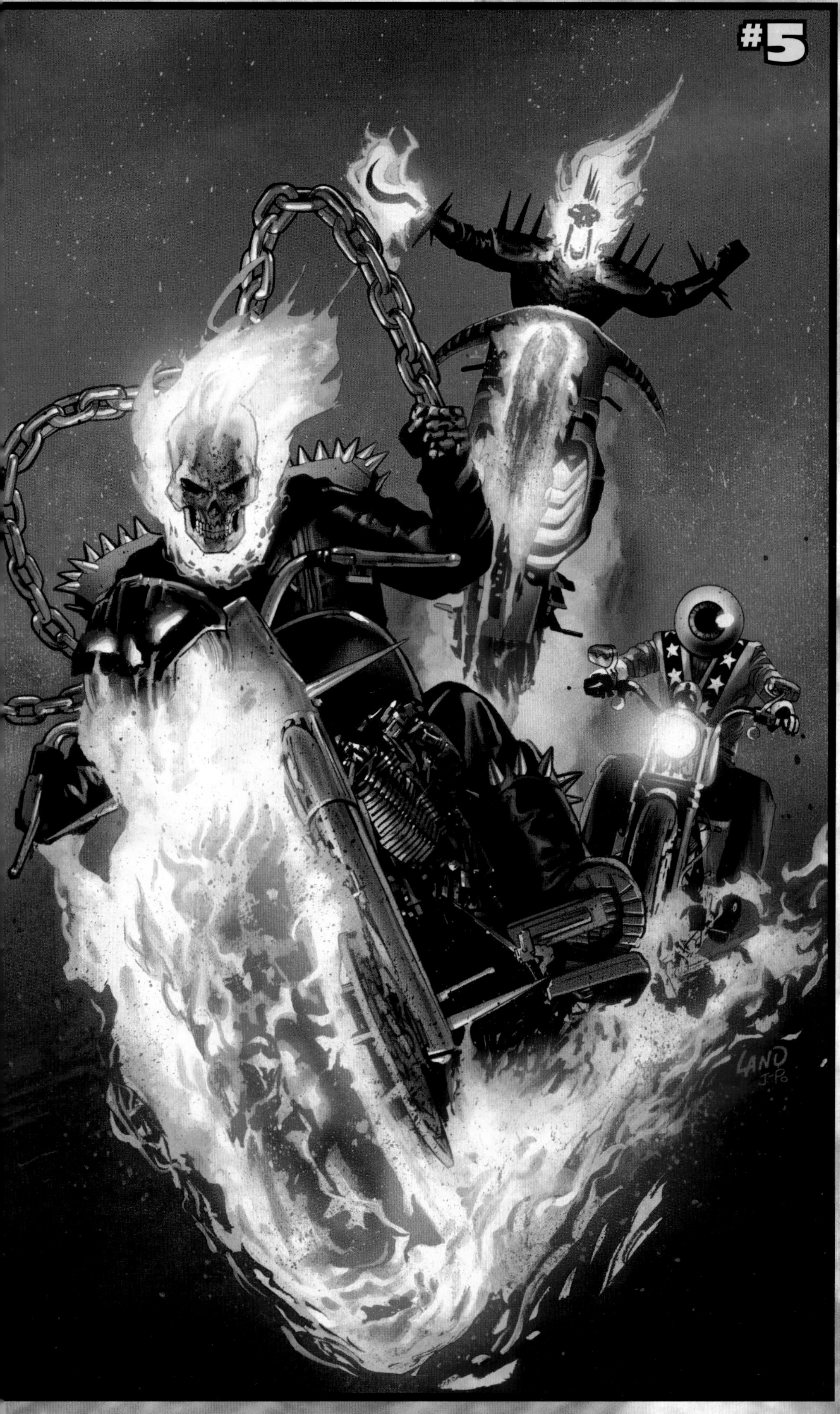
#5
LAND
J-Po

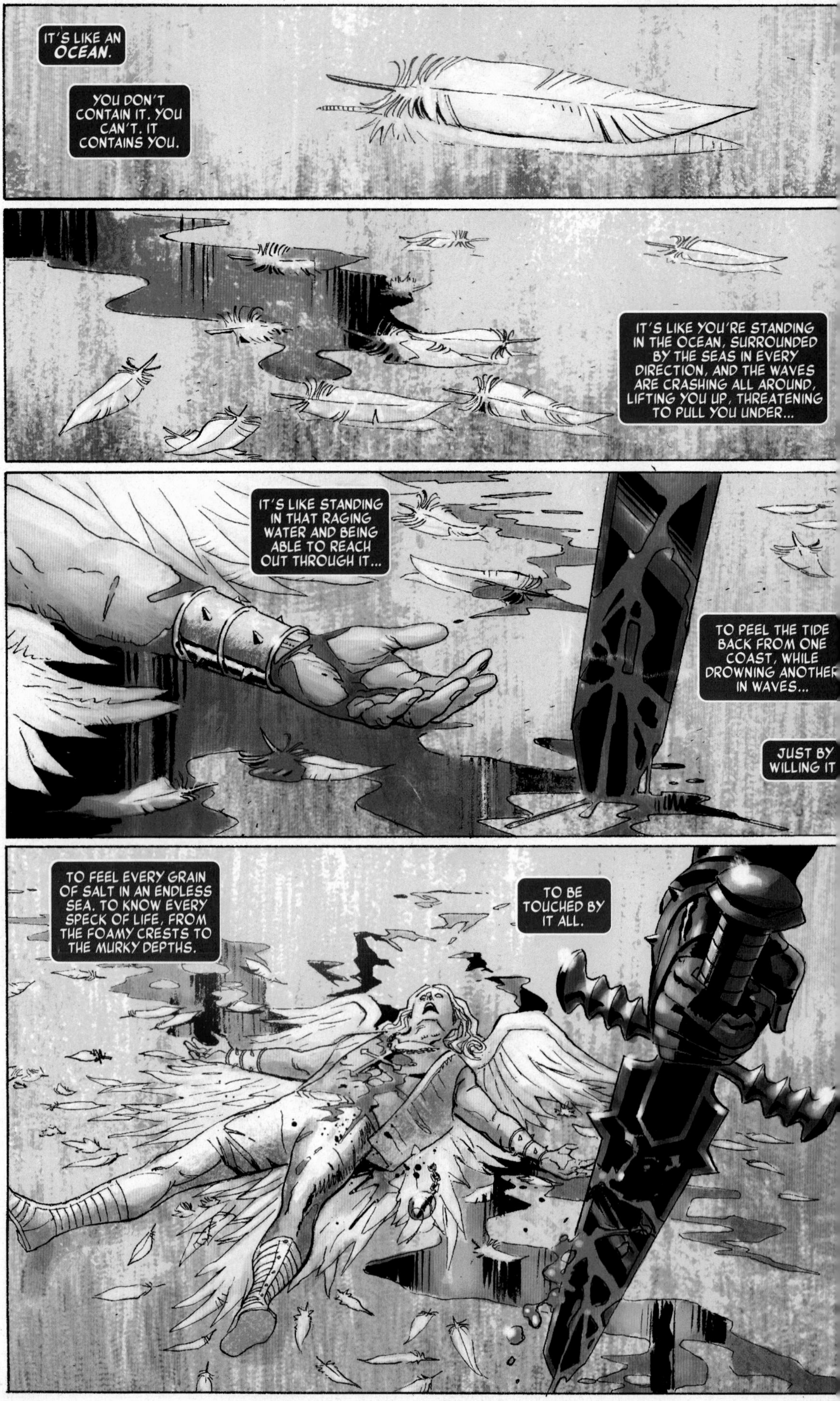
IT'S LIKE AN OCEAN.
YOU DON'T CONTAIN IT. YOU CAN'T. IT CONTAINS YOU.
IT'S LIKE YOU'RE STANDING IN THE OCEAN, SURROUNDED BY THE SEAS IN EVERY DIRECTION, AND THE WAVES ARE CRASHING ALL AROUND, LIFTING YOU UP, THREATENING TO PULL YOU UNDER...
IT'S LIKE STANDING IN THAT RAGING WATER AND BEING ABLE TO REACH OUT THROUGH IT...
TO PEEL THE TIDE BACK FROM ONE COAST, WHILE DROWNING ANOTHER IN WAVES...
JUST BY WILLING IT
TO FEEL EVERY GRAIN OF SALT IN AN ENDLESS SEA, TO KNOW EVERY SPECK OF LIFE, FROM THE FOAMY CRESTS TO THE MURKY DEPTHS.
TO BE TOUCHED BY IT ALL.

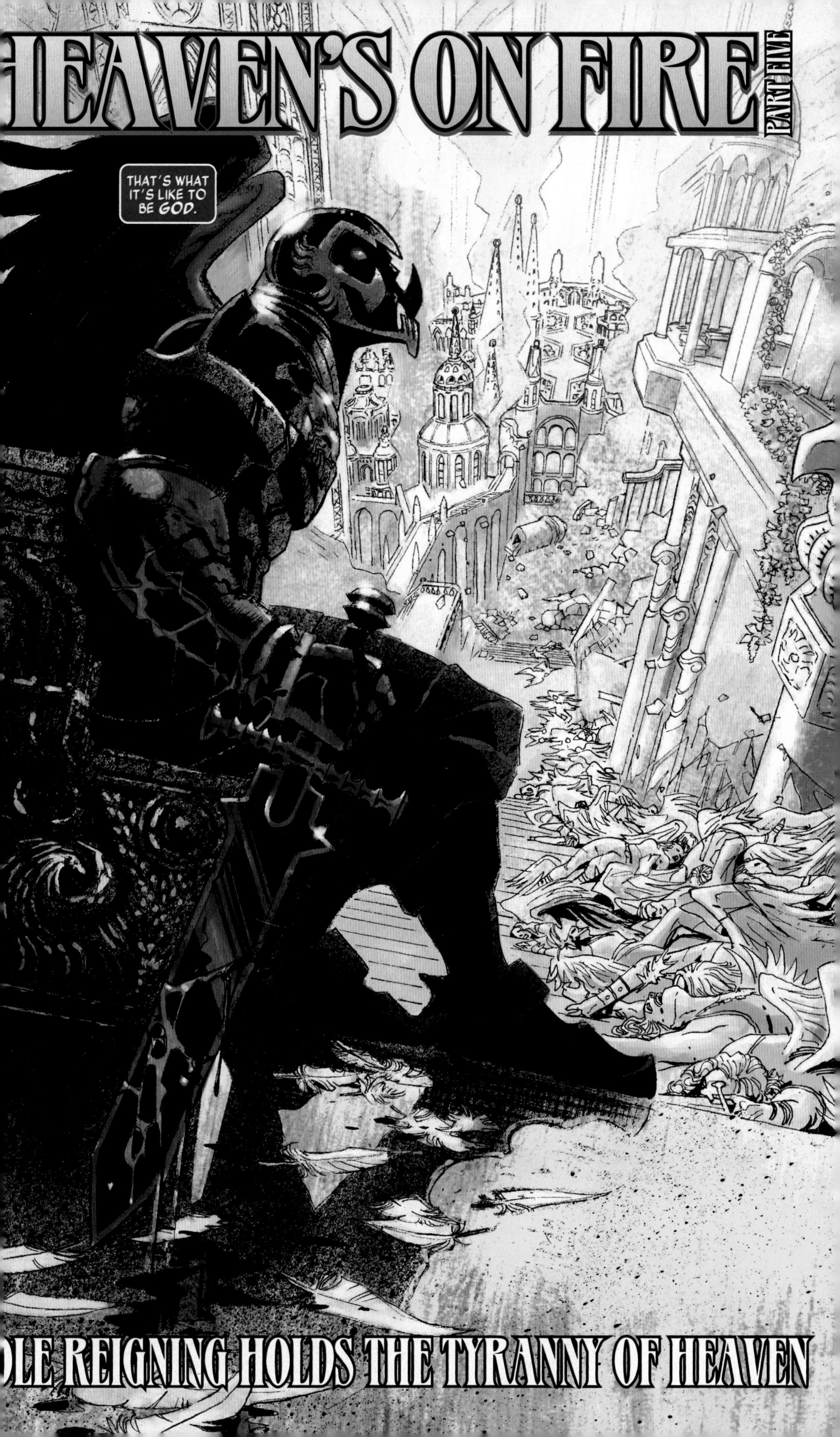
HEAVEN'S ON FIRE
PART FIVE
THAT'S WHAT IT'S LIKE TO BE GOD.
OLE REIGNING HOLDS THE TYRANNY OF HEAVEN

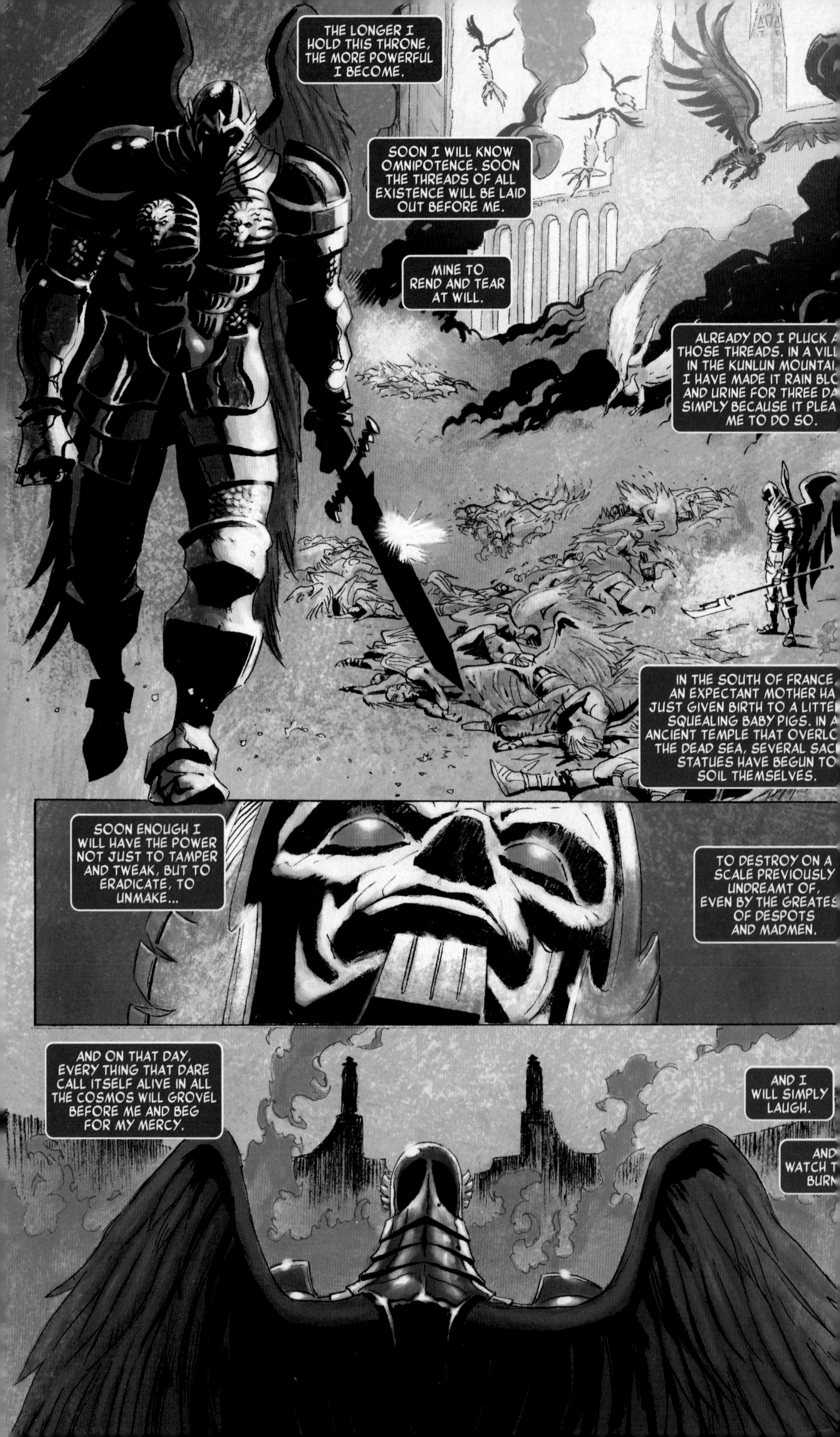

THE LONGER I HOLD THIS THRONE, THE MORE POWERFUL I BECOME.
SOON I WILL KNOW OMNIPOTENCE. SOON THE THREADS OF ALL EXISTENCE WILL BE LAID OUT BEFORE ME.
MINE TO REND AND TEAR AT WILL.
ALREADY DO I PLUCK A THOSE THREADS. IN A VILL IN THE KUNLUN MOUNTAI I HAVE MADE IT RAIN BLO AND URINE FOR THREE DA SIMPLY BECAUSE IT PLEA ME TO DO SO.
IN THE SOUTH OF FRANCE, AN EXPECTANT MOTHER HA JUST GIVEN BIRTH TO A LITTE SQUEALING BABY PIGS. IN A ANCIENT TEMPLE THAT OVERLO THE DEAD SEA, SEVERAL SAC STATUES HAVE BEGUN TO SOIL THEMSELVES.
SOON ENOUGH I WILL HAVE THE POWER NOT JUST TO TAMPER AND TWEAK, BUT TO ERADICATE, TO UNMAKE...
TO DESTROY ON A SCALE PREVIOUSLY UNDREAMT OF, EVEN BY THE GREATES OF DESPOTS AND MADMEN.
AND ON THAT DAY, EVERY THING THAT DARE CALL ITSELF ALIVE IN ALL THE COSMOS WILL GROVEL BEFORE ME AND BEG FOR MY MERCY.
AND I WILL SIMPLY LAUGH.
AND WATCH T BURN

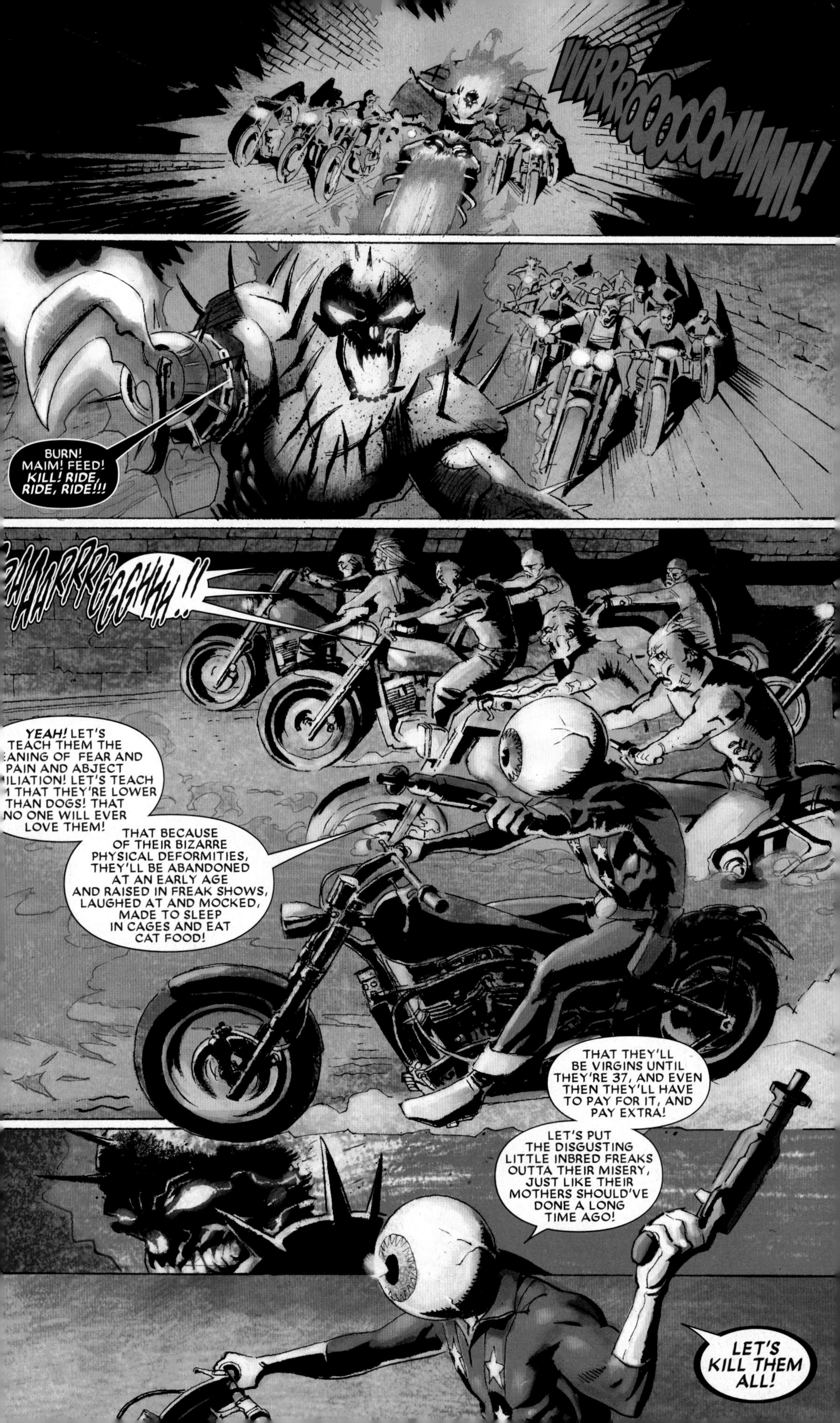
VVRRROOOOOOMMMM!
BURN! MAIM! FEED! KILL! RIDE, RIDE, RIDE!!!
AAARRRGGGHHH!!
YEAH! LET'S TEACH THEM THE EANING OF FEAR AND PAIN AND ABJECT ILIATION! LET'S TEACH THAT THEY'RE LOWER THAN DOGS! THAT NO ONE WILL EVER LOVE THEM!
THAT BECAUSE OF THEIR BIZARRE PHYSICAL DEFORMITIES, THEY'LL BE ABANDONED AT AN EARLY AGE AND RAISED IN FREAK SHOWS, LAUGHED AT AND MOCKED, MADE TO SLEEP IN CAGES AND EAT CAT FOOD!
THAT THEY'LL BE VIRGINS UNTIL THEY'RE 37, AND EVEN THEN THEY'LL HAVE TO PAY FOR IT, AND PAY EXTRA!
LET'S PUT THE DISGUSTING LITTLE INBRED FREAKS OUTTA THEIR MISERY, JUST LIKE THEIR MOTHERS SHOULD'VE DONE A LONG TIME AGO!
LET'S KILL THEM ALL!

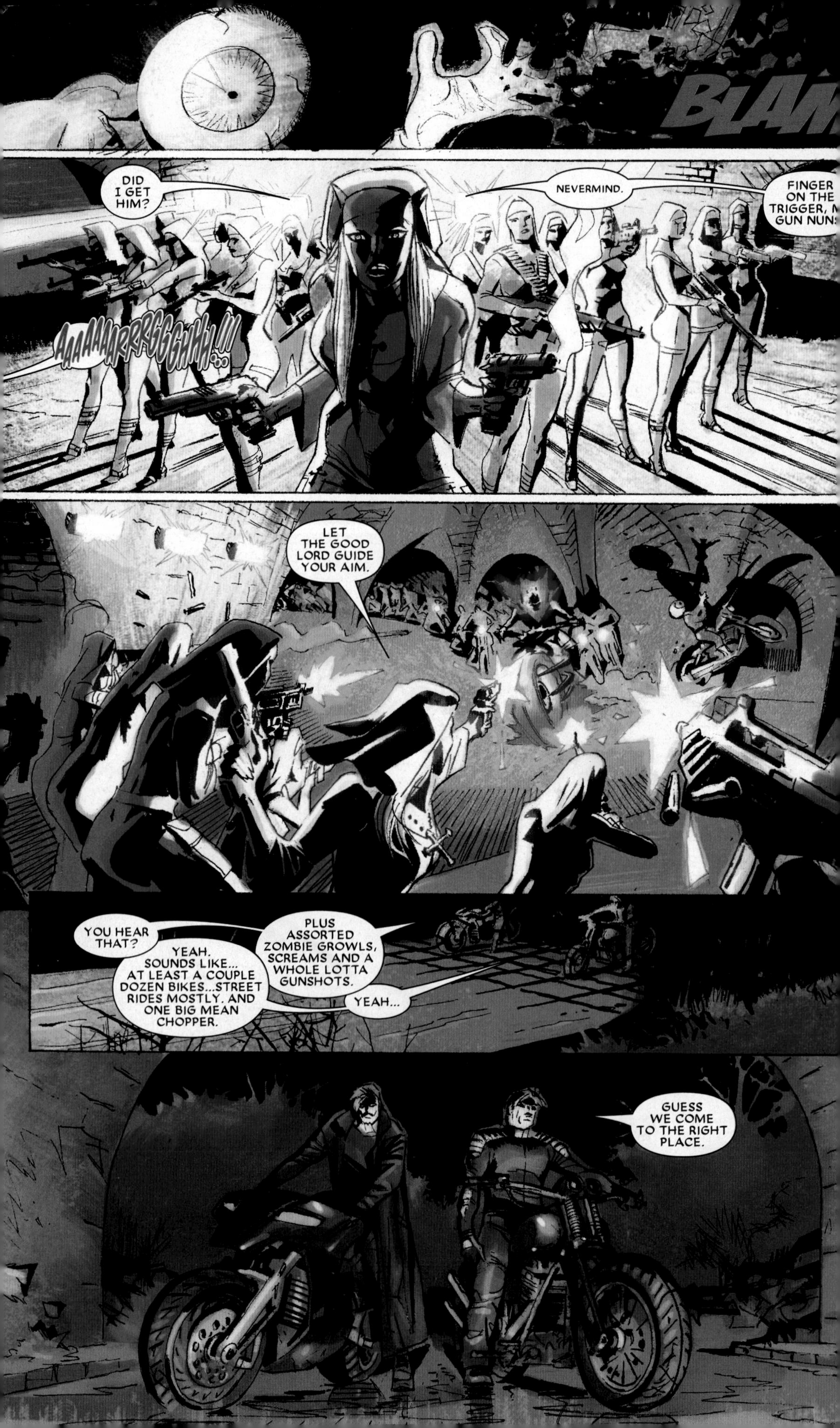
BLAM
DID I GET HIM?
NEVERMIND.
FINGER ON THE TRIGGER, M
GUN NUNS
AAAAAAARRRGGGHHH!!!
LET THE GOOD LORD GUIDE YOUR AIM.
YOU HEAR THAT?
YEAH. SOUNDS LIKE... AT LEAST A COUPLE DOZEN BIKES...STREET RIDES MOSTLY. AND ONE BIG MEAN CHOPPER.
PLUS ASSORTED ZOMBIE GROWLS, SCREAMS AND A WHOLE LOTTA GUNSHOTS.
YEAH...
GUESS WE COME TO THE RIGHT PLACE.

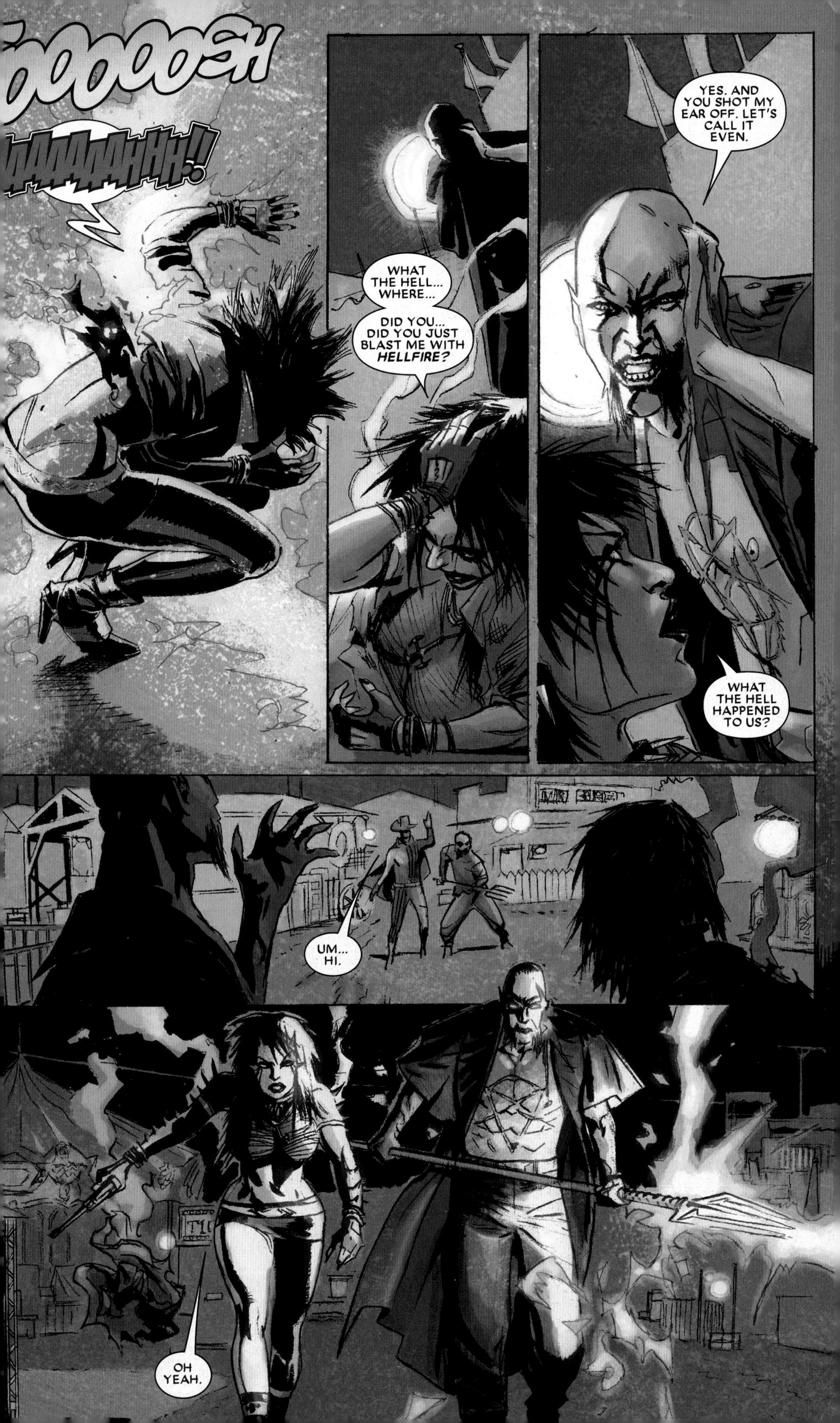
OOOOOSH
AAAAAAHH!!
WHAT THE HELL... WHERE...
DID YOU... DID YOU JUST BLAST ME WITH HELLFIRE?
YES. AND YOU SHOT MY EAR OFF. LET'S CALL IT EVEN.
WHAT THE HELL HAPPENED TO US?
UM... HI.
OH YEAH.

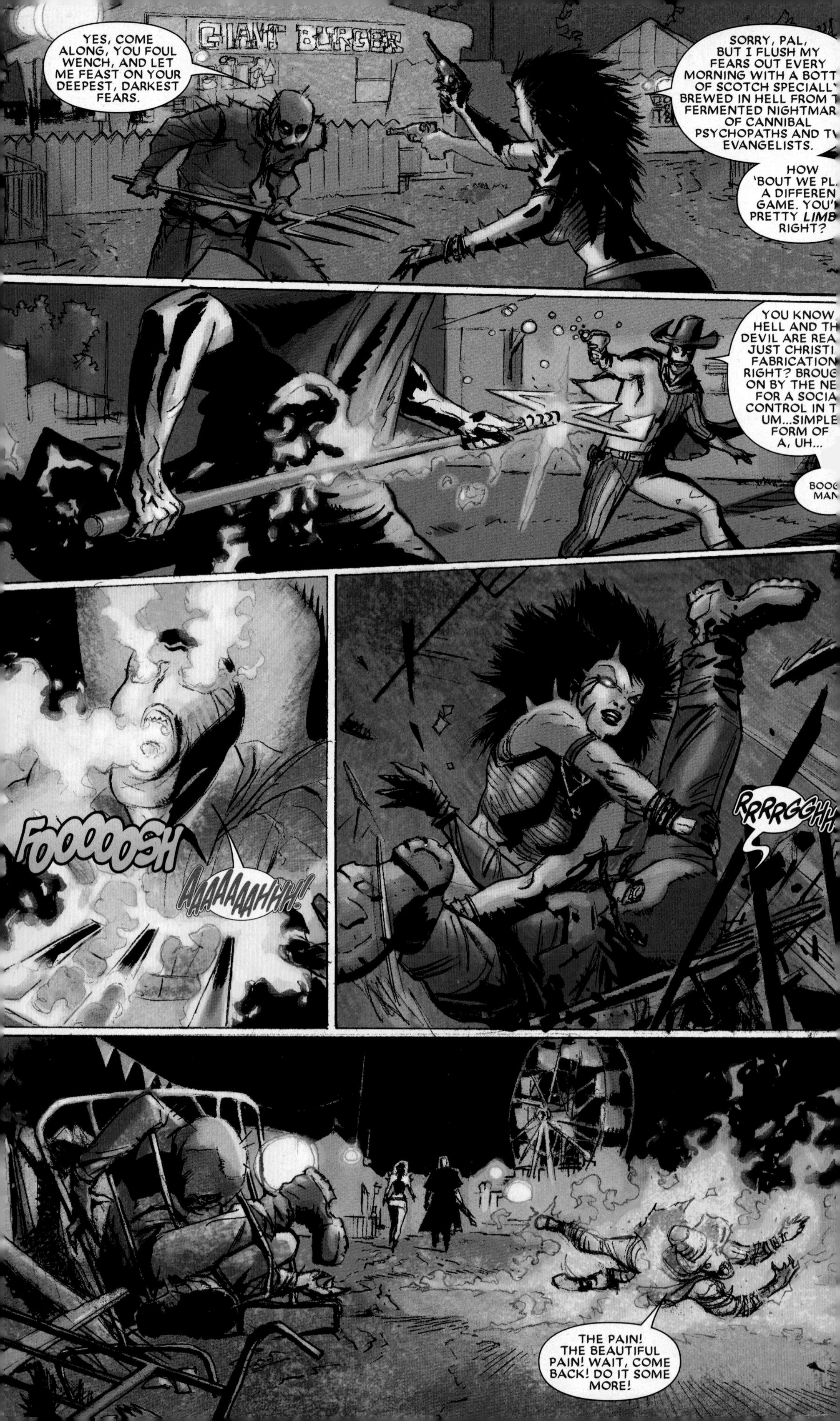
GIANT BURGER
YES, COME ALONG, YOU FOUL WENCH, AND LET ME FEAST ON YOUR DEEPEST, DARKEST FEARS.
SORRY, PAL, BUT I FLUSH MY FEARS OUT EVERY MORNING WITH A BOTT OF SCOTCH SPECIALL BREWED IN HELL FROM T FERMENTED NIGHTMAR OF CANNIBAL PSYCHOPATHS AND T EVANGELISTS.
HOW 'BOUT WE PL A DIFFEREN GAME. YOU' PRETTY LIMB RIGHT?
YOU KNOW HELL AND TH DEVIL ARE REA JUST CHRIST FABRICATION RIGHT? BROUG ON BY THE NE FOR A SOCIA CONTROL IN T UM...SIMPLE FORM OF A, UH...
BOOG MAN
FOOOOOSH
AAAAAAAHHH!
RRRRGGHH
THE PAIN! THE BEAUTIFUL PAIN! WAIT, COME BACK! DO IT SOME MORE!

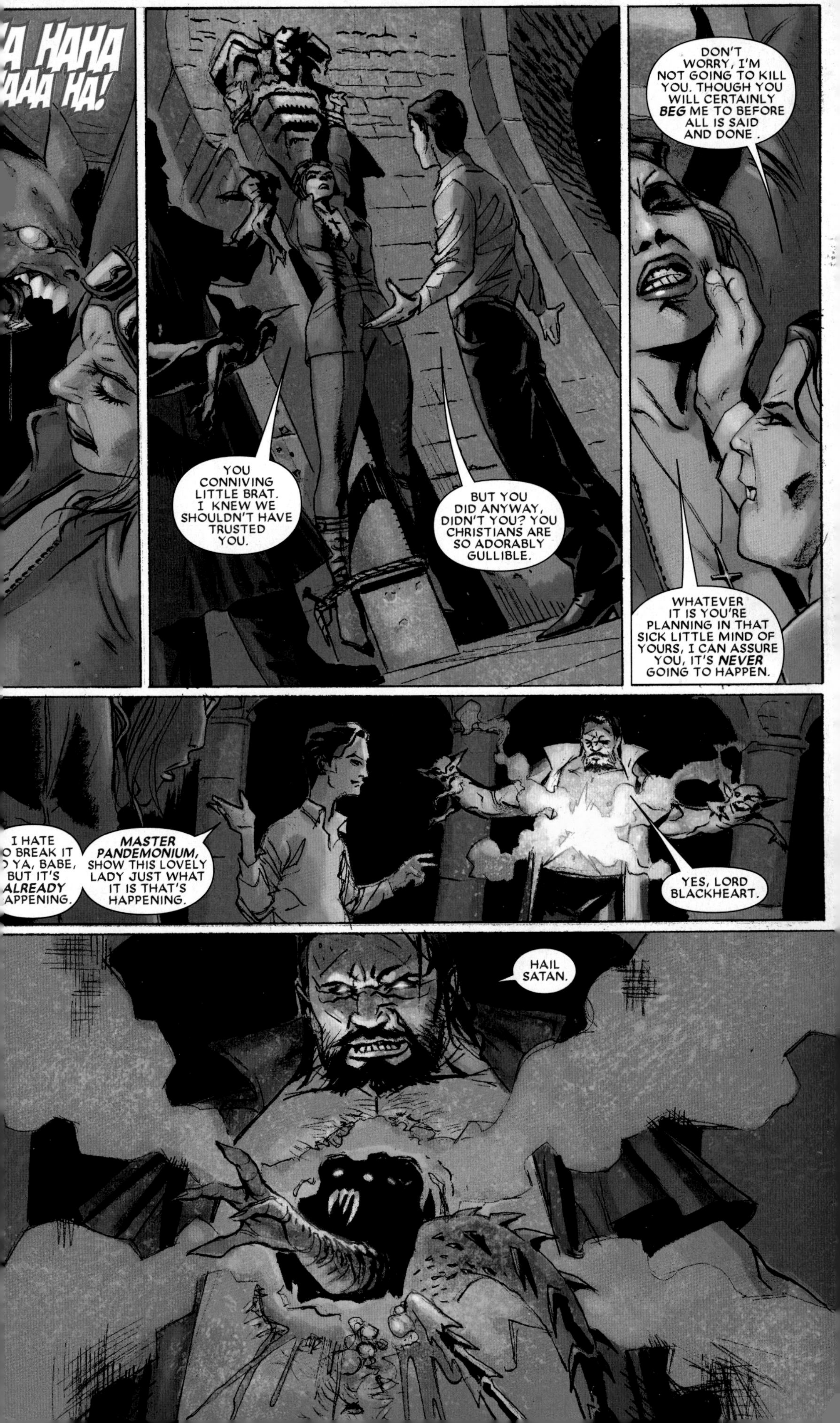
A HAHA
AAA HA!
YOU CONNIVING LITTLE BRAT. I KNEW WE SHOULDN'T HAVE TRUSTED YOU.
BUT YOU DID ANYWAY, DIDN'T YOU? YOU CHRISTIANS ARE SO ADORABLY GULLIBLE.
DON'T WORRY, I'M NOT GOING TO KILL YOU. THOUGH YOU WILL CERTAINLY BEG ME TO BEFORE ALL IS SAID AND DONE.
WHATEVER IT IS YOU'RE PLANNING IN THAT SICK LITTLE MIND OF YOURS, I CAN ASSURE YOU, IT'S NEVER GOING TO HAPPEN.
I HATE O BREAK IT D YA, BABE, BUT IT'S ALREADY APPENING.
MASTER PANDEMONIUM, SHOW THIS LOVELY LADY JUST WHAT IT IS THAT'S HAPPENING.
YES, LORD BLACKHEART.
HAIL SATAN.

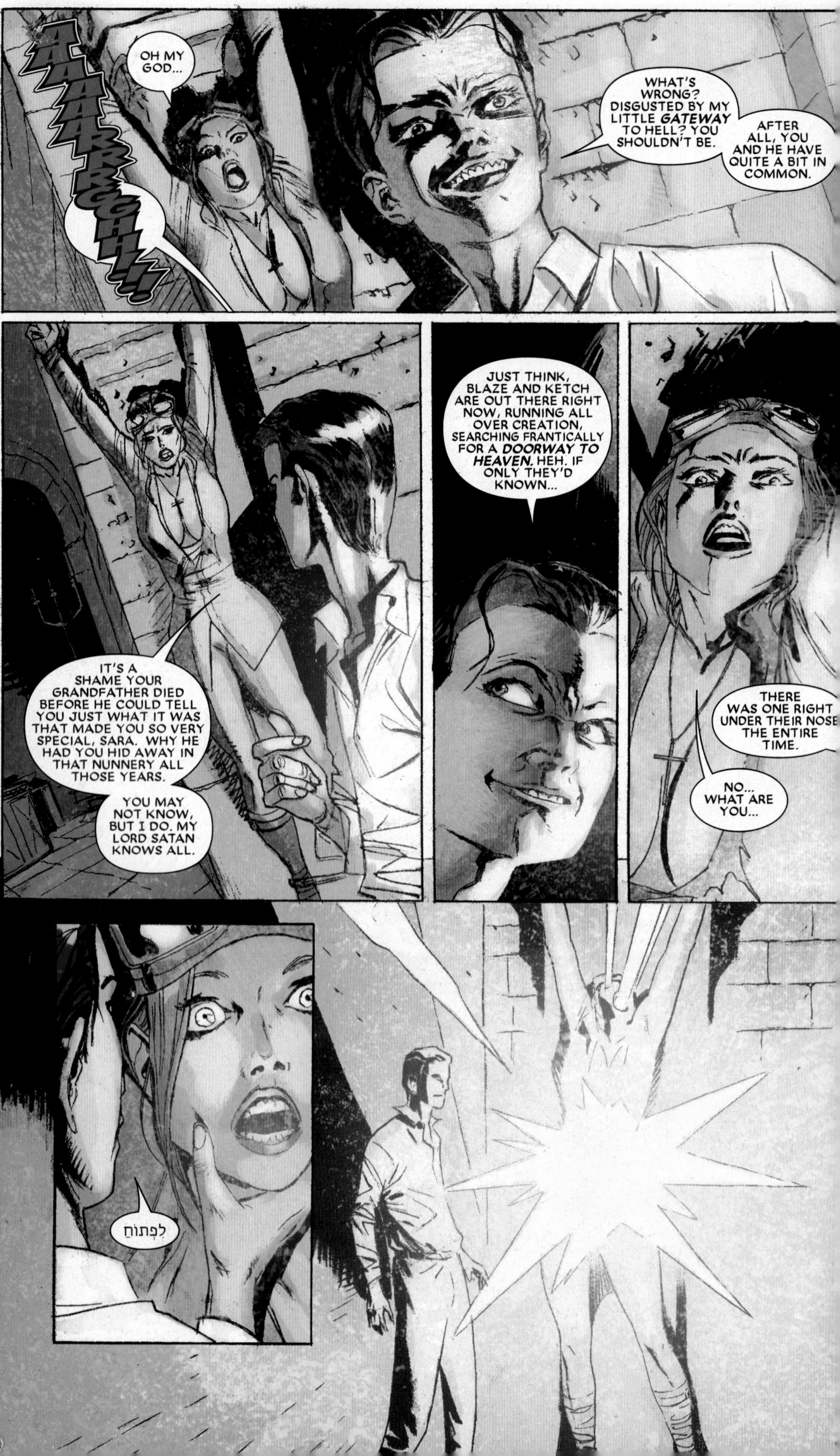
AAAAARRGGHH!!
OH MY GOD...
WHAT'S WRONG? DISGUSTED BY MY LITTLE GATEWAY TO HELL? YOU SHOULDN'T BE.
AFTER ALL, YOU AND HE HAVE QUITE A BIT IN COMMON.
IT'S A SHAME YOUR GRANDFATHER DIED BEFORE HE COULD TELL YOU JUST WHAT IT WAS THAT MADE YOU SO VERY SPECIAL, SARA. WHY HE HAD YOU HID AWAY IN THAT NUNNERY ALL THOSE YEARS.
YOU MAY NOT KNOW, BUT I DO. MY LORD SATAN KNOWS ALL.
JUST THINK, BLAZE AND KETCH ARE OUT THERE RIGHT NOW, RUNNING ALL OVER CREATION, SEARCHING FRANTICALLY FOR A DOORWAY TO HEAVEN. HEH. IF ONLY THEY'D KNOWN...
THERE WAS ONE RIGHT UNDER THEIR NOSE THE ENTIRE TIME.
NO... WHAT ARE YOU...
לִפְתּוֹחַ

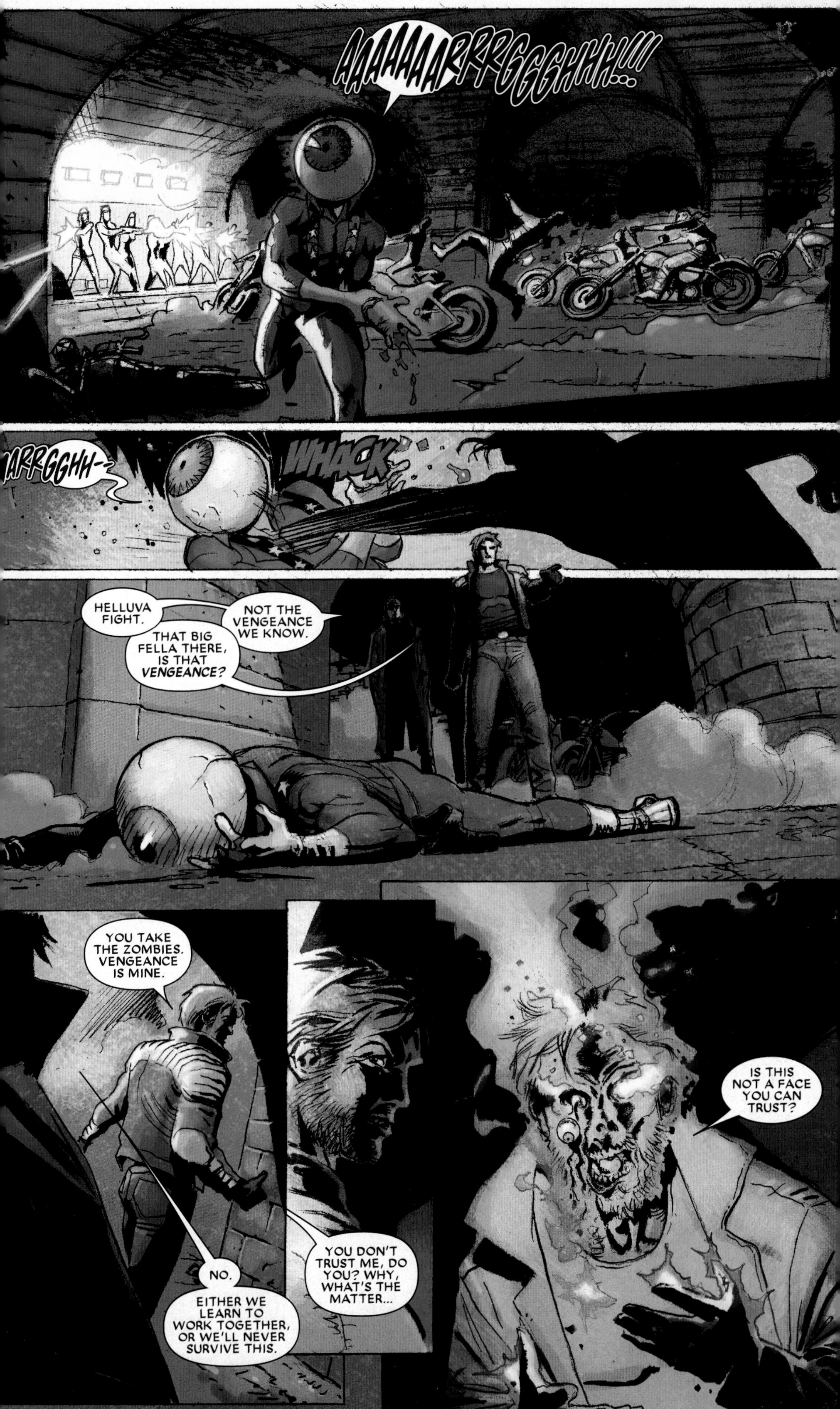
AAAAAAARRRGGGHHH!!!...
ARRGGHH--
WHACK
HELLUVA FIGHT.
THAT BIG FELLA THERE, IS THAT *VENGEANCE?*
NOT THE VENGEANCE WE KNOW.
YOU TAKE THE ZOMBIES. VENGEANCE IS MINE.
NO.
EITHER WE LEARN TO WORK TOGETHER, OR WE'LL NEVER SURVIVE THIS.
YOU DON'T TRUST ME, DO YOU? WHY, WHAT'S THE MATTER...
IS THIS NOT A FACE YOU CAN TRUST?

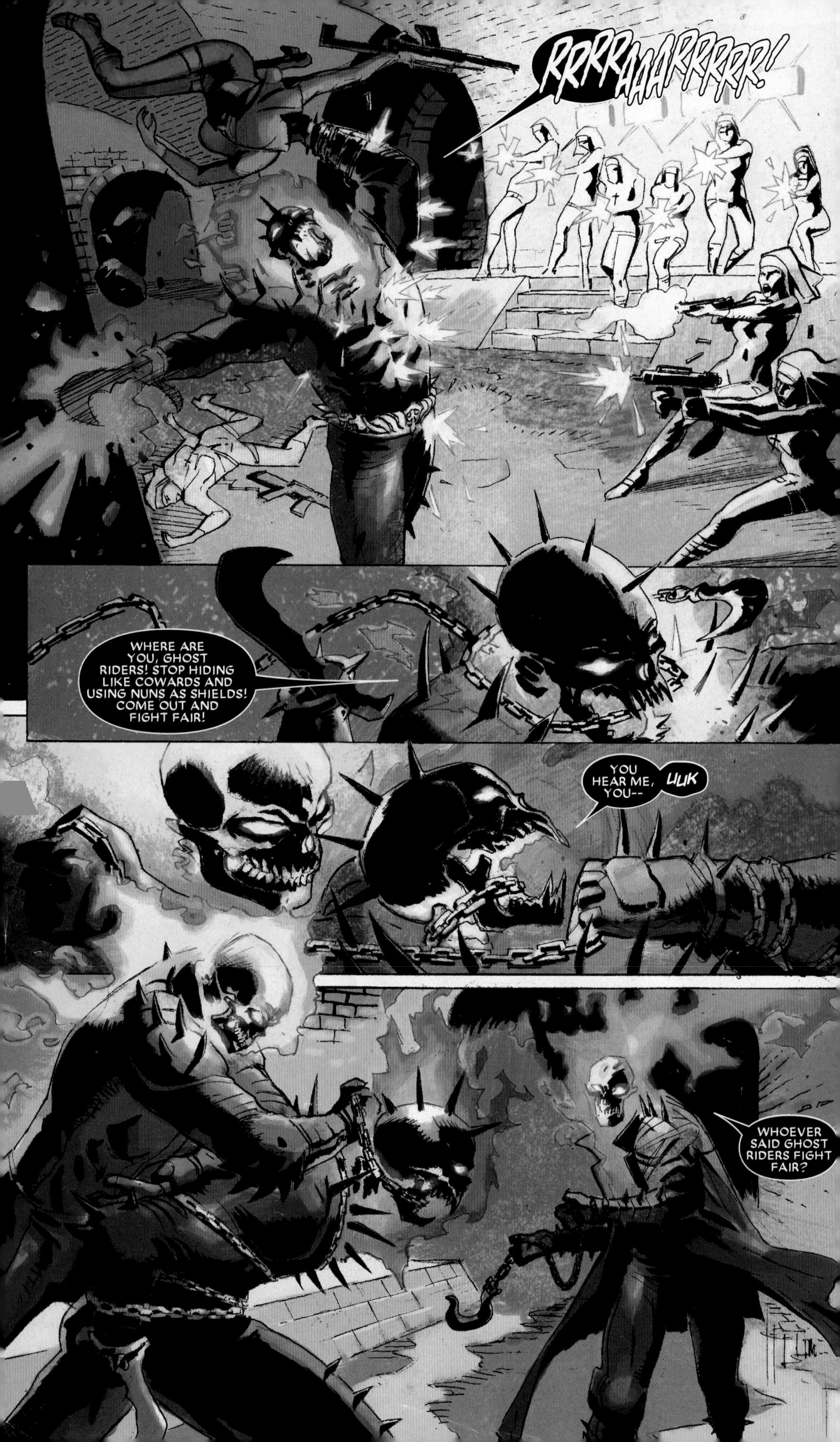
RRRRAAARRRRR!
WHERE ARE YOU, GHOST RIDERS! STOP HIDING LIKE COWARDS AND USING NUNS AS SHIELDS! COME OUT AND FIGHT FAIR!
YOU HEAR ME, YOU--
UUK
WHOEVER SAID GHOST RIDERS FIGHT FAIR?

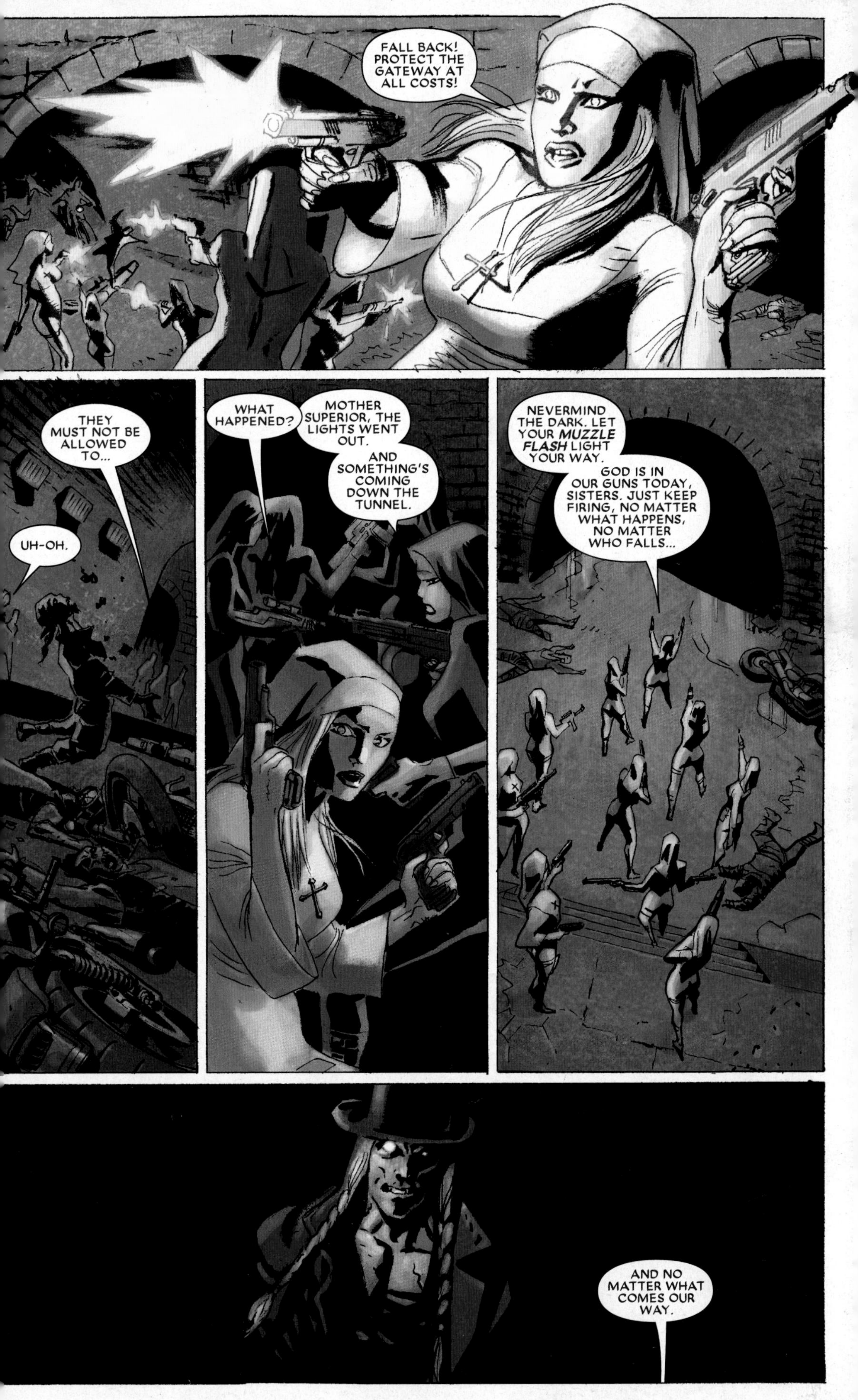
FALL BACK! PROTECT THE GATEWAY AT ALL COSTS!
THEY MUST NOT BE ALLOWED TO...
UH-OH.
WHAT HAPPENED?
MOTHER SUPERIOR, THE LIGHTS WENT OUT.
AND SOMETHING'S COMING DOWN THE TUNNEL.
NEVERMIND THE DARK. LET YOUR MUZZLE FLASH LIGHT YOUR WAY.
GOD IS IN OUR GUNS TODAY, SISTERS. JUST KEEP FIRING, NO MATTER WHAT HAPPENS, NO MATTER WHO FALLS...
AND NO MATTER WHAT COMES OUR WAY.

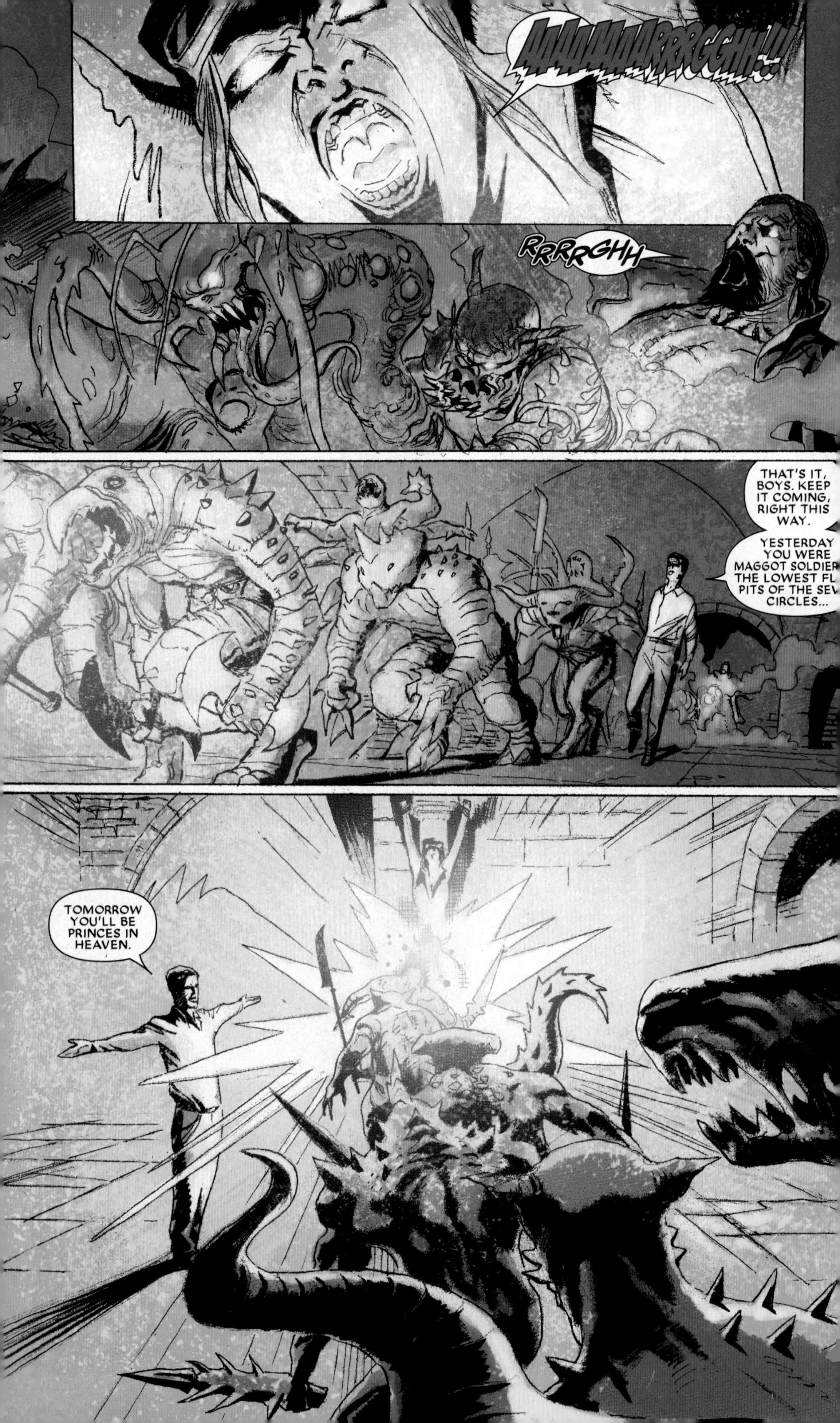
AAAAAAARRRGGHH!!!
RRRRGHH
THAT'S IT, BOYS. KEEP IT COMING, RIGHT THIS WAY.
YESTERDAY YOU WERE MAGGOT SOLDIER THE LOWEST FL PITS OF THE SEV CIRCLES...
TOMORROW YOU'LL BE PRINCES IN HEAVEN.

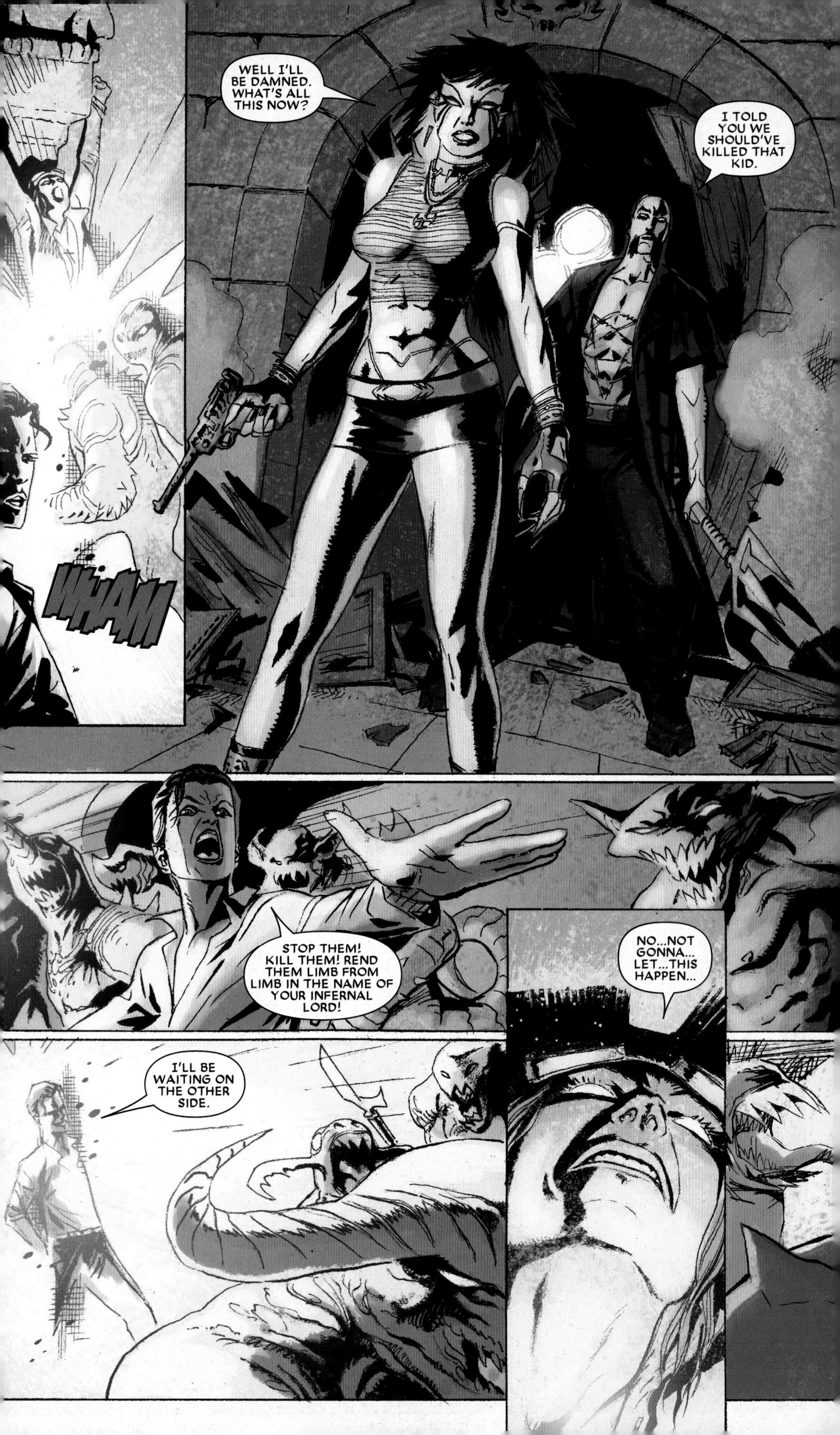
WHAM
WELL I'LL BE DAMNED. WHAT'S ALL THIS NOW?
I TOLD YOU WE SHOULD'VE KILLED THAT KID.
STOP THEM! KILL THEM! REND THEM LIMB FROM LIMB IN THE NAME OF YOUR INFERNAL LORD!
NO...NOT GONNA... LET...THIS HAPPEN...
I'LL BE WAITING ON THE OTHER SIDE.

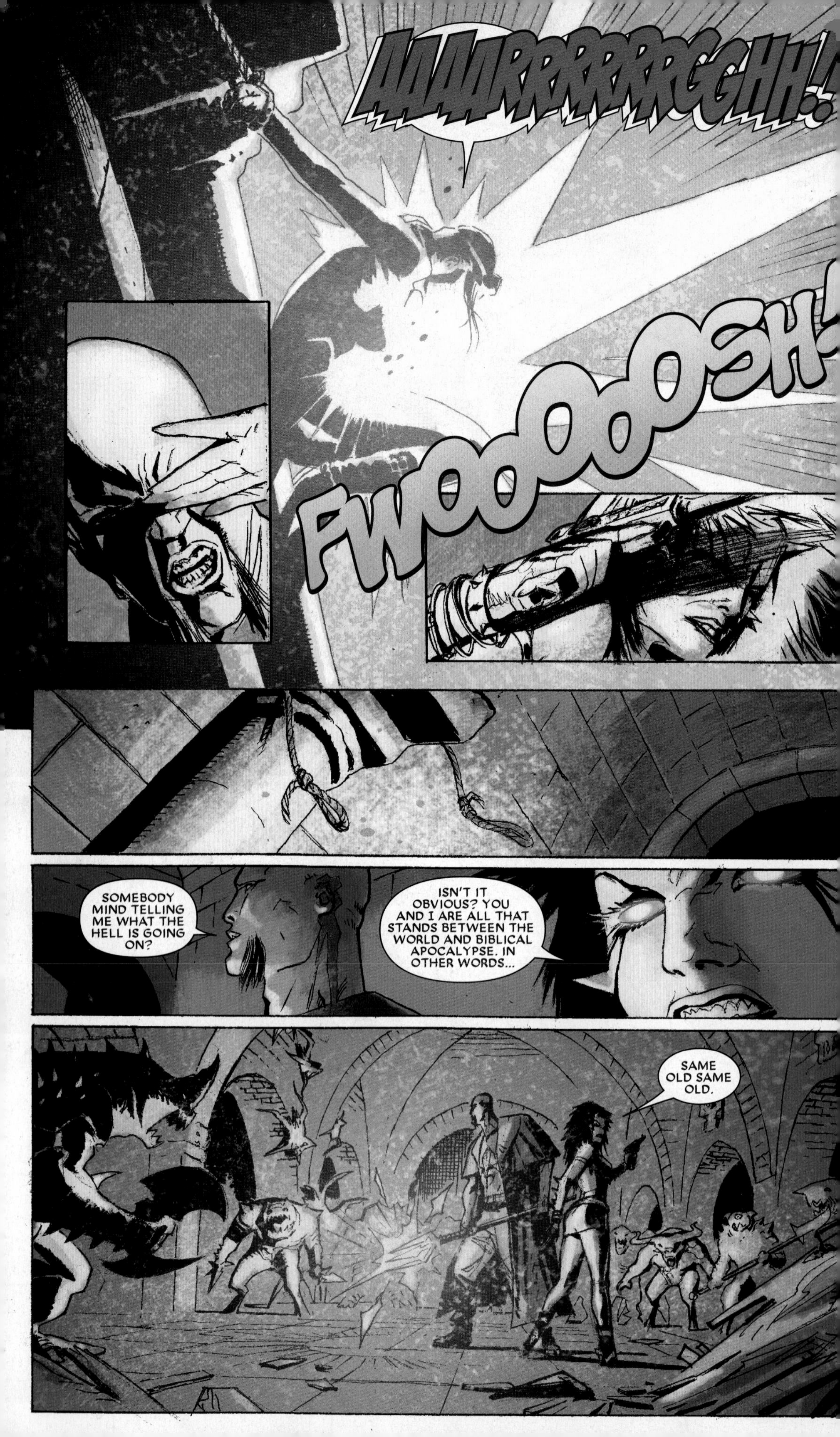
AAAARRRRRRGGHH!!
FWOOOOOOSH!!
SOMEBODY MIND TELLING ME WHAT THE HELL IS GOING ON?
ISN'T IT OBVIOUS? YOU AND I ARE ALL THAT STANDS BETWEEN THE WORLD AND BIBLICAL APOCALYPSE. IN OTHER WORDS...
SAME OLD SAME OLD.

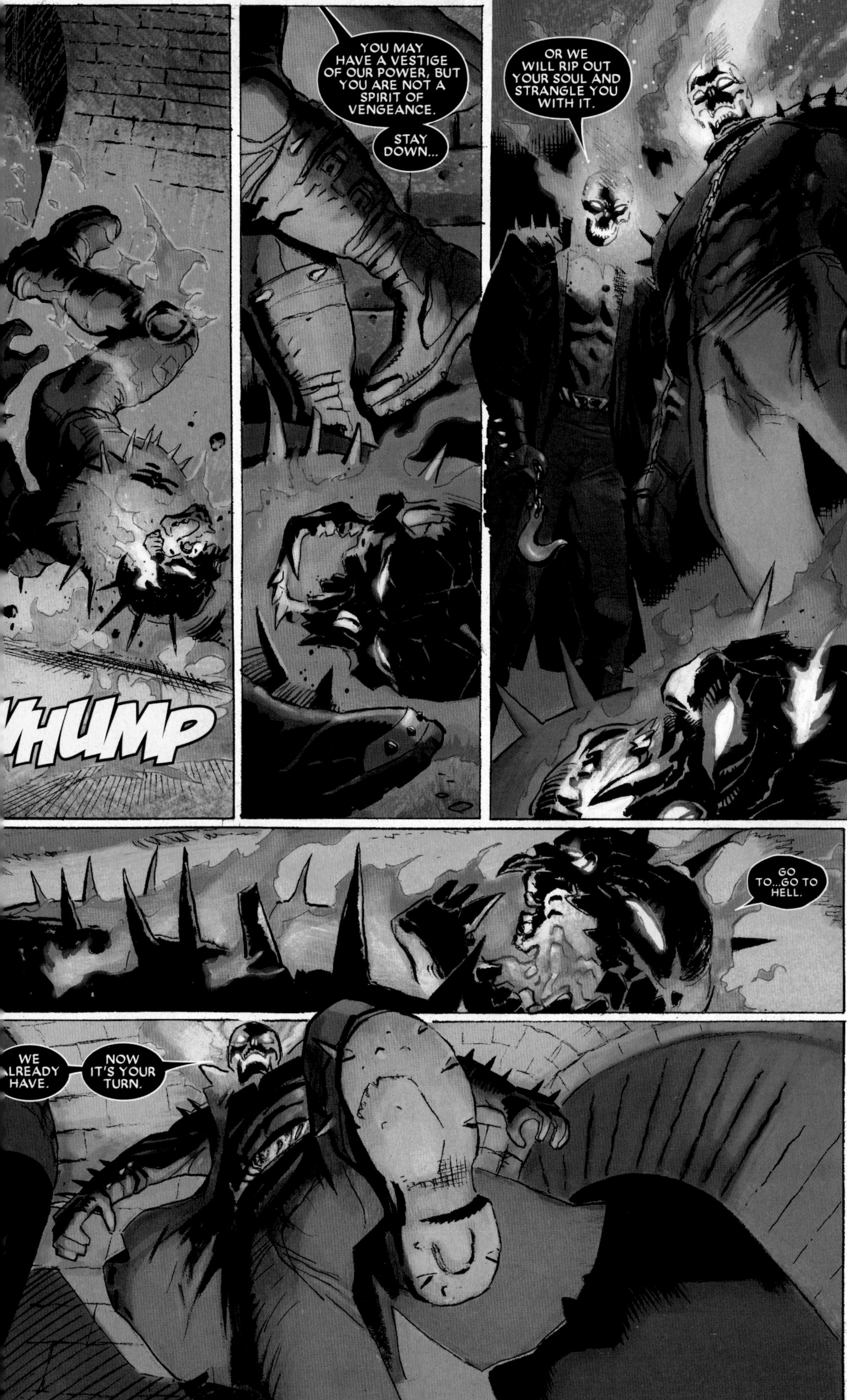

WHUMP
YOU MAY HAVE A VESTIGE OF OUR POWER, BUT YOU ARE NOT A SPIRIT OF VENGEANCE.
STAY DOWN...
OR WE WILL RIP OUT YOUR SOUL AND STRANGLE YOU WITH IT.
GO TO...GO TO HELL.
WE ALREADY HAVE.
NOW IT'S YOUR TURN.

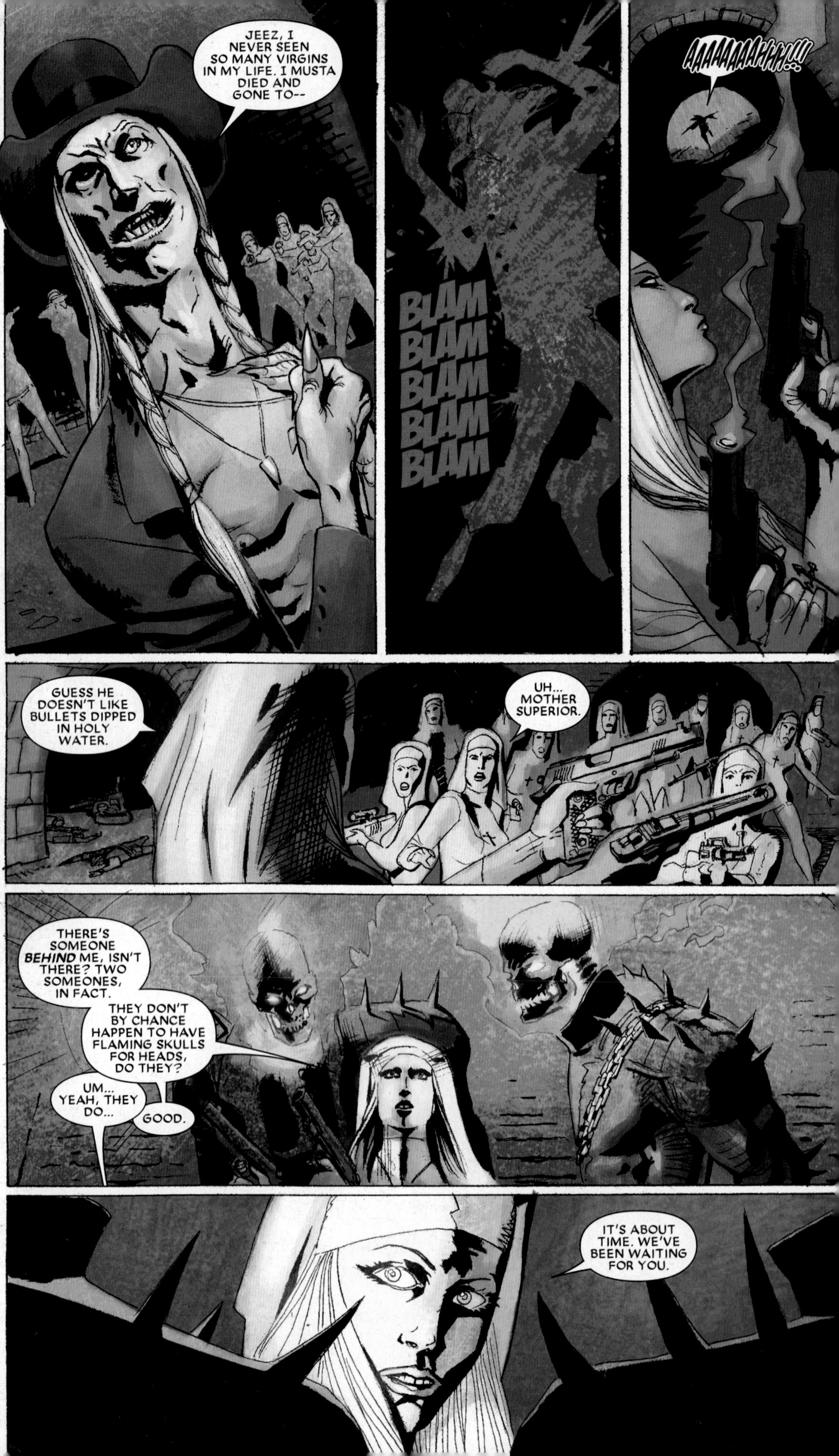
JEEZ, I NEVER SEEN SO MANY VIRGINS IN MY LIFE. I MUSTA DIED AND GONE TO--
BLAM
BLAM
BLAM
BLAM
BLAM
AAAAAAAAHHH!!!
GUESS HE DOESN'T LIKE BULLETS DIPPED IN HOLY WATER.
UH... MOTHER SUPERIOR.
THERE'S SOMEONE *BEHIND* ME, ISN'T THERE? TWO SOMEONES, IN FACT.
THEY DON'T BY CHANCE HAPPEN TO HAVE FLAMING SKULLS FOR HEADS, DO THEY?
UM... YEAH, THEY DO...
GOOD.
IT'S ABOUT TIME. WE'VE BEEN WAITING FOR YOU.

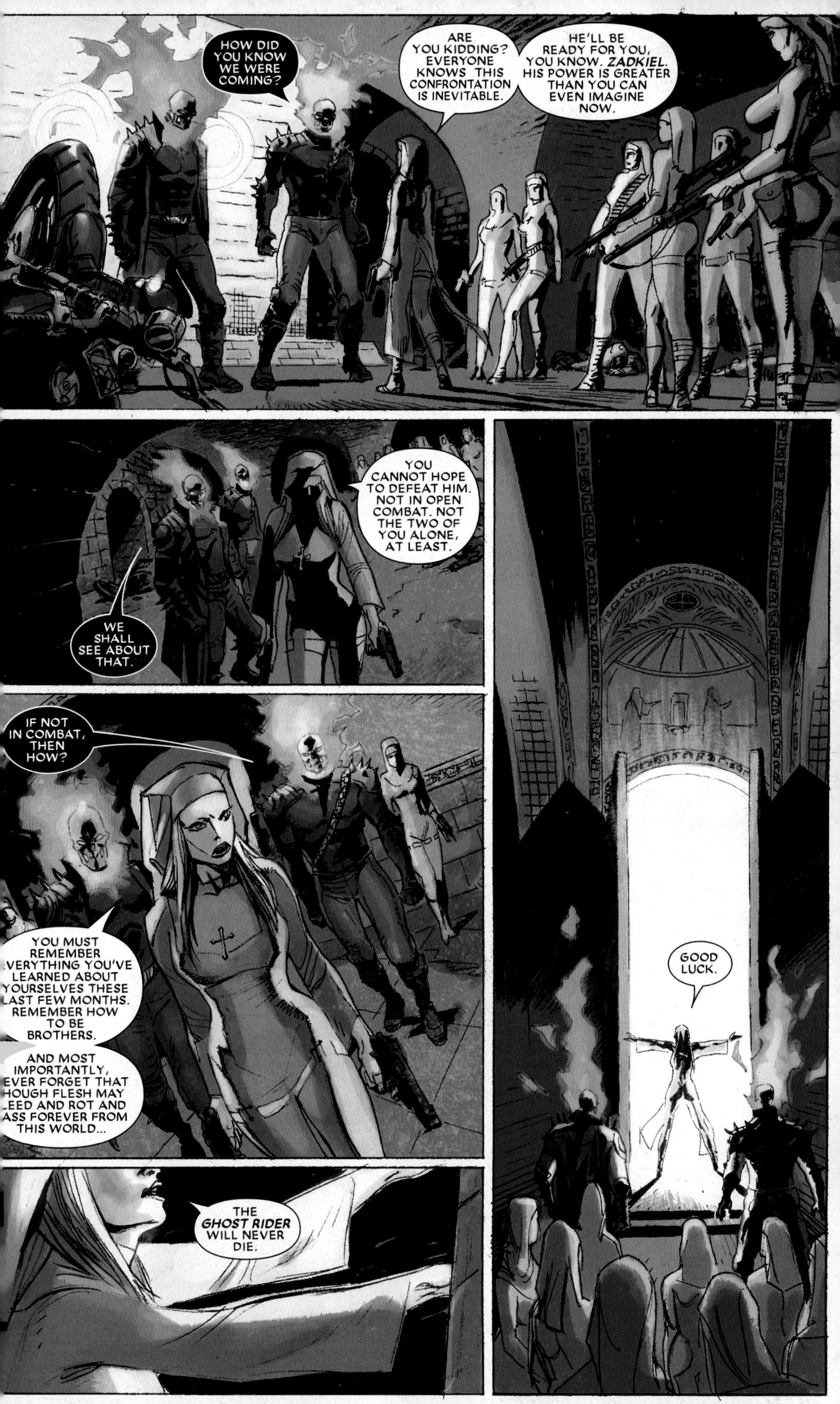
HOW DID YOU KNOW WE WERE COMING?
ARE YOU KIDDING? EVERYONE KNOWS THIS CONFRONTATION IS INEVITABLE.
HE'LL BE READY FOR YOU, YOU KNOW. *ZADKIEL.* HIS POWER IS GREATER THAN YOU CAN EVEN IMAGINE NOW.
YOU CANNOT HOPE TO DEFEAT HIM. NOT IN OPEN COMBAT. NOT THE TWO OF YOU ALONE, AT LEAST.
WE SHALL SEE ABOUT THAT.
IF NOT IN COMBAT, THEN HOW?
YOU MUST REMEMBER EVERYTHING YOU'VE LEARNED ABOUT YOURSELVES THESE LAST FEW MONTHS. REMEMBER HOW TO BE BROTHERS.
AND MOST IMPORTANTLY, NEVER FORGET THAT THOUGH FLESH MAY BLEED AND ROT AND PASS FOREVER FROM THIS WORLD...
THE *GHOST RIDER* WILL NEVER DIE.
GOOD LUCK.

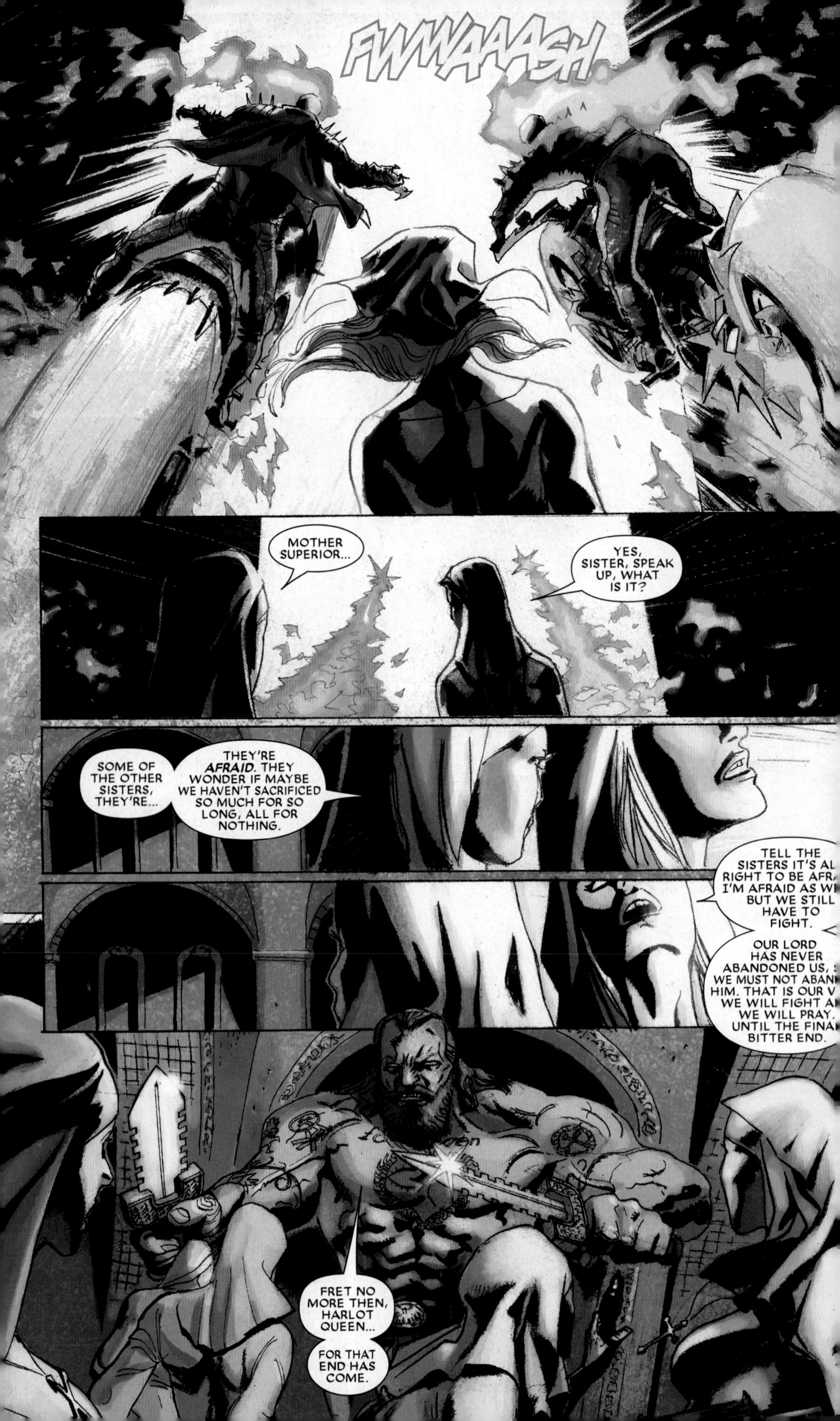
FWWAAASH
MOTHER SUPERIOR...
YES, SISTER, SPEAK UP, WHAT IS IT?
SOME OF THE OTHER SISTERS, THEY'RE...
THEY'RE *AFRAID.* THEY WONDER IF MAYBE WE HAVEN'T SACRIFICED SO MUCH FOR SO LONG, ALL FOR NOTHING.
TELL THE SISTERS IT'S AL RIGHT TO BE AFR I'M AFRAID AS W BUT WE STILL HAVE TO FIGHT.
OUR LORD HAS NEVER ABANDONED US, WE MUST NOT ABAN HIM. THAT IS OUR V WE WILL FIGHT A WE WILL PRAY. UNTIL THE FINA BITTER END.
FRET NO MORE THEN, HARLOT QUEEN...
FOR THAT END HAS COME.

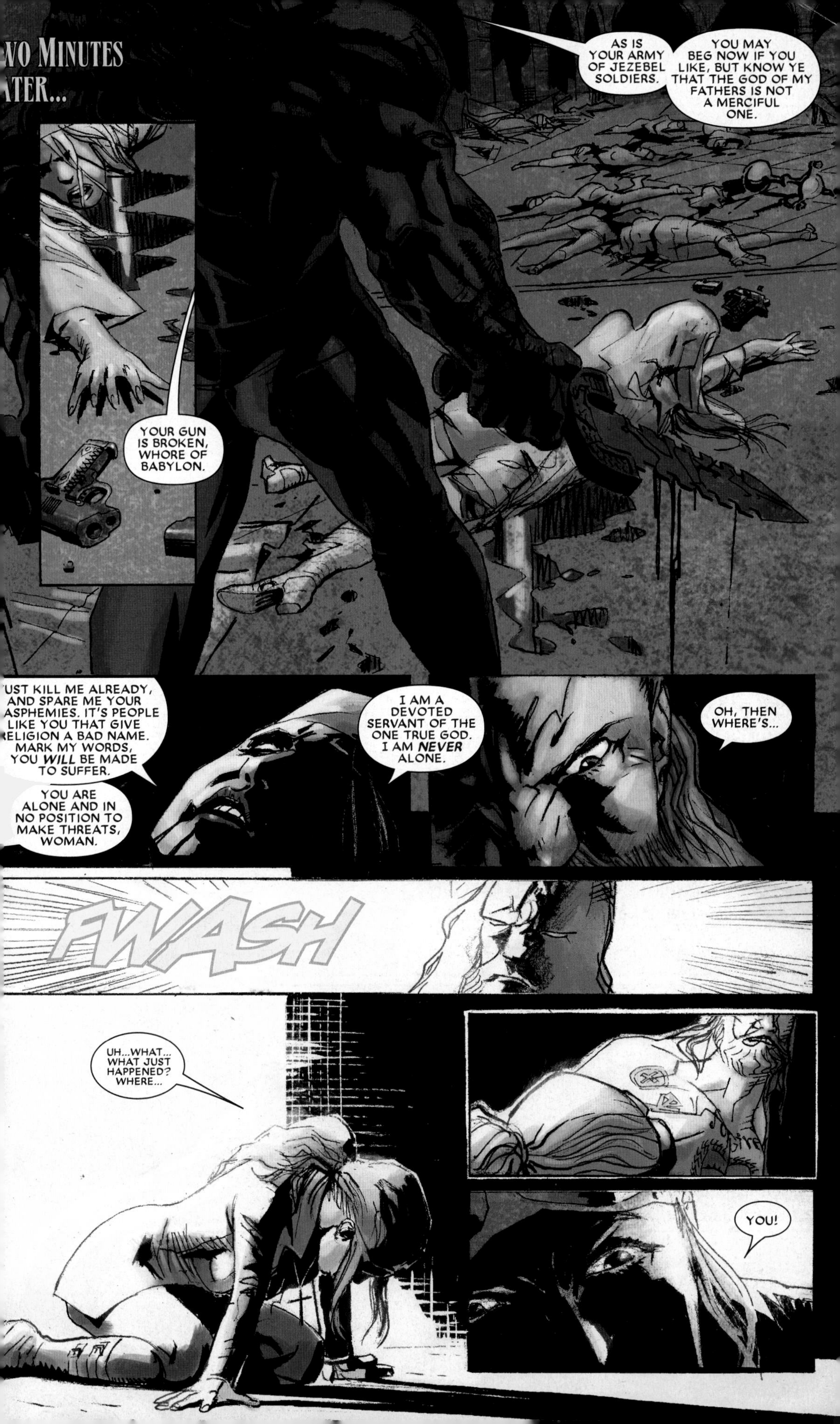

VO MINUTES
ATER...
AS IS YOUR ARMY OF JEZEBEL SOLDIERS.
YOU MAY BEG NOW IF YOU LIKE, BUT KNOW YE THAT THE GOD OF MY FATHERS IS NOT A MERCIFUL ONE.
YOUR GUN IS BROKEN, WHORE OF BABYLON.
UST KILL ME ALREADY, AND SPARE ME YOUR ASPHEMIES. IT'S PEOPLE LIKE YOU THAT GIVE RELIGION A BAD NAME. MARK MY WORDS, YOU *WILL* BE MADE TO SUFFER.
YOU ARE ALONE AND IN NO POSITION TO MAKE THREATS, WOMAN.
I AM A DEVOTED SERVANT OF THE ONE TRUE GOD. I AM *NEVER* ALONE.
OH, THEN WHERE'S...
FWASH
UH...WHAT... WHAT JUST HAPPENED? WHERE...
YOU!

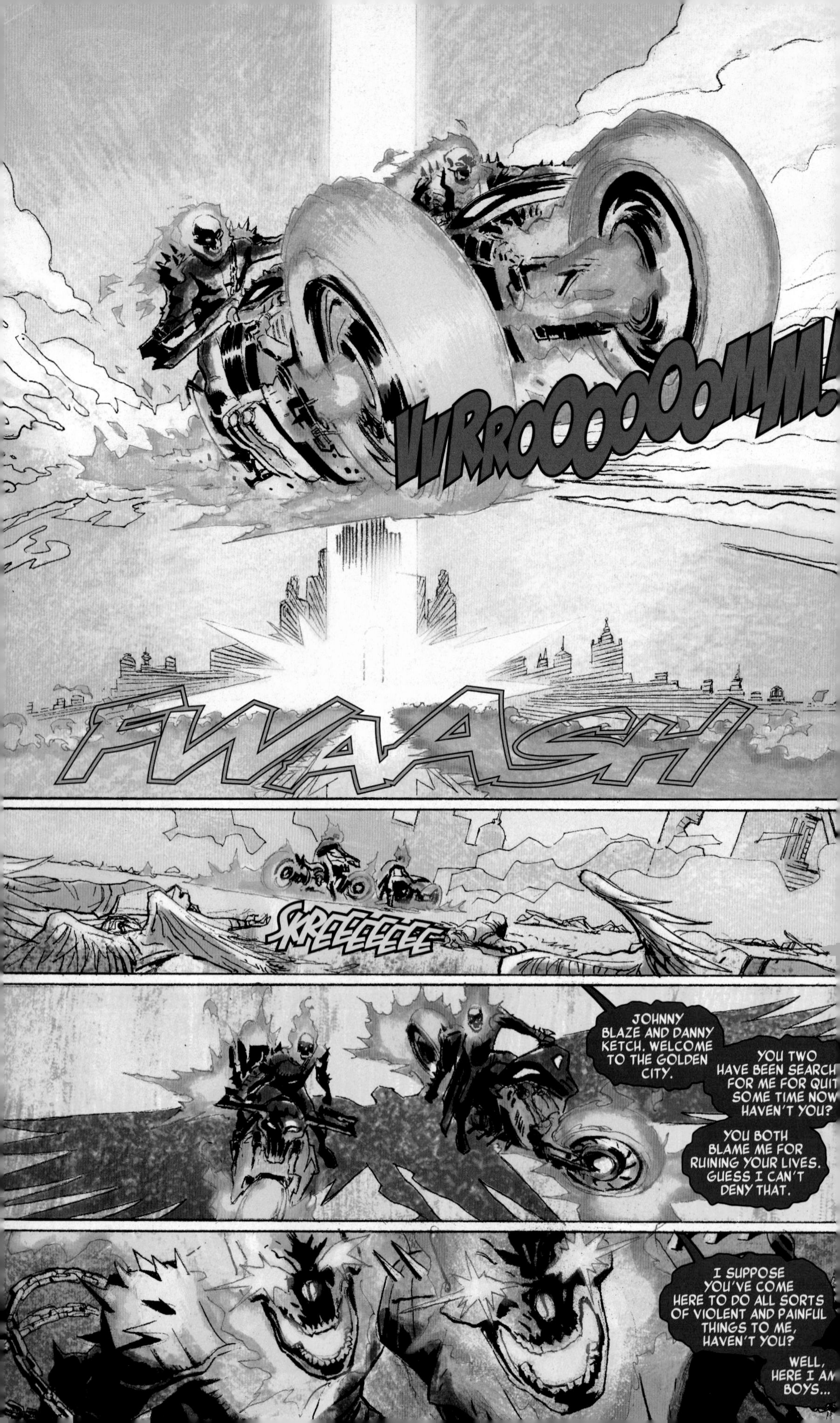
VVRROOOOOOOMMM!
FWACH
SKREEEEEEE
JOHNNY BLAZE AND DANNY KETCH. WELCOME TO THE GOLDEN CITY.
YOU TWO HAVE BEEN SEARCH FOR ME FOR QUIT SOME TIME NOW HAVEN'T YOU?
YOU BOTH BLAME ME FOR RUINING YOUR LIVES. GUESS I CAN'T DENY THAT.
I SUPPOSE YOU'VE COME HERE TO DO ALL SORTS OF VIOLENT AND PAINFUL THINGS TO ME, HAVEN'T YOU?
WELL, HERE I AM BOYS...

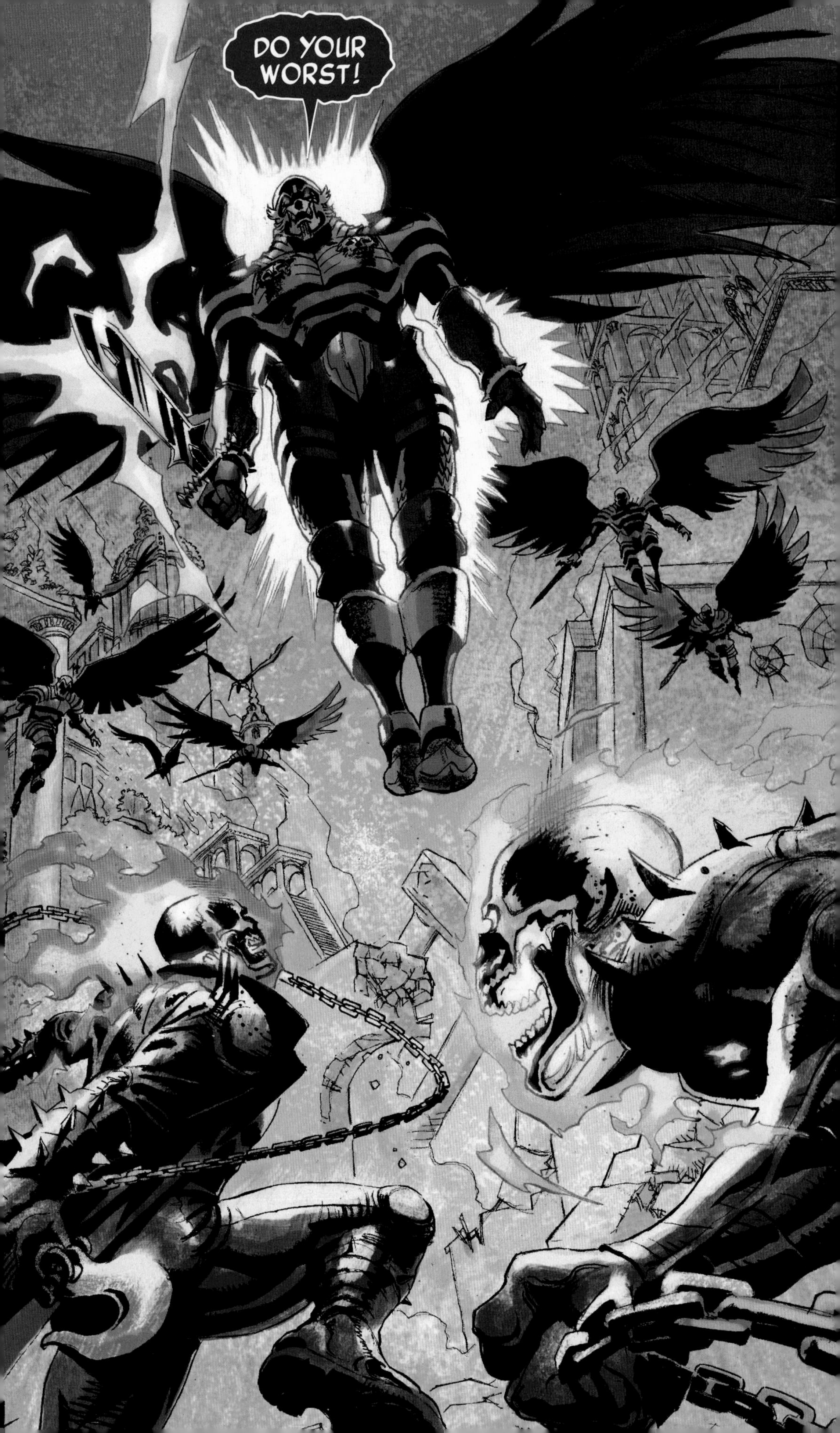
DO YOUR WORST!

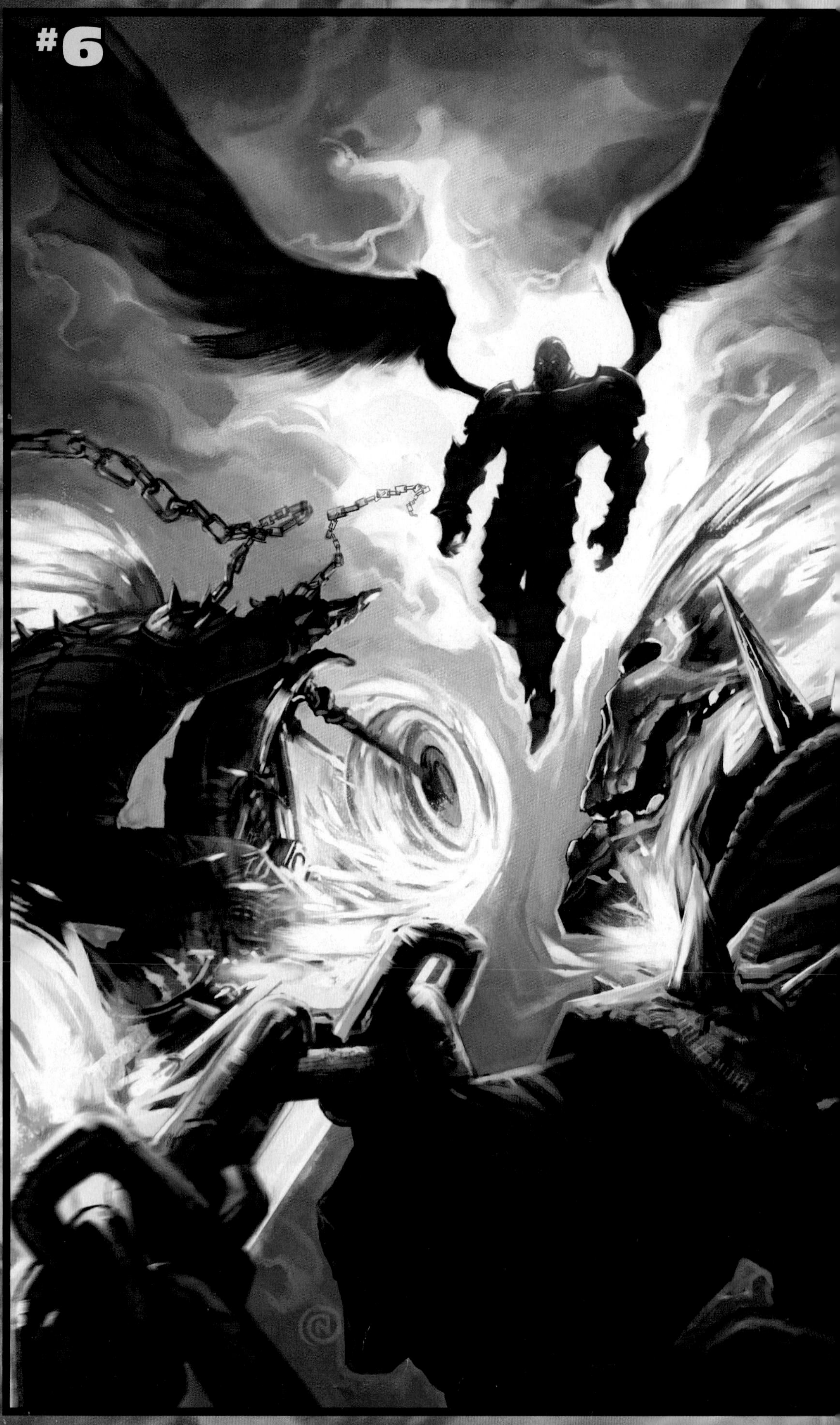
#6

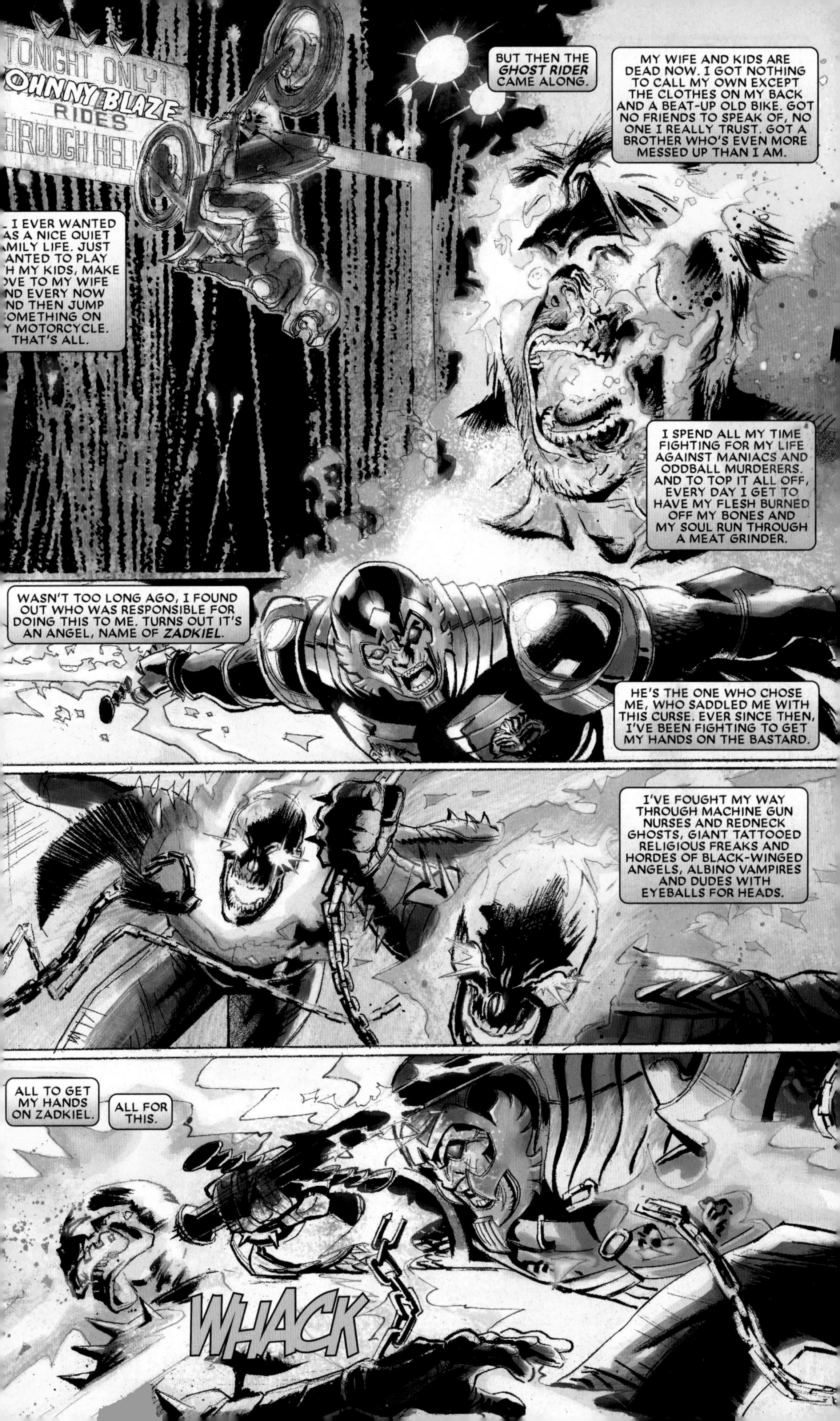
TONIGHT ONLY!
OHNNY BLAZE
RIDES
HROUGH HELL
L I EVER WANTED AS A NICE QUIET AMILY LIFE. JUST ANTED TO PLAY H MY KIDS, MAKE OVE TO MY WIFE ND EVERY NOW ND THEN JUMP OMETHING ON Y MOTORCYCLE. THAT'S ALL.
BUT THEN THE GHOST RIDER CAME ALONG.
MY WIFE AND KIDS ARE DEAD NOW. I GOT NOTHING TO CALL MY OWN EXCEPT THE CLOTHES ON MY BACK AND A BEAT-UP OLD BIKE. GOT NO FRIENDS TO SPEAK OF, NO ONE I REALLY TRUST. GOT A BROTHER WHO'S EVEN MORE MESSED UP THAN I AM.
I SPEND ALL MY TIME FIGHTING FOR MY LIFE AGAINST MANIACS AND ODDBALL MURDERERS. AND TO TOP IT ALL OFF, EVERY DAY I GET TO HAVE MY FLESH BURNED OFF MY BONES AND MY SOUL RUN THROUGH A MEAT GRINDER.
WASN'T TOO LONG AGO, I FOUND OUT WHO WAS RESPONSIBLE FOR DOING THIS TO ME. TURNS OUT IT'S AN ANGEL, NAME OF ZADKIEL.
HE'S THE ONE WHO CHOSE ME, WHO SADDLED ME WITH THIS CURSE. EVER SINCE THEN, I'VE BEEN FIGHTING TO GET MY HANDS ON THE BASTARD.
I'VE FOUGHT MY WAY THROUGH MACHINE GUN NURSES AND REDNECK GHOSTS, GIANT TATTOOED RELIGIOUS FREAKS AND HORDES OF BLACK-WINGED ANGELS, ALBINO VAMPIRES AND DUDES WITH EYEBALLS FOR HEADS.
ALL TO GET MY HANDS ON ZADKIEL.
ALL FOR THIS.
WHACK

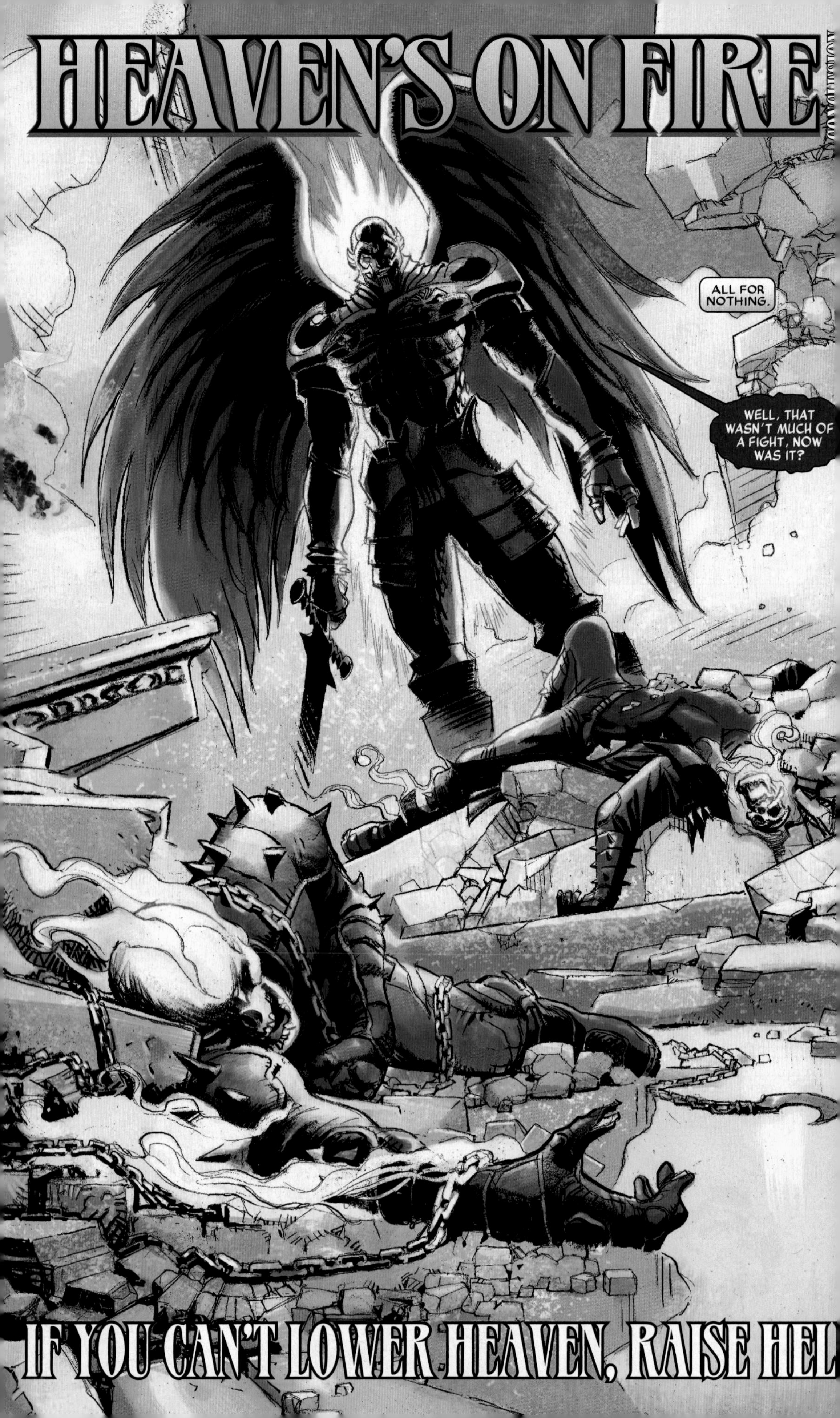
HEAVEN'S ON FIRE
ALL FOR NOTHING.
WELL, THAT WASN'T MUCH OF A FIGHT, NOW WAS IT?
IF YOU CAN'T LOWER HEAVEN, RAISE HEL

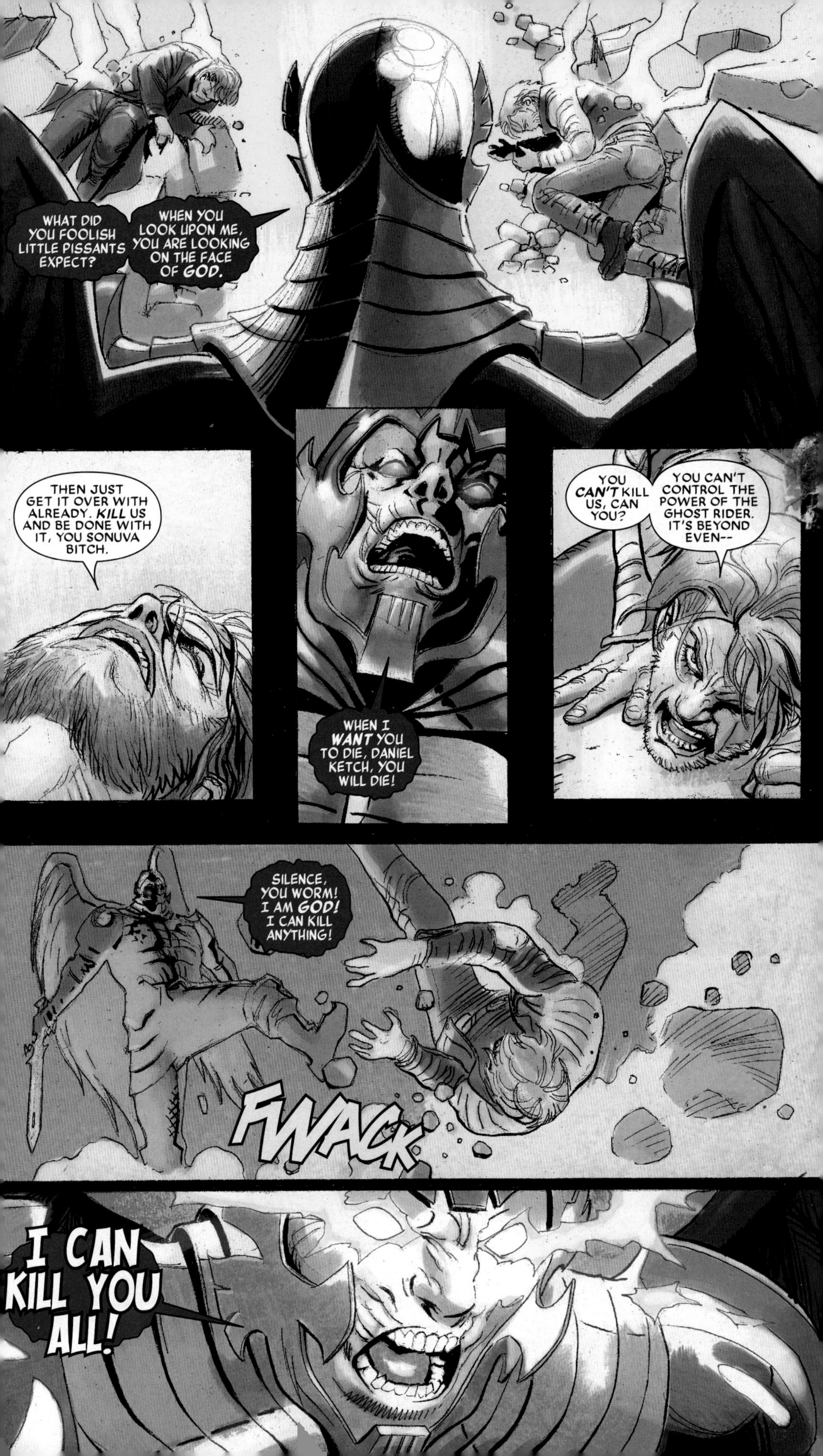
WHAT DID YOU FOOLISH LITTLE PISSANTS EXPECT?
WHEN YOU LOOK UPON ME, YOU ARE LOOKING ON THE FACE OF GOD.
THEN JUST GET IT OVER WITH ALREADY. KILL US AND BE DONE WITH IT, YOU SONUVA BITCH.
WHEN I WANT YOU TO DIE, DANIEL KETCH, YOU WILL DIE!
YOU CAN'T KILL US, CAN YOU?
YOU CAN'T CONTROL THE POWER OF THE GHOST RIDER. IT'S BEYOND EVEN--
SILENCE, YOU WORM! I AM GOD! I CAN KILL ANYTHING!
FWACK
I CAN KILL YOU ALL!

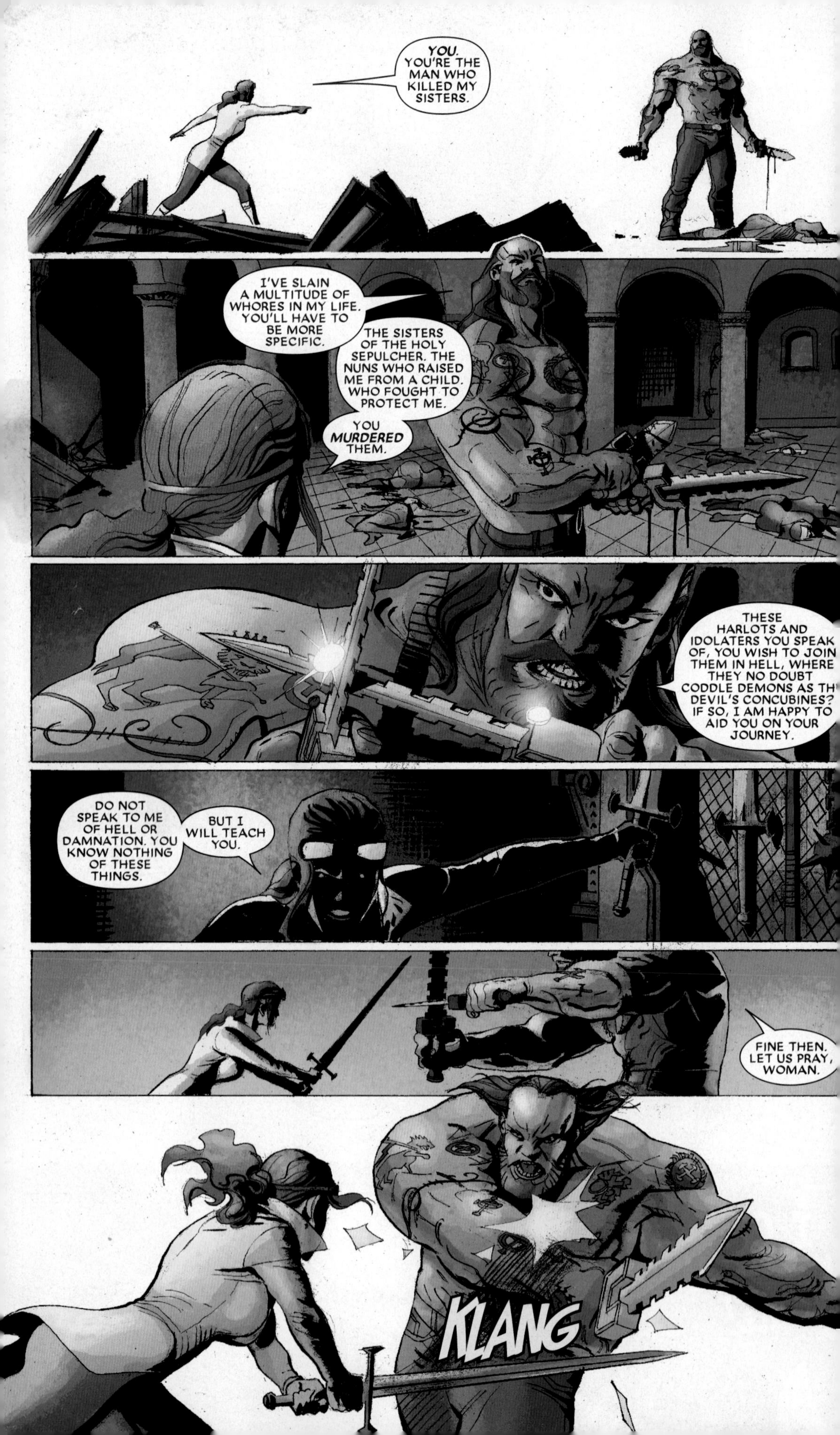

YOU. YOU'RE THE MAN WHO KILLED MY SISTERS.
I'VE SLAIN A MULTITUDE OF WHORES IN MY LIFE. YOU'LL HAVE TO BE MORE SPECIFIC.
THE SISTERS OF THE HOLY SEPULCHER. THE NUNS WHO RAISED ME FROM A CHILD. WHO FOUGHT TO PROTECT ME.
YOU ***MURDERED*** THEM.
THESE HARLOTS AND IDOLATERS YOU SPEAK OF, YOU WISH TO JOIN THEM IN HELL, WHERE THEY NO DOUBT CODDLE DEMONS AS TH DEVIL'S CONCUBINES? IF SO, I AM HAPPY TO AID YOU ON YOUR JOURNEY.
DO NOT SPEAK TO ME OF HELL OR DAMNATION. YOU KNOW NOTHING OF THESE THINGS.
BUT I WILL TEACH YOU.
FINE THEN. LET US PRAY, WOMAN.
KLANG

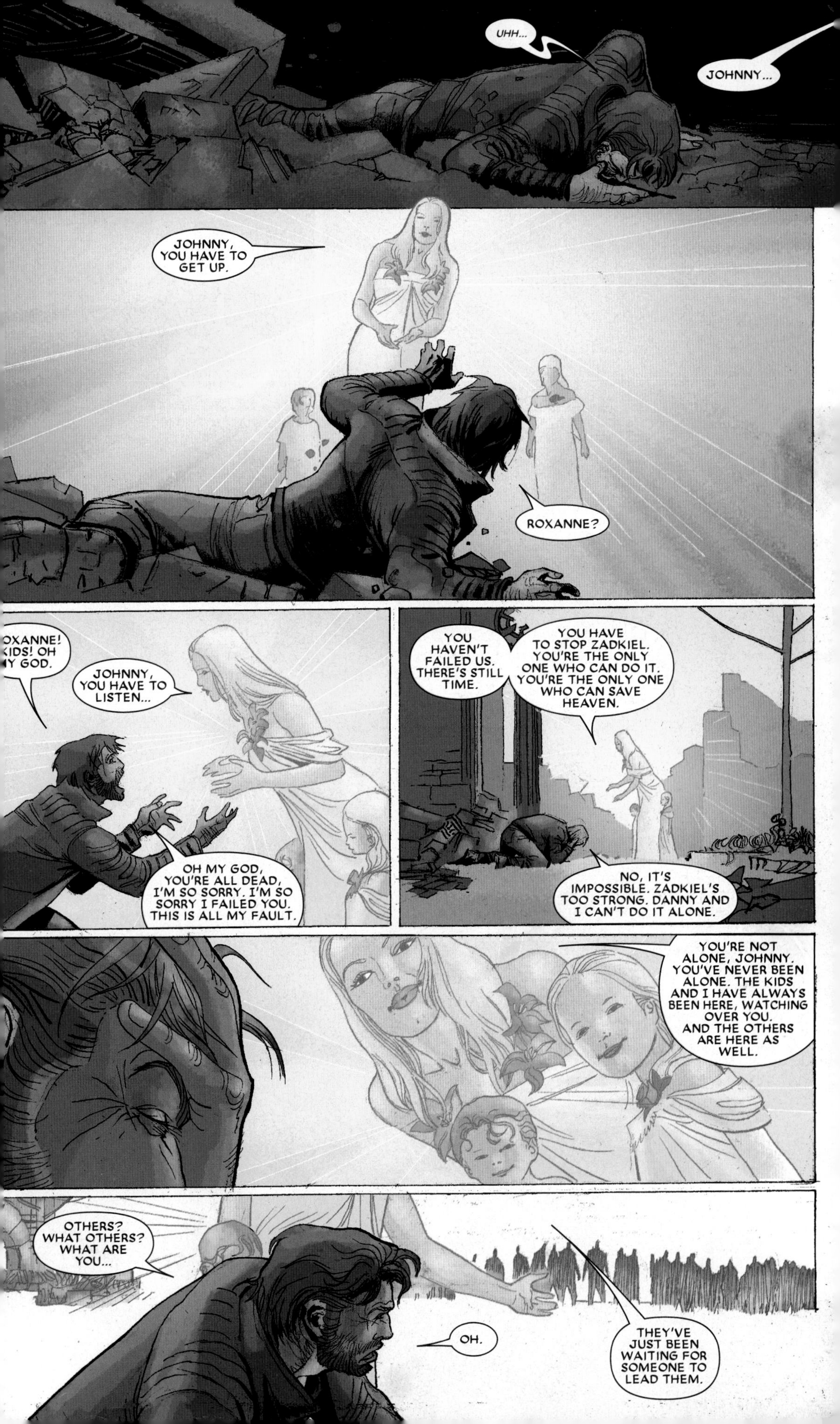
UHH...
JOHNNY...
JOHNNY, YOU HAVE TO GET UP.
ROXANNE?
OXANNE! KIDS! OH Y GOD.
JOHNNY, YOU HAVE TO LISTEN...
OH MY GOD, YOU'RE ALL DEAD, I'M SO SORRY. I'M SO SORRY I FAILED YOU. THIS IS ALL MY FAULT.
YOU HAVEN'T FAILED US. THERE'S STILL TIME.
YOU HAVE TO STOP ZADKIEL. YOU'RE THE ONLY ONE WHO CAN DO IT. YOU'RE THE ONLY ONE WHO CAN SAVE HEAVEN.
NO, IT'S IMPOSSIBLE. ZADKIEL'S TOO STRONG. DANNY AND I CAN'T DO IT ALONE.
YOU'RE NOT ALONE, JOHNNY. YOU'VE NEVER BEEN ALONE. THE KIDS AND I HAVE ALWAYS BEEN HERE, WATCHING OVER YOU. AND THE OTHERS ARE HERE AS WELL.
OTHERS? WHAT OTHERS? WHAT ARE YOU...
OH.
THEY'VE JUST BEEN WAITING FOR SOMEONE TO LEAD THEM.

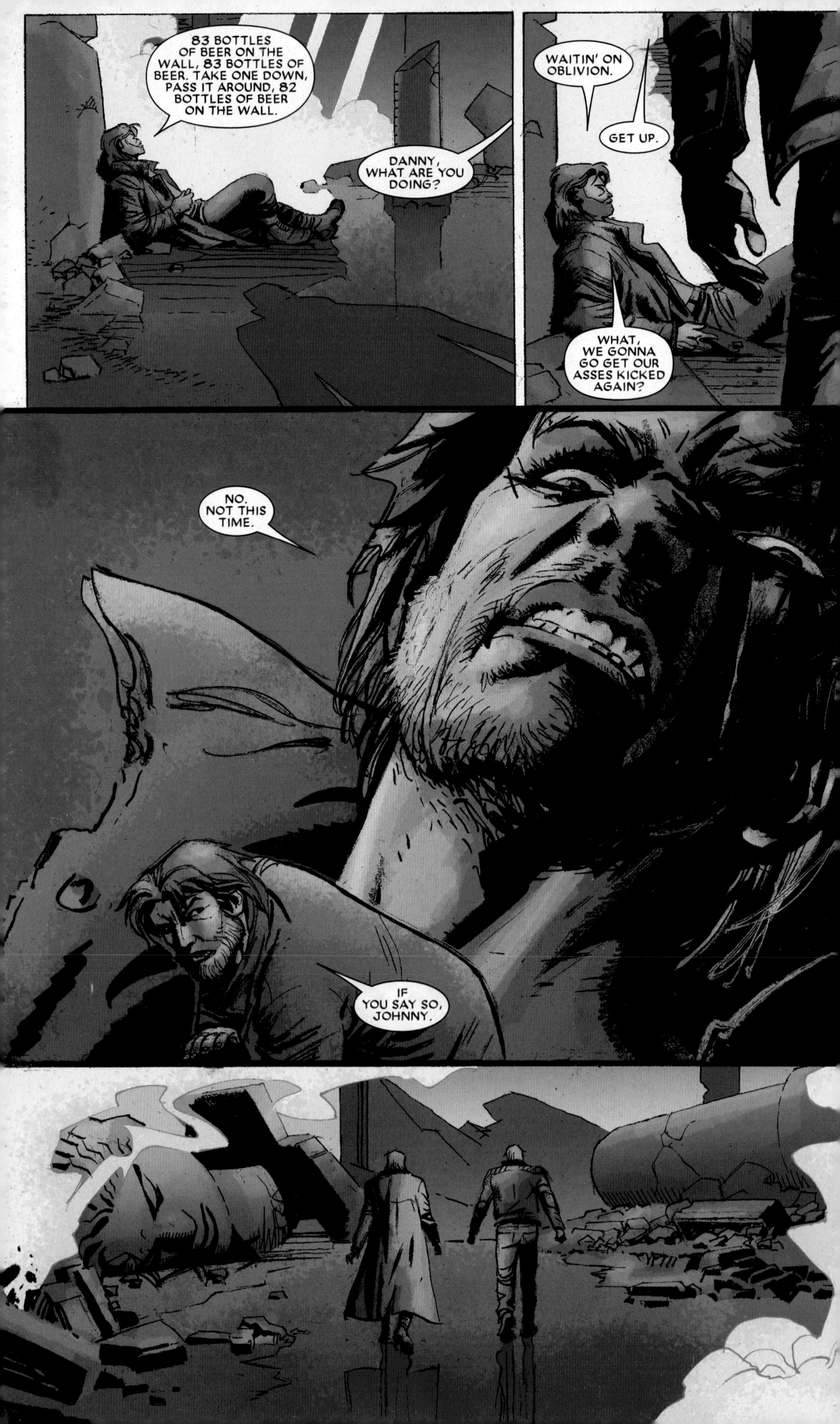
83 BOTTLES OF BEER ON THE WALL, 83 BOTTLES OF BEER. TAKE ONE DOWN, PASS IT AROUND, 82 BOTTLES OF BEER ON THE WALL.
DANNY, WHAT ARE YOU DOING?
WAITIN' ON OBLIVION.
GET UP.
WHAT, WE GONNA GO GET OUR ASSES KICKED AGAIN?
NO. NOT THIS TIME.
IF YOU SAY SO, JOHNNY.

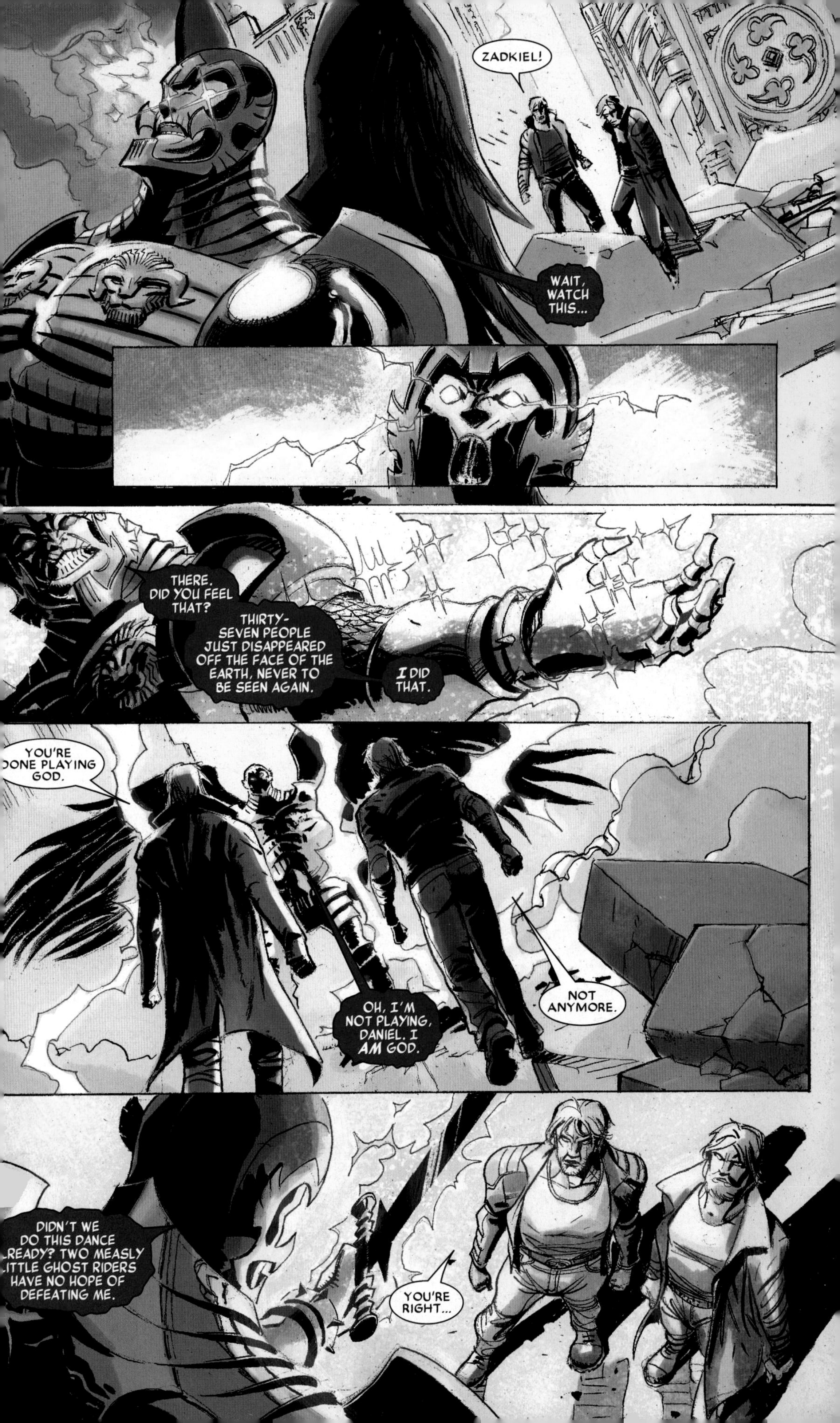
ZADKIEL!
WAIT, WATCH THIS...
THERE. DID YOU FEEL THAT?
THIRTY-SEVEN PEOPLE JUST DISAPPEARED OFF THE FACE OF THE EARTH, NEVER TO BE SEEN AGAIN.
I DID THAT.
YOU'RE DONE PLAYING GOD.
OH, I'M NOT PLAYING, DANIEL. I AM GOD.
NOT ANYMORE.
DIDN'T WE DO THIS DANCE ALREADY? TWO MEASLY LITTLE GHOST RIDERS HAVE NO HOPE OF DEFEATING ME.
YOU'RE RIGHT...

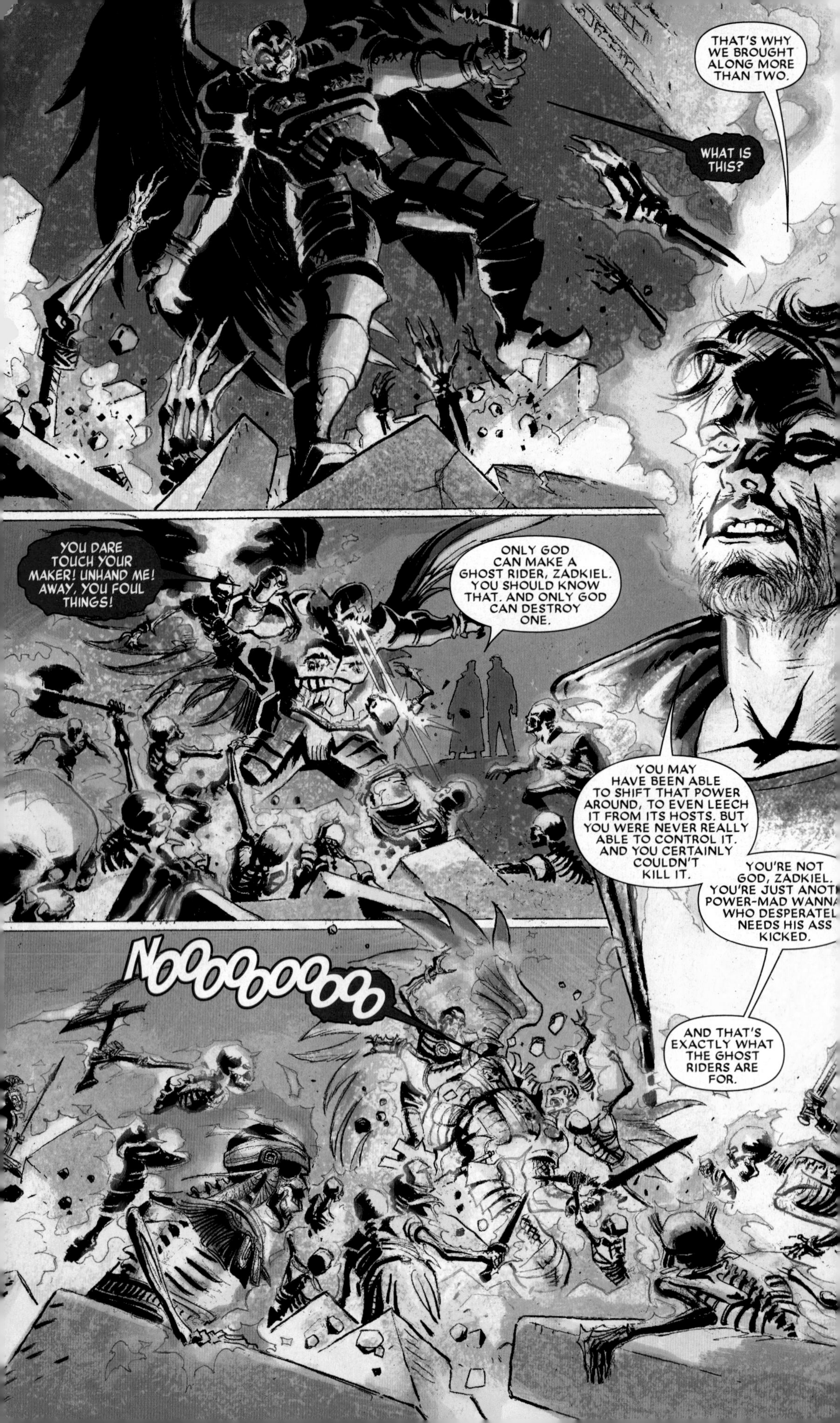
THAT'S WHY WE BROUGHT ALONG MORE THAN TWO.
WHAT IS THIS?
YOU DARE TOUCH YOUR MAKER! UNHAND ME! AWAY, YOU FOUL THINGS!
ONLY GOD CAN MAKE A GHOST RIDER, ZADKIEL. YOU SHOULD KNOW THAT. AND ONLY GOD CAN DESTROY ONE.
YOU MAY HAVE BEEN ABLE TO SHIFT THAT POWER AROUND, TO EVEN LEECH IT FROM ITS HOSTS. BUT YOU WERE NEVER REALLY ABLE TO CONTROL IT. AND YOU CERTAINLY COULDN'T KILL IT.
YOU'RE NOT GOD, ZADKIEL. YOU'RE JUST ANOT POWER-MAD WANNA WHO DESPERATEL NEEDS HIS ASS KICKED.
NOOOOOOOOO
AND THAT'S EXACTLY WHAT THE GHOST RIDERS ARE FOR.

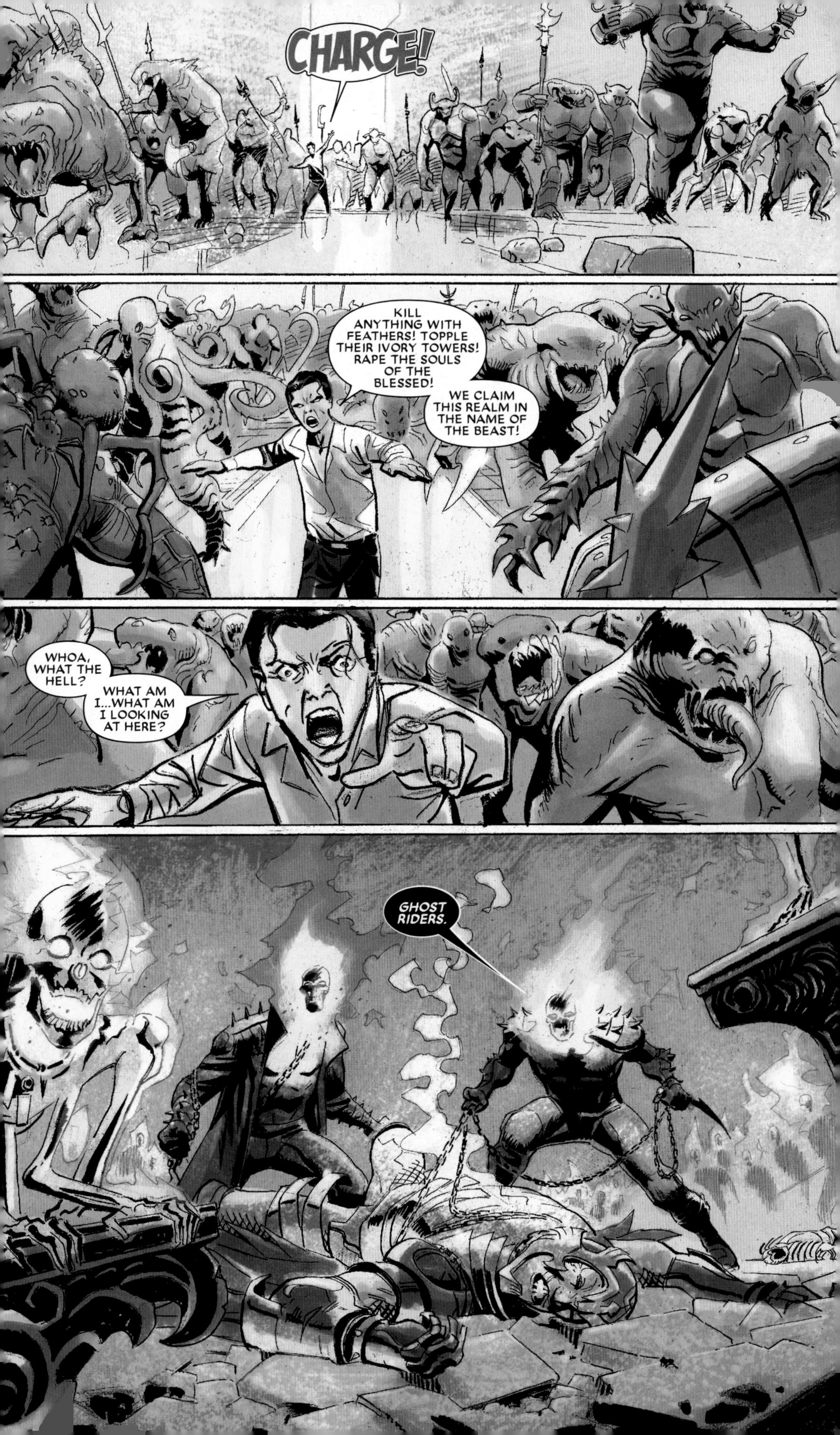
CHARGE!
KILL ANYTHING WITH FEATHERS! TOPPLE THEIR IVORY TOWERS! RAPE THE SOULS OF THE BLESSED!
WE CLAIM THIS REALM IN THE NAME OF THE BEAST!
WHOA, WHAT THE HELL?
WHAT AM I...WHAT AM I LOOKING AT HERE?
GHOST RIDERS.

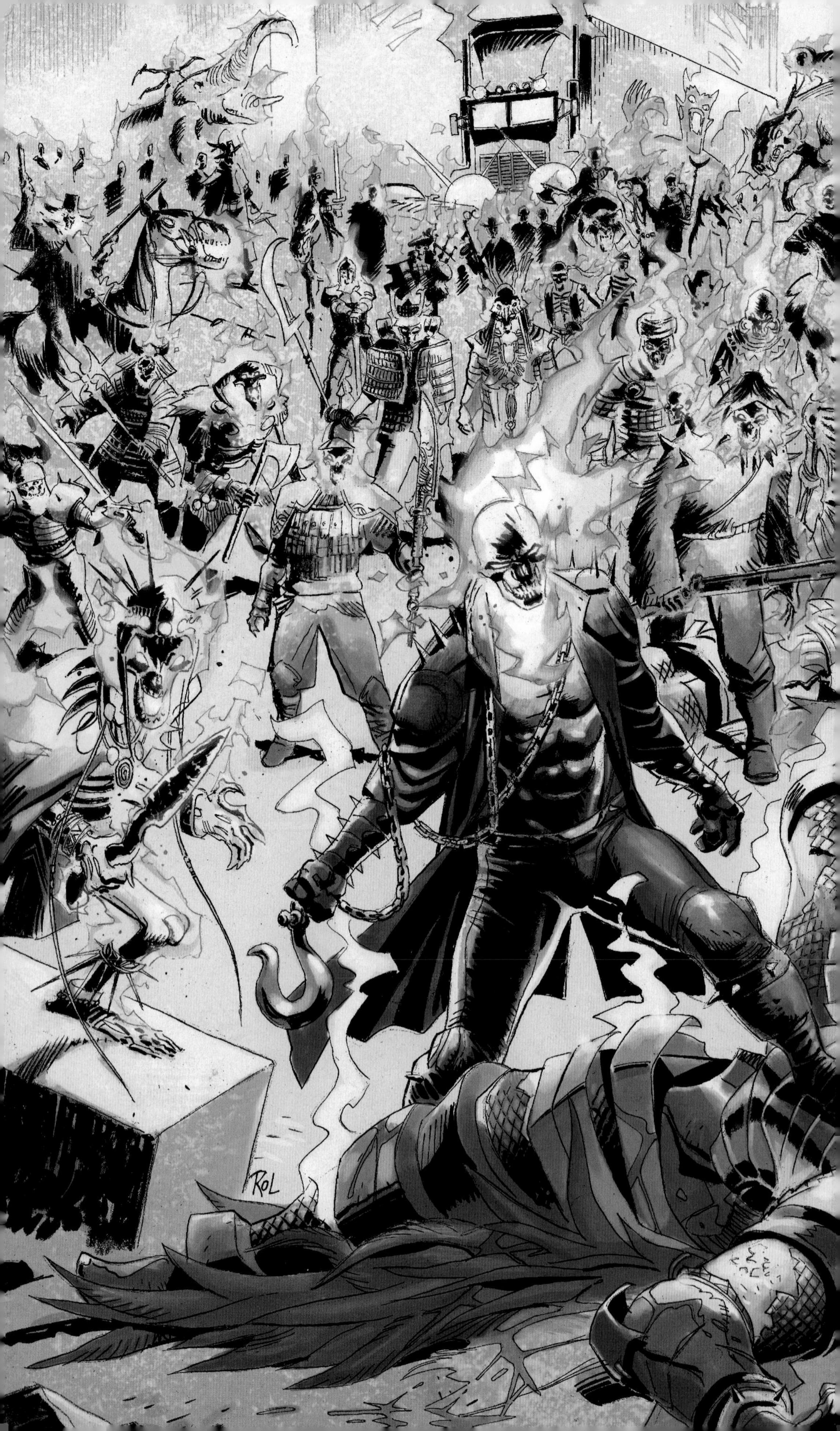
ROL

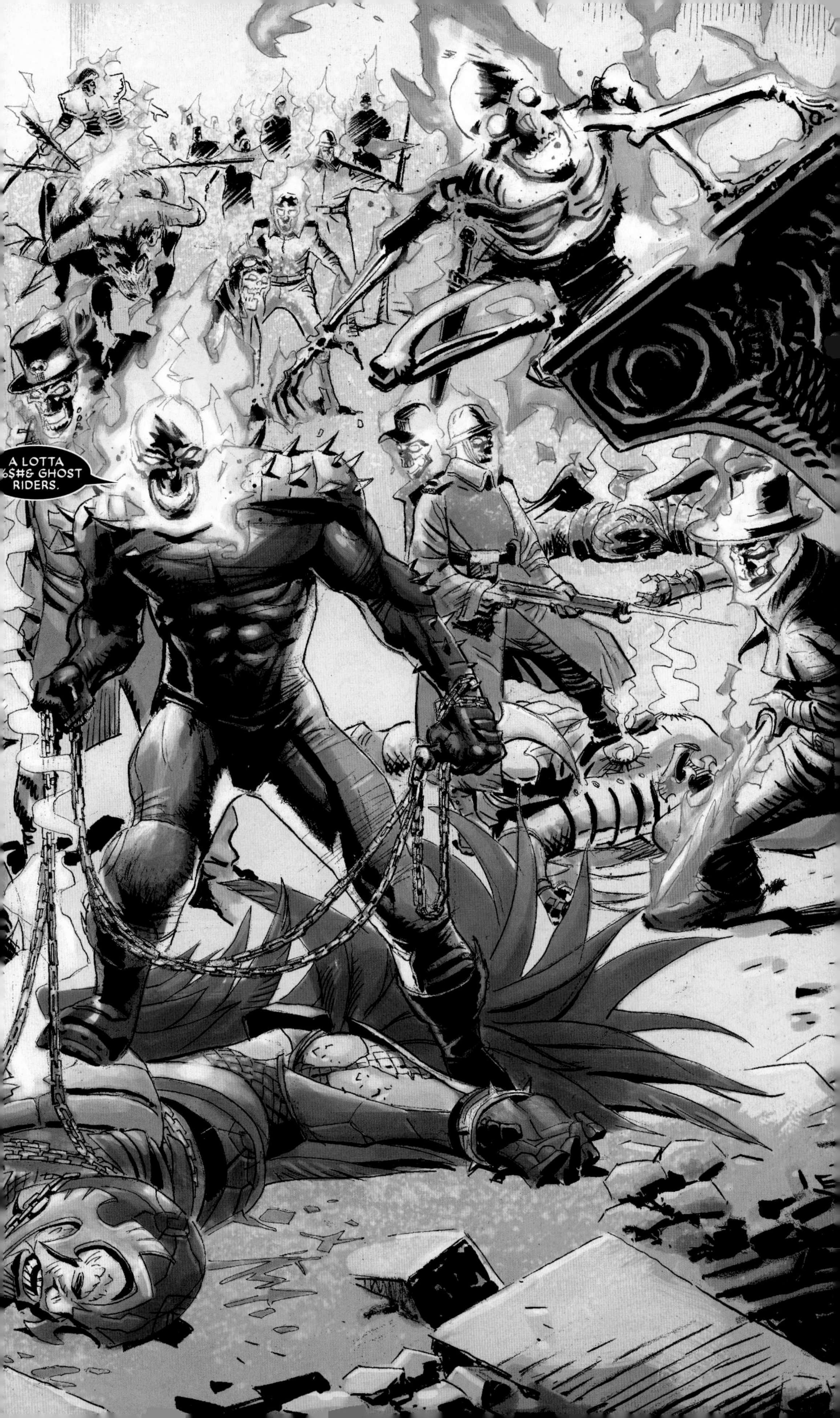

A LOTTA
%$#& GHOST
RIDERS.

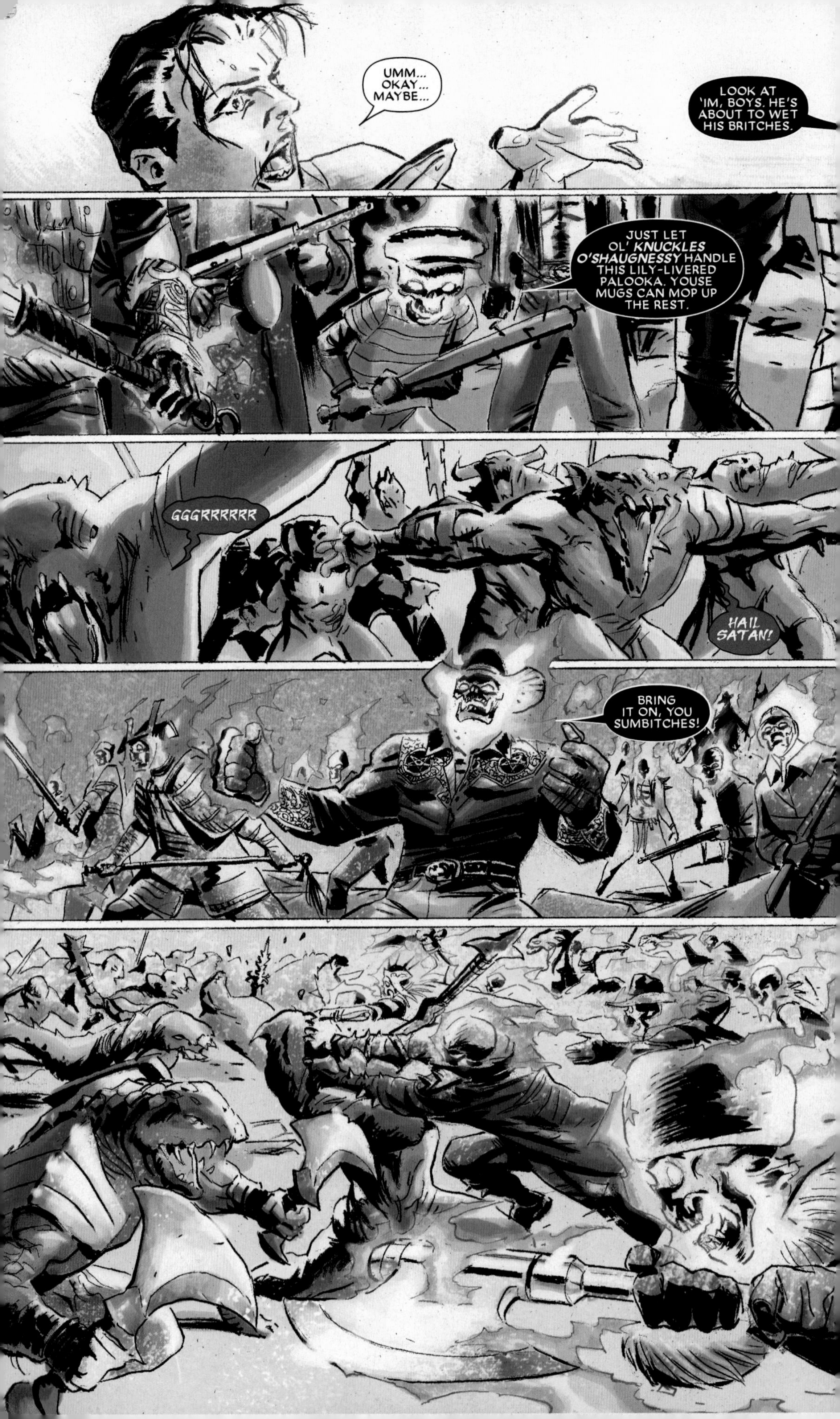
UMM... OKAY... MAYBE...
LOOK AT 'IM, BOYS. HE'S ABOUT TO WET HIS BRITCHES.
JUST LET OL' KNUCKLES O'SHAUGNESSY HANDLE THIS LILY-LIVERED PALOOKA. YOUSE MUGS CAN MOP UP THE REST.
GGGRRRRRR
HAIL SATAN!
BRING IT ON, YOU SUMBITCHES!

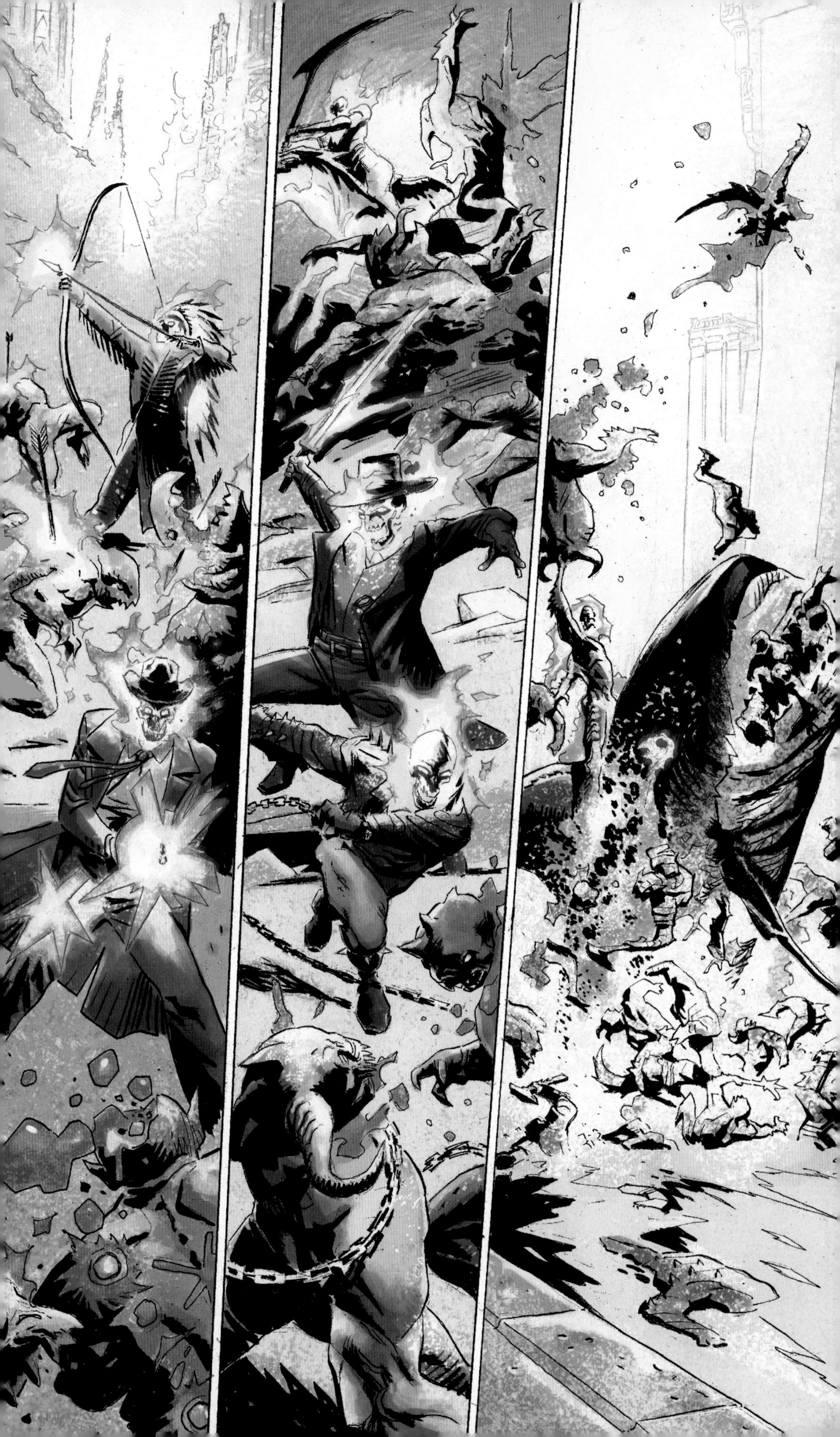

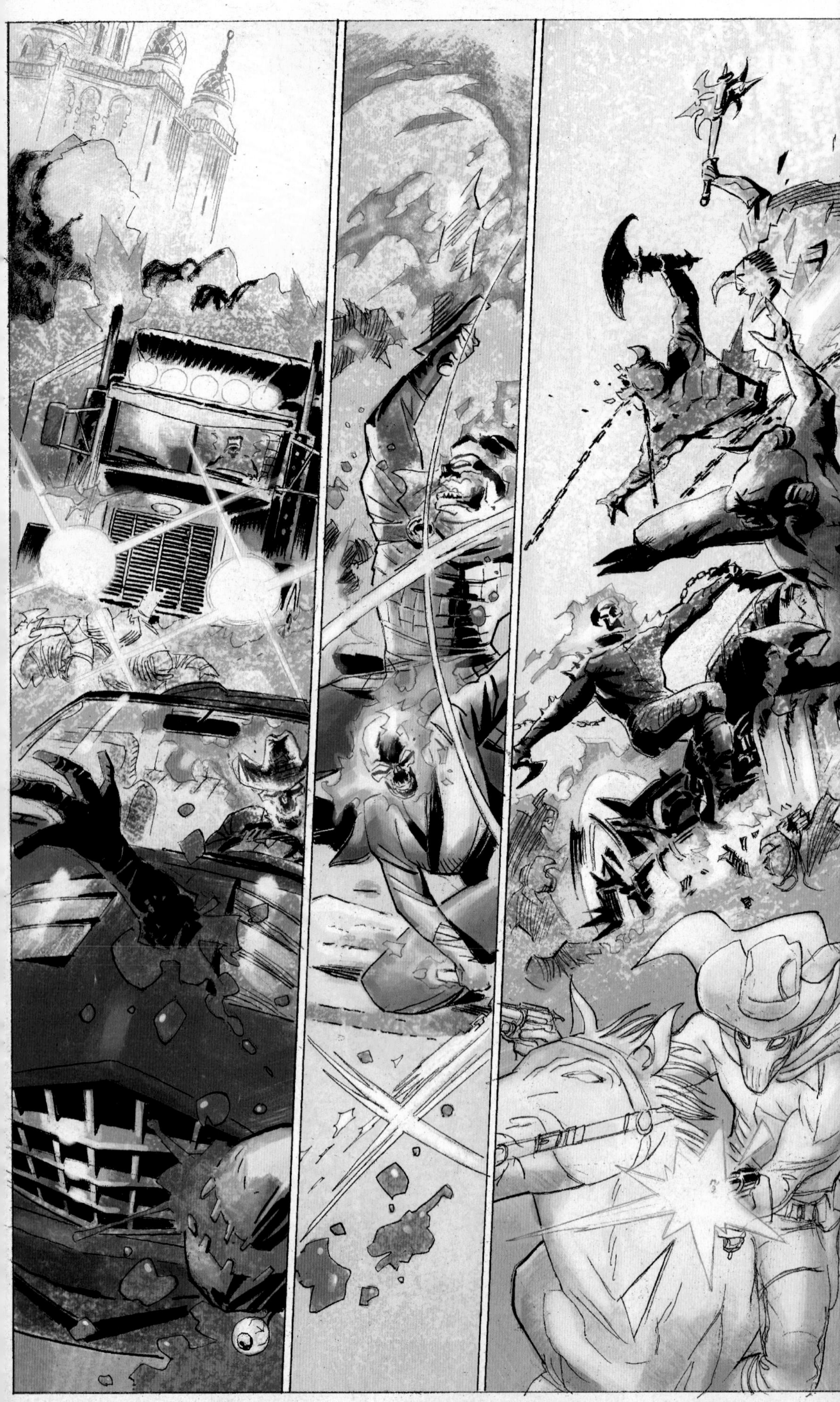

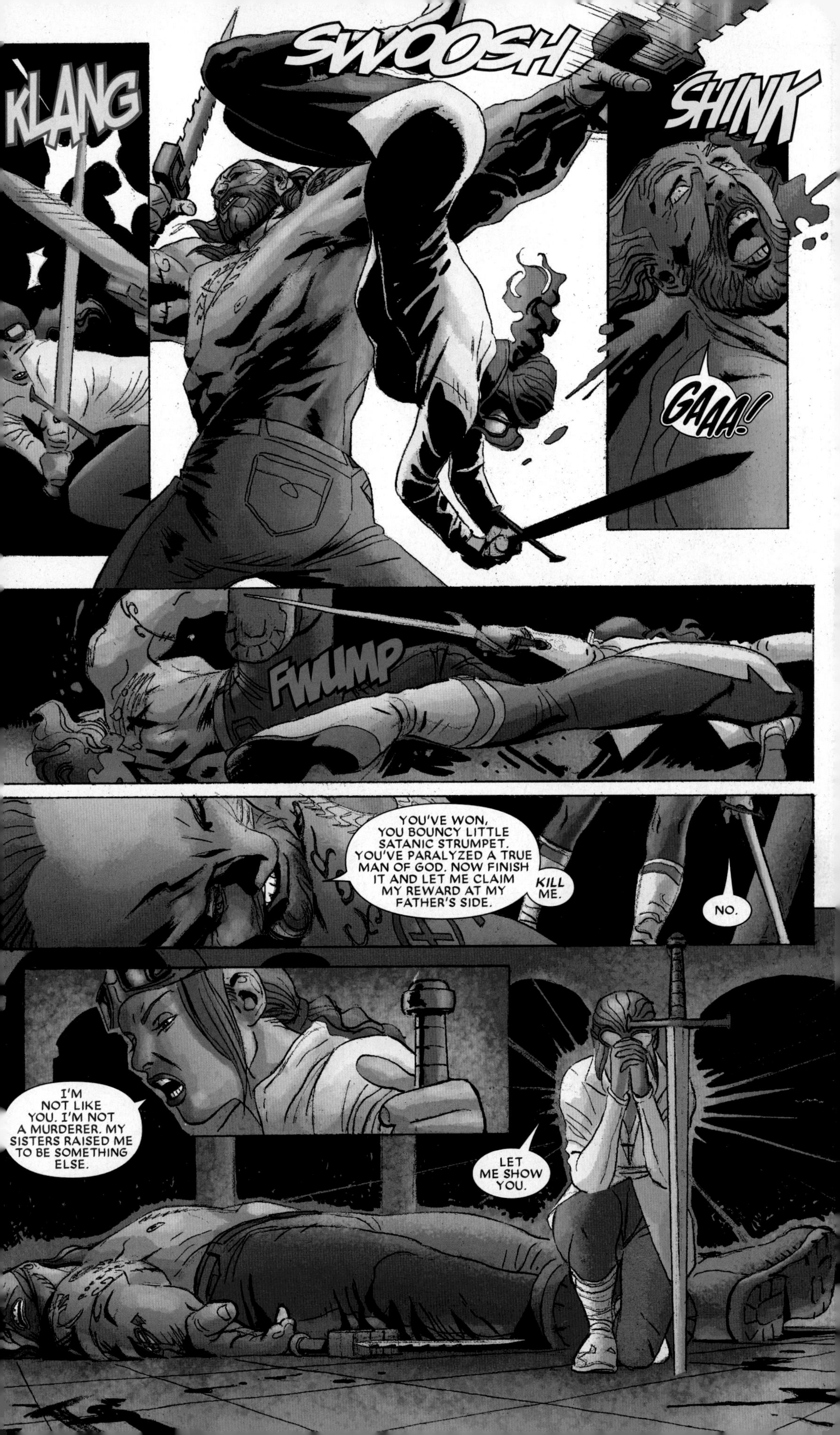
SWOOSH
KLANG
SHINK
GAAA!
FWUMP
YOU'VE WON, YOU BOUNCY LITTLE SATANIC STRUMPET. YOU'VE PARALYZED A TRUE MAN OF GOD. NOW FINISH IT AND LET ME CLAIM MY REWARD AT MY FATHER'S SIDE.
KILL ME.
NO.
I'M NOT LIKE YOU. I'M NOT A MURDERER. MY SISTERS RAISED ME TO BE SOMETHING ELSE.
LET ME SHOW YOU.

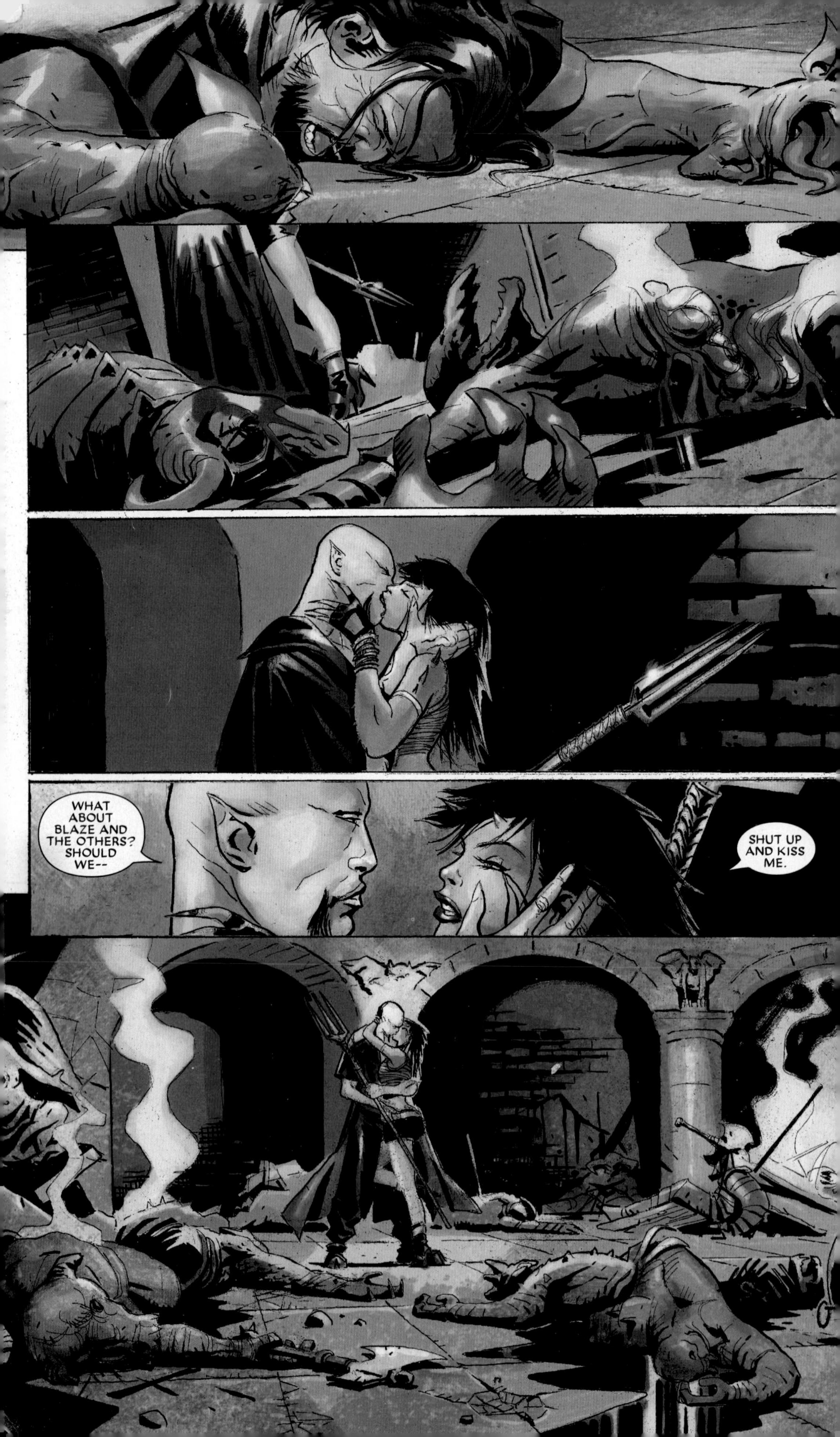
WHAT ABOUT BLAZE AND THE OTHERS? SHOULD WE--
SHUT UP AND KISS ME.

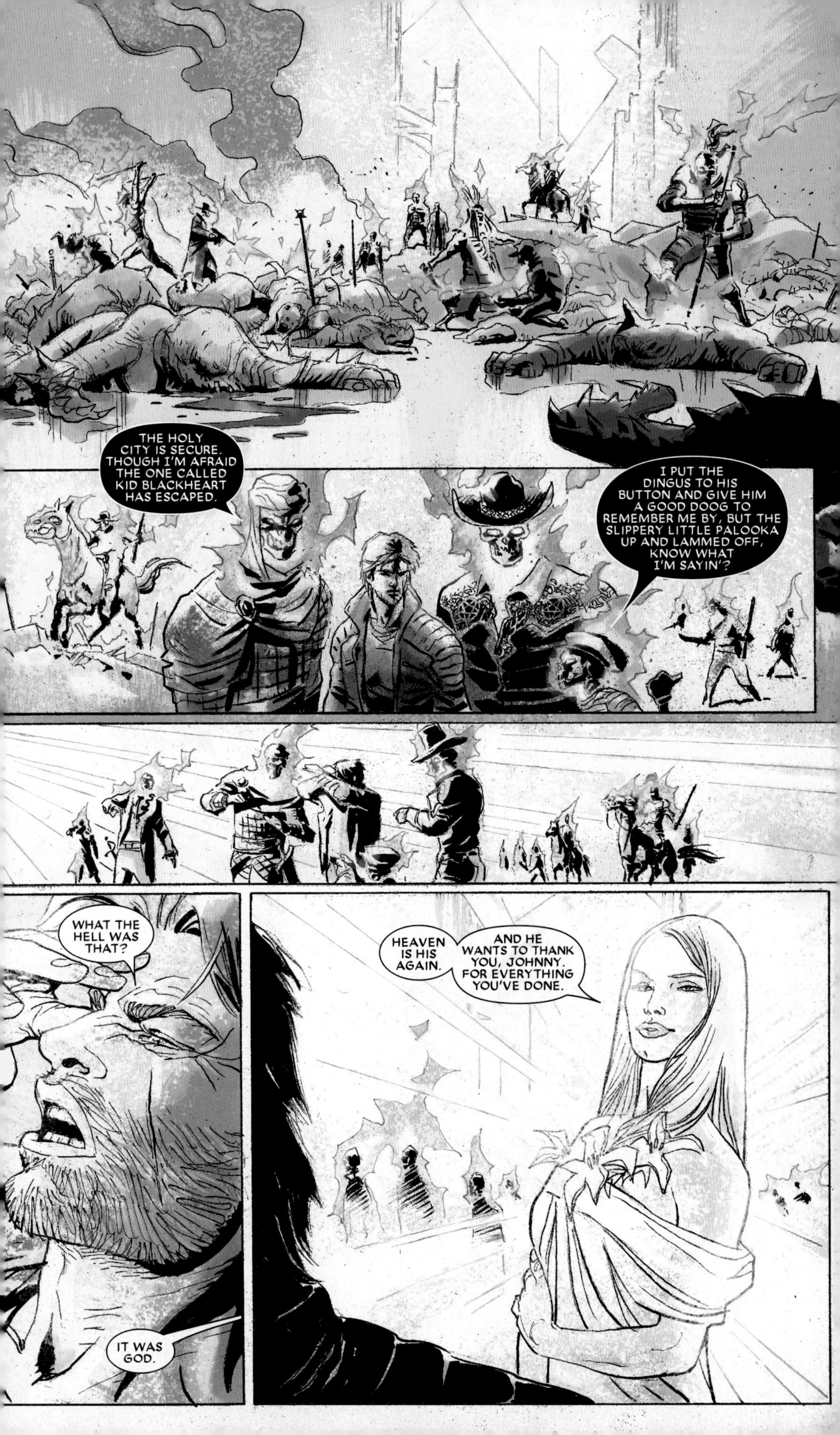
THE HOLY CITY IS SECURE. THOUGH I'M AFRAID THE ONE CALLED KID BLACKHEART HAS ESCAPED.
I PUT THE DINGUS TO HIS BUTTON AND GIVE HIM A GOOD DOOG TO REMEMBER ME BY, BUT THE SLIPPERY LITTLE PALOOKA UP AND LAMMED OFF, KNOW WHAT I'M SAYIN'?
WHAT THE HELL WAS THAT?
IT WAS GOD.
HEAVEN IS HIS AGAIN.
AND HE WANTS TO THANK YOU, JOHNNY. FOR EVERYTHING YOU'VE DONE.

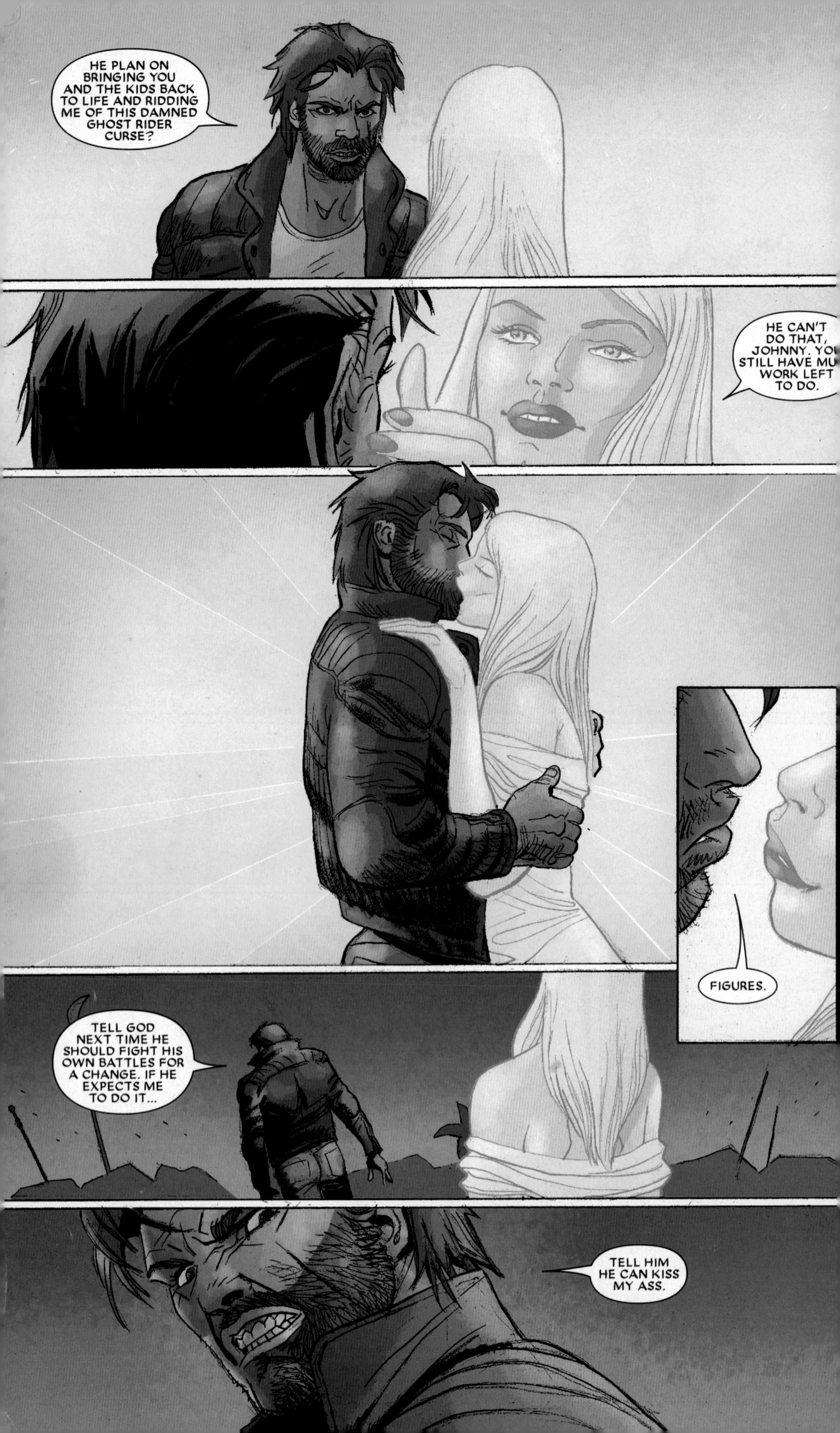
HE PLAN ON BRINGING YOU AND THE KIDS BACK TO LIFE AND RIDDING ME OF THIS DAMNED GHOST RIDER CURSE?
HE CAN'T DO THAT, JOHNNY. YOU STILL HAVE MU WORK LEFT TO DO.
FIGURES.
TELL GOD NEXT TIME HE SHOULD FIGHT HIS OWN BATTLES FOR A CHANGE. IF HE EXPECTS ME TO DO IT...
TELL HIM HE CAN KISS MY ASS.

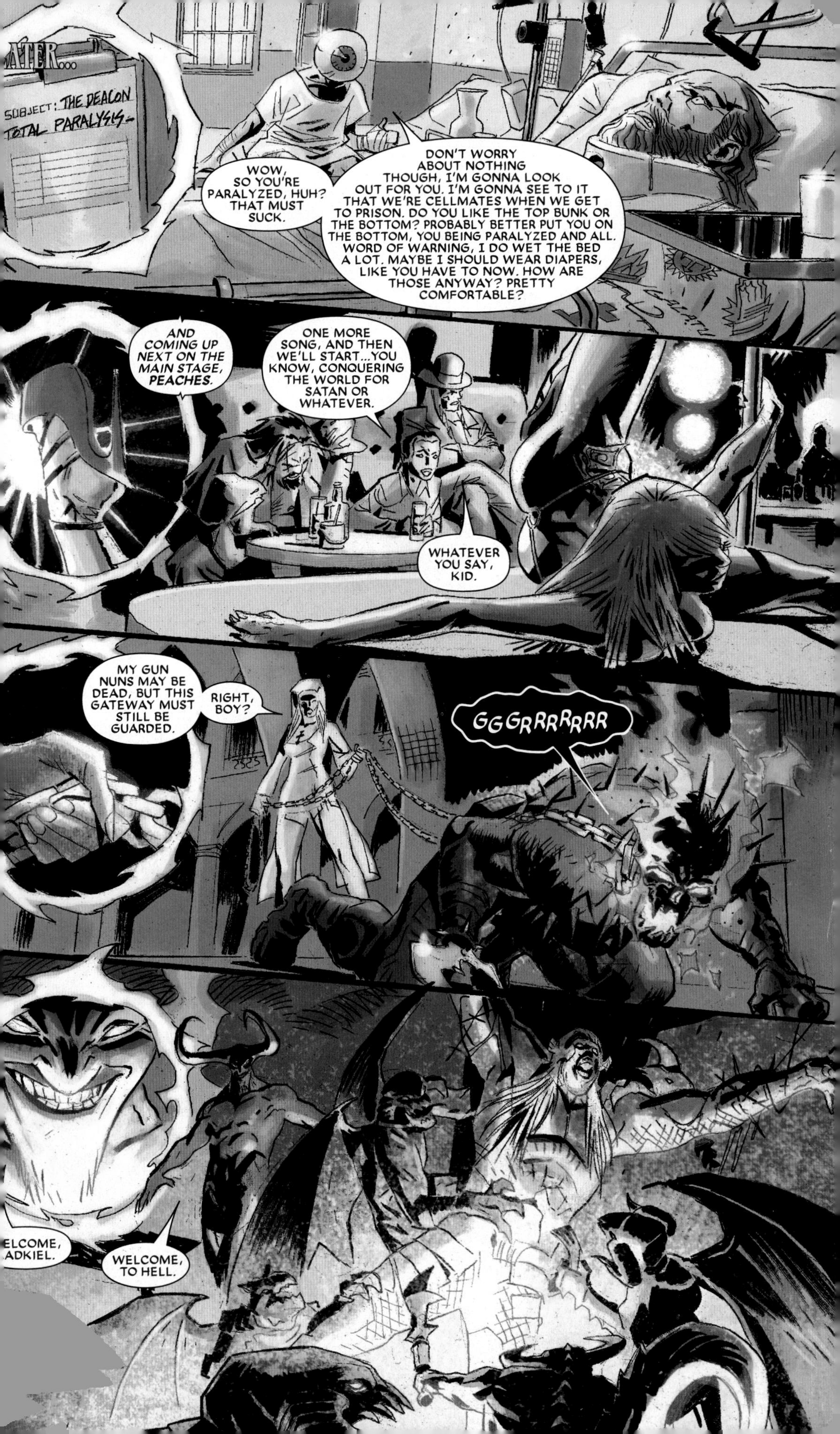
LATER...
SUBJECT: THE DEACON
TOTAL PARALYSIS
WOW, SO YOU'RE PARALYZED, HUH? THAT MUST SUCK.
DON'T WORRY ABOUT NOTHING THOUGH, I'M GONNA LOOK OUT FOR YOU. I'M GONNA SEE TO IT THAT WE'RE CELLMATES WHEN WE GET TO PRISON. DO YOU LIKE THE TOP BUNK OR THE BOTTOM? PROBABLY BETTER PUT YOU ON THE BOTTOM, YOU BEING PARALYZED AND ALL. WORD OF WARNING, I DO WET THE BED A LOT. MAYBE I SHOULD WEAR DIAPERS, LIKE YOU HAVE TO NOW. HOW ARE THOSE ANYWAY? PRETTY COMFORTABLE?
AND COMING UP NEXT ON THE MAIN STAGE, PEACHES.
ONE MORE SONG, AND THEN WE'LL START...YOU KNOW, CONQUERING THE WORLD FOR SATAN OR WHATEVER.
WHATEVER YOU SAY, KID.
MY GUN NUNS MAY BE DEAD, BUT THIS GATEWAY MUST STILL BE GUARDED.
RIGHT, BOY?
GGGRRRRRRR
ELCOME, ADKIEL.
WELCOME, TO HELL.

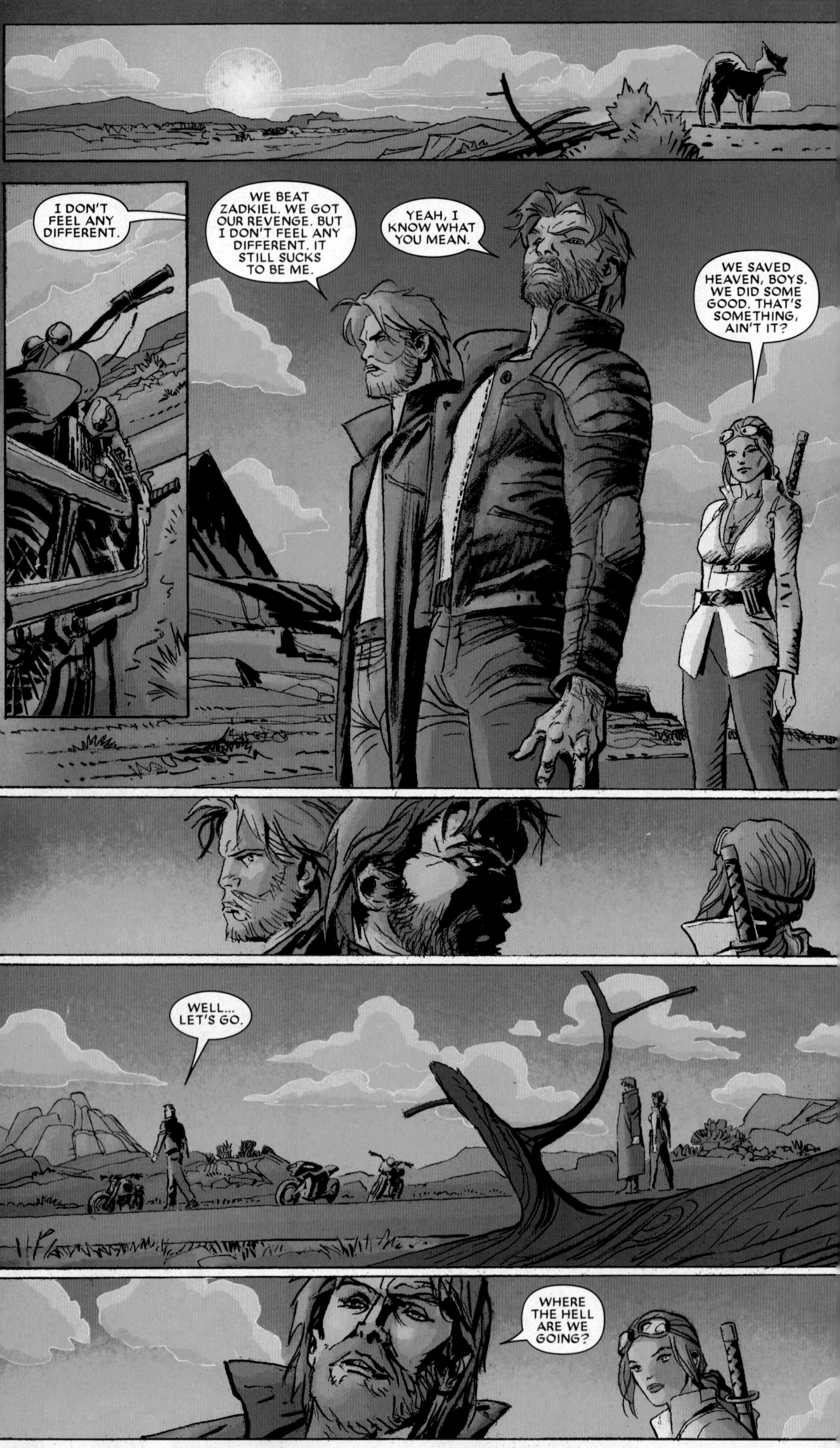
I DON'T FEEL ANY DIFFERENT.
WE BEAT ZADKIEL. WE GOT OUR REVENGE. BUT I DON'T FEEL ANY DIFFERENT. IT STILL SUCKS TO BE ME.
YEAH, I KNOW WHAT YOU MEAN.
WE SAVED HEAVEN, BOYS. WE DID SOME GOOD. THAT'S SOMETHING, AIN'T IT?
WELL... LET'S GO.
WHERE THE HELL ARE WE GOING?

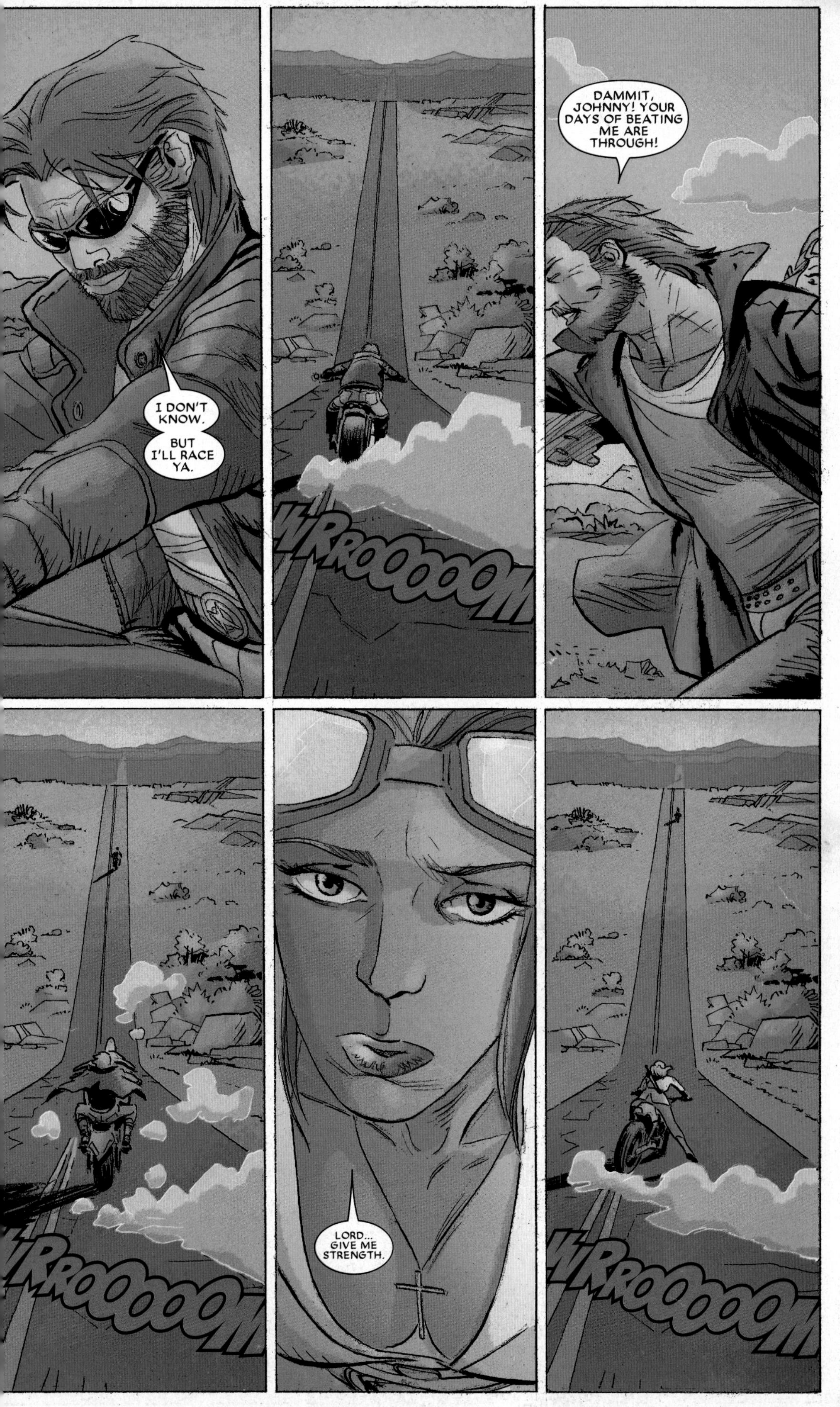
I DON'T KNOW.
BUT I'LL RACE YA.
WRROOOOOOM
DAMMIT, JOHNNY! YOUR DAYS OF BEATING ME ARE THROUGH!
WRROOOOOOM
LORD... GIVE ME STRENGTH.
WRROOOOOOM

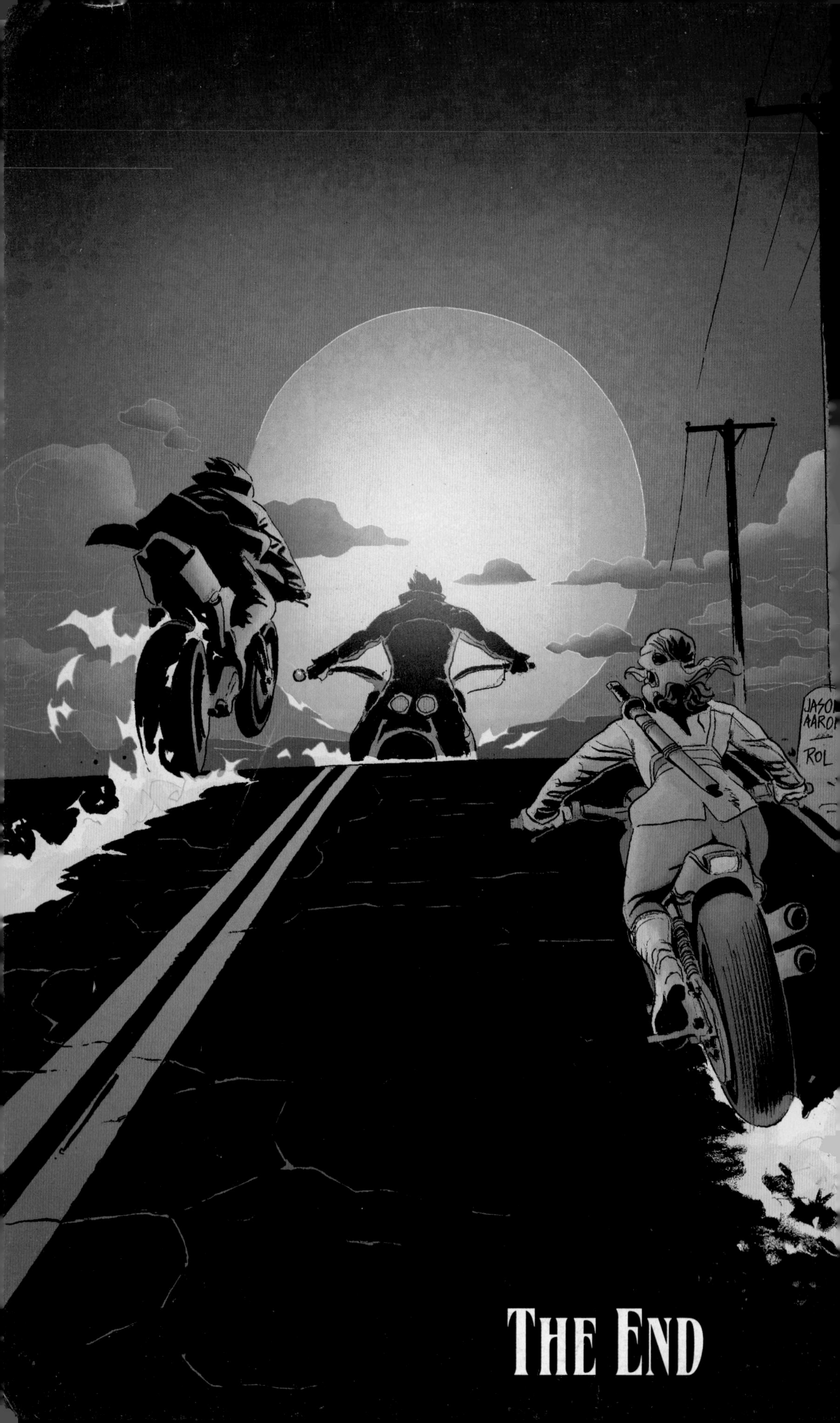
THE END

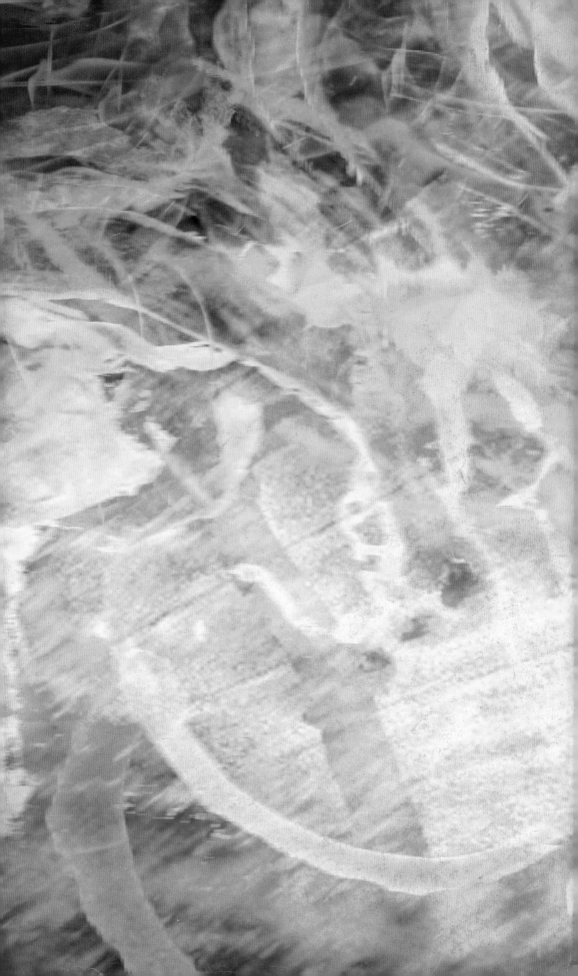

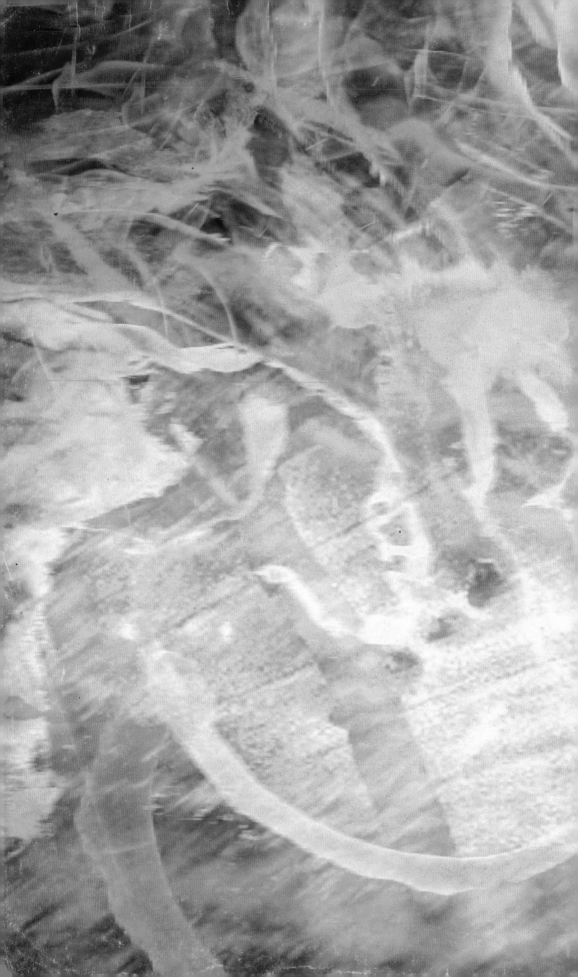